THE
BOOK OF
CATHOLIC AUTHORS

(First Series)

*Informal self-portraits of famous
modern Catholic writers, edited
with preface and notes*

by

WALTER ROMIG

fully illustrated by portraits

WALTER ROMIG, Publisher
979 LAKEPOINTE ROAD
GROSSE POINTE 30, MICHIGAN

COPYRIGHT, 1942
BY
WALTER ROMIG & COMPANY

Publishers of
The Guide to Catholic Literature
The American Catholic Who's Who
The Book of Catholic Authors
The Catholic Bookman

TYPOGRAPHY, PRINTING, AND BINDING IN THE U. S. A. BY
KINGSPORT PRESS, INC., KINGSPORT, TENNESSEE

To

Right Reverend Monsignor
EDWARD J. HICKEY, Ph.D.
Chancellor of the Archdiocese of Detroit
Churchman and Scholar

PREFACE

LATE LAST FALL, one of the authors in this book was a guest in my home. He was friendly, genial, conversational. The next day I secured those of his books which were not already in my library. And some evenings later, while reading one of them, I thought of that consequence of his visit. The attractiveness of his personality had invited continued acquaintance with the man; and this is easily and always available through his books. How fine it would be, I thought, if the talented minds and noble hearts of our Catholic writers could be made informally familiar—at home, I might say—to the multitudes of their potential readers. Surely such acquaintance would transform those potential readers into actual readers, into enthusiastic, devoted, receptive readers. To so bring Catholic writers before their audience—informally, genially, conversationally, in as much like a personal visit as possible—such is the purpose of this book. If it is met with a fraction of the enthusiasm the authors themselves brought to its making, the second series of *The Book of Catholic Authors* will be demanded before the ink in this first is scarcely dry. The demand will be easily met, for the second series is now ready for press. And a third is in preparation.

Except where otherwise noted, all the chapters in this book, even those written in the third person, were written by the authors themselves, and were written expressly for this book. Thus you have here autobiographies, self-portraits, more intimate, more colorful, more truly reflecting the personality of each author than would be possible for anyone else to write them.

Each author's chapter is accompanied by his portrait, and each of these, too, was made expressly for this book.

The book-lists at the end of the chapters invite you to further continue your happy acquaintance with the author through his other writings, as I did in the instance which led to this series of books.

The writers in this volume vary in the amount and the preciseness of the factual autobiographical detail they give. Readers who desire more are referred to the current edition of *The American Catholic Who's Who.* And those who also wish for more material on each of the author's books are referred to *The Guide to Catholic Literature, 1888–1940.* These two references are made here in preference to repeating them after each of the writer's chapters in *The Book of Catholic Authors.*

For continuous assistance in the preparation of this volume, I am indebted to my wife, Madeleine Collins Romig, a former member of the Staff of the Detroit Public Library.

W. R.

CONTENTS

of the first three series of *The Book of Catholic Authors,* with the number preceding the name indicating in which series the author's chapter is to be found

CONTENTS

CONTENTS

JULIE BEDIER

In Religion, Sister M. Juliana, O.P.

I WAS BORN of poor but Protestant parents and brought up in the Rocky Mountain country, among cowboys, Indians, horses, prospectors, six-shooters, and cows. (No sheep or sheep men. We always killed 'em off in our section.) Early memories: bearded gent sitting in our parlor telling tall tales about panning gold and drawing a bead on claim-jumper around corner of bunk house; Mom driving prowling Indian out of kitchen with broomstick; the howl of a timber wolf; a dark-eyed little antelope that looked in at my playhouse window!

Education: Appleton's Readers, given in large doses by Mom while mixing cakes or kneading bread at the kitchen table. I learned to read the old-fashioned way by spelling every word, and have ever since been able to spell (an accomplishment that I understand is falling into disuse). As soon as I was able to read, no printed matter could be kept from me except by force. When everything else was read, I went to the bookcase and read all over again *Robinson Crusoe,* the *Bible for Children, Black*

Beauty, and *Pilgrim's Progress.* (I thought *Pilgrim's Progress* pretty dull, but anything will do in a pinch.)

Music: Harmonica, learned by trial-and-error method while sitting in an empty buggy out by the corral. Also yodeling, copied from Swiss records on our phonograph.

Art: coloring pictures in Montgomery Ward's catalog. Mom got me a box of paints by sending away soap wrappers.

Mathematics, etc.: none till much later.

After I had attained to some size without ever having gained what my father thought were ladylike accomplishments, he sent me to a small boarding academy run by the Sisters of the Holy Cross—a place much frequented by daughters of ranchers. Here Pop hoped that I would learn to sew and embroider and be a lady. I learned something else besides, for I wanted to see what it was all about, so borrowed a catechism from one of the Catholic girls and for the first time in my life was up against *Logic,* cold, hard, somewhat frightening. And there was our Lady. I prayed to her. And the Blessed Sacrament, for we had Mass and Benediction. And of course one asked questions.

So, at seventeen, I became a Catholic, without too much opposition at home. And in due time I ran across a copy of *The Field Afar*—and I wrote and asked to join that new little community of Sisters. They let me in, and what is more, they put on me the gray habit of Maryknoll, my mark of distinction. While I was a postulant they sent their first Sisters to China, and their first Sisters made final vows. Now we have all grown up a great deal.

As soon as possible after my profession, they sent me as far away as they could, in the first group of Sisters to Korea. And in the Orient I stayed for thirteen years—a while in Korea, a while in Hong-kong, most of the time in Dairen, Manchuko. I know children in all these countries: Koreans and Japanese and Chinese and Russians, even a few brown little Hindus.

I was brought back to the United States to attend a General Chapter meeting of our Community, and here I stay, trying to tell the young folks of America something about Catholic children—and others who ought to be Catholic—in the places I know. People are so much alike everywhere, when you get to

know them! Race prejudice is such a narrow, twisted thing.
And every Catholic has a job that will never be finished as long
as there is a non-Catholic or an uninstructed Catholic left in the
world. That is what I am trying to say, as I write for Maryknoll.
And that is Maryknoll's message.

EDITOR'S NOTE: The author's Units of Study and other school materials have
been usually published under her religious name, Sister M. Juliana; while her
books for the general public have been issued under her family name, Julie
Bedier. These latter include the two mission stories for young readers: *The
Long Road to Lo-Ting*, 1941, Longmans; and *Thomas the Good Thief*, 1942,
Longmans.

REVEREND FRANCIS E. BENZ

Children's Books

DAD PASSED OUT THE cigars on election day at the turn of the century and predicted that I was to be a great politician. He must have given away more than the usual number of cigars on the day of my birth, for, years ago, business on election day was at a standstill. Men congregated at the polls, made bets on the outcome of the election, and forgot about their daily tasks. So I started out in life being more of an expense than usual and continued to be so for many years to come.

After successfully negotiating practically every disease for children known to the medical world at that time, I entered high school, and when studies and athletics permitted I wrote poetry. My first published poem appeared in the school magazine. And was I thrilled! A second followed the first, and then I seemed to have only sporadic outbursts of courting the poetic muse. Most of my later attempts were never submitted to any publication. One poem, however, "Mother," has appeared in print more than a million times.

Upon entering college I became a member of the staff of the college publication. During the Fall of my last year, I broke my collarbone in a football game and one day, after a few weeks of inactivity, I was wandering downtown and the idea struck me of obtaining a job as a reporter on the St. Paul *Dispatch and Pioneer Press*. Accordingly I entered the "sanctum sanctorum" of the managing editor and, much to my surprise, I was told to report for work the following afternoon. At home, that evening, I read every line in the paper, and pounded out imaginary "scoops" until the wee hours of the morning.

The next afternoon I reported for work, a little puffed up with my own importance as a reporter, I must admit. But the inflated feeling did not last long. A few weeks of covering a beat of hotels, clubs, and the Union Station, checking new arrivals, was not the exciting life of a reporter that I had imagined. My hours were from 5:00 P.M. to about 1:00 A.M. My school hours were from 9:30 to 3:30. A busy day.

Reporting, however, was not all routine. I remember the night of the Armistice of the First World War. News of its signing was expected momentarily, and the entire staff was waiting. Every reporter had a definite phase to cover, and when the news was flashed over the wires there was no sleep for us for more than twenty-four hours.

One incident that taught me a lesson, and which I shall never forget, was when I was told to go to a certain place where a group of natives of India were assembled. I hurried to the spot and endeavored to converse with various members of the group; but with no success. Finally, a man who said he was in charge came up to me and told me what great personages were in the group. He said they were a "sensation" on their trip across the country. He gave me photographs of all kinds. I hurried back to my typewriter and pounded out pages of copy. Proudly I placed my story, together with the photographs, on the city editor's desk. A short time later I heard a gruff voice shout: "Benz, come here! What do you think you are doing? Cut this down to about twenty lines." Slowly I returned to my desk with my precious story. Only then did I realize that the man to whom

I had spoken was the press agent for the group, and I had fallen for his chatter.

Another time I was assigned to cover a special meeting of a certain labor organization which was at odds with my paper. I was about to enter the main door with two reporters from other papers when I was stopped and told that, because of my paper's stand, I was not welcome. I wandered around the building and finally spied a fire escape that led to a window right behind the speakers' platform. Up the fire escape I climbed and perched beneath the window. I listened to the speeches. Then I hurried back to the city room and reported the proceedings. A word of commendation from the city editor? No. Just part of the night's work.

After working for some months as a reporter, I was offered the position of covering college sports. I accepted, for it allowed me more time for athletics and study as the hours were not so exciting.

The following September, I entered the St. Paul Seminary and had little time for outside writing. I covered the seminary news and conducted a column in the diocesan paper. During those six years I also managed to have a few articles published in various magazines.

After ordination to the priesthood I became interested in youth activities. I coached athletic teams and organized young people's groups, sodalities, boys' clubs, summer camps, etc. During these years I attended some literature and jouralism classes at the University of Minnesota and at Columbia University in New York. Finally, after a physical breakdown, I was ordered to take a rest. This I did, but continued to attend a few classes in journalism as a sort of diversion.

After hearing a certain lecturer, I conceived the idea of starting a magazine for Catholic boys. I realized the need for it from my contacts with boys. After receiving the necessary permission from Archbishop John G. Murray, *The Catholic Boy* magazine was launched.

Soon after this my only novel, *The Red Flame of Sound*, was published by Benziger Brothers. Analyzing the field of books for Catholic boys and girls, I came to the conclusion that there was a definite need for good biographies written in a popular style. There was no doubt in my mind but that my first attempt should be the life of that famous Catholic scientist, Louis Pasteur. This was published under the title, *Pasteur: Knight of the Laboratory*, by Dodd, Mead & Co. Next came the story of the famous engineer and builder of the Suez Canal, Ferninand de Lesseps. The title of this book is *On to Suez*. The subject is particularly timely because of its importance in the present war.

At the request of Dodd, Mead & Co., my next book was a venture into the field of communication. Miss Dorothy Bryan of that company desired that someone, not connected with the telephone company, write a non-technical book on the invention of the telephone and the life of Alexander Graham Bell. After much research in a field foreign to me *Talking Round the Earth* resulted. At present I am working on the life of Captain John Barry, Father of the American Navy. I hope I can complete it before the end of 1942.

In February of 1942 I began another publication. This time one for girls and called it *The Catholic Miss of America*. The following month I took over *The Catholic Woman's World* changing the name to *Poise*.

During these last ten years most of my life has been concerned with writing for boys and girls. Editorials, fiction, articles and pamphlets are turned out regularly. Then too, there is the most important task of examining material submitted by others, encouraging talent where it exists, assisting and in general advancing the cause of the Catholic Press.

Father Benz' books for young readers include *Pasteur: Knight of the Laboratory*, 1938, Dodd; *The Red Flame of Sound*, 1937, Benziger; *On to Suez*, 1941, Dodd; *Talking Round the Earth*, 1942, Dodd; and, with John S. Gibbons, a pamphlet life of St. John Nepomucene, for boys, *A Martyr to the Seal of Confession*, 1936, Our Sunday Visitor Press.

REVEREND HUGH FRANCIS BLUNT, LL.D.

Poet and Religious Writer

FOR THE PAST forty years the name of Father Blunt has been a familiar one in Catholic literature. More than thirty books— poetry, fiction, essays, spiritual studies—as well as innumerable contributions to both the Catholic and the secular press have flowed from his pen. Many of his poems have become household words, and he has attained, what he feels is a great distinction, the inclusion of his verses in the school reading-books. In regard to that, Father Blunt gets a laugh out of the fact that people who learned his poems in their readers some thirty years ago think of him as an ante-deluvian. Recently a woman who met him for the first time asked him if by any chance he was the Father Blunt who wrote poetry. When he admitted the charge she said, "Why, I thought you died in 1877." Father Blunt is not dead yet. He is still going strong, turning out book after book, sometimes two in one year, from the store of information he has gathered in his sixty-five years of life; not that he takes

his literary life too seriously, but because he is convinced that
the cause of Catholic literature is of supreme importance.

Hugh Francis Blunt was born January 20, 1877, in the small
town of Medway, Massachusetts. His father, Patrick Blunt,
was born in County Sligo, Ireland, and came to this country at
the age of fourteen, an orphan. He served all through the Civil
War, as Sergeant in the famous Irish Ninth, and then in the
twenty-sixth Massachusetts Volunteer Veterans. Father Blunt,
who prizes as his greatest possession his father's gun, wrote one
of his most popular poems, "The Irish Ninth," published in his
first volume of poems, as a tribute to his father's service in the
war. With little formal schooling, his father was a self-educated
man. There were not the opportunities for education in those
days, especially for a poor boy. But he loved books and was always reading. Father Blunt's mother, Ann Mahon, was also born
in Ireland, County Westmeath. As a young girl she came to
America in a sailing vessel, that took eight weeks for the voyage.
Her father was a noted Irish piper who once played his pipes before Queen Victoria. A set of his pipes is now in the British
museum. His was a large Irish family and every member of it
had a special love for the old Irish poetry and music. Father
Blunt considers that another rich inheritance. Music is his
hobby. He still delights in playing the piano. For many years
he lectured on Irish music and poetry in many states of the Union. Thus when he began to write he had the fine equipment
of music and poetry which had come from his Irish blood.

Medway, where Father Blunt was born, is a lovely New England town. Outside the village proper were endless fields and
woods and streams, and the lovely Charles River, which had its
source a few miles away. It was an ideal place for a boy who
loved nature. There he learned to appreciate the marvels of
God's creation, and in much of his poetry you will find the reflections of the secrets of nature learned in his Medway boyhood.
But just as literature has been only a side issue in the life of
Father Blunt, so in his boyhood everything was secondary to the
Catholic life of the town. There were no parish schools, only

the public schools, which, like all the New England schools of the day, were excellent, confining themselves to the fundamental studies. In those days boys and girls were especially taught how to read, and how to appreciate poetry. There was no end to the memorizing of poems, especially the poems of Longfellow and the other poets of the New England school. It was a fine training, and it was the beginning of Father Blunt's love of books. Besides that the parish church had an excellent library, and it was a common thing for the boys and girls to read four or five books every week, the books of Oliver Optic, who had been born in Medway, and the other juvenile writers of the time. The parish was actively Catholic. Catholic action was in vogue then, even though the name was not known. It was a fine atmosphere in which to grow up, under excellent, zealous priests who made up for the lack of parish schools by driving the catechism incessantly into the minds of the children. Hugh Blunt was made an altar-boy, and he ascribes to that fact the awakening of his future vocation. When he finished the grammar school, he was sent to Boston College, twenty-five miles away, making the trip every day. It was too hard a grind for a growing boy. At the end of the year he became ill with pneumonia almost to death (his father died at that time) and due to the interest of the pastor, Father Lowney, it was decided to send him to St. Laurent College, near Montreal, where several of the Medway boys were studying already. St. Laurent was an excellent school, conducted by the Holy Cross Fathers, with boys from all over Canada and the United States. One thing instilled there, second only to the piety which was taken as a matter of fact by the boys as the duty of every Catholic, was a love of books. There was an excellent library, and every boy was expected to know the English classics, especially Dickens, Scott and Thackeray. Father Blunt still maintains that the boys of those years knew more about the English classics than most of the university students of today. But it was not reading alone. The professors, particularly Father Carrier and Father Condon, insisted in season and out of season in drilling the students in writing. Every day there was an English theme, and the ideal of authorship was held up before the boys. It was active authorship, too, and some of the students had the great satisfaction of seeing their work published in the Catholic papers: no mean accomplishment for lads in their teens. One boy in particular was pointed out with pride as having had a sonnet published in the *Catholic World*.

So that it was at St. Laurent that Hugh Blunt made his first plunge into literature with a full page story in one of the Catholic papers. He laughs at the story today, but it had a thrill then. But it was the beginning, and when he left the college after four years, he took with him, more than all, a passion for reading and writing, a passion second only to the vocation to the priesthood which had been fostered by the thoroughly Catholic life of the college. He had a bundle of poems, mostly poor stuff, as he knew, but many of which he later redrafted and turned into good poetry.

He entered St. John's Seminary, Brighton, Massachusetts, in the September of 1896 to begin his special studies for the priesthood. By the side of that great vocation the study of letters amounted to little according to his way of thinking. The studies were hard. It is amazing the amount of study that is demanded of a young seminarian. But there were recreation days when the main studies could be put aside and attention be given to the magazines and the classics. In his offtime, spared from the more strenuous studies, Hugh Blunt still kept at his poetry, now entirely of a religious nature, and thus kept alive the love for Catholic letters for which he was to do so much after his ordination.

Ordained to the priesthood, December 20, 1901, he was appointed temporarily to the church at Stoneham, Massachusetts. In May, 1902, he was appointed an assistant at St. Peter's, Dorchester, Massachusetts. It was then he began to write in earnest. His first little poem, "Love," was submitted to *Donahue's Magazine,* and accepted by the editor, Miss Mary B. O'Sullivan, who for years as writer and editor made her magazine one of the best Catholic publications. Miss O'Sullivan recognized Father Blunt's talents and encouraged him to accept the assignments for articles, short stories, poems, which now began to appear regularly. Father Blunt's popularity as a writer of short stories is evidenced by his scrap-book which has hundreds of his stories and poems copied from *Donahue's* by the Catholic papers of the country. Another writer who encouraged Father Blunt at the time was Miss Susan L. Emery, who lived then in St. Peter's parish. A convert, known as the author of that spiritual classic, *Inner Life of the Soul,* she was working on the *Sacred Heart Review,* one of our best weeklies. Through her persuasion, Father Blunt submitted to the Review some of his poems, such as "An Old Woman's Rosary," which made a success at once and is still widely quoted. Miss Emery was a stern critic, and Father Blunt still treasures dozens of letters containing her helpful suggestions to one beginning the profession in which she had attained eminence. It was Miss Emery that brought Father Blunt in contact with the noted Jesuit, Father Matthew Russell, who became an admirer of the younger priest's work and invited him to contribute to his magazine, the *Irish Monthly,* for which Father Blunt wrote some of his best poems.

When Father Blunt published his first book, *Poems,* in 1911, Father Russell wrote: "The book is far superior to most of the collections of verse that are published nowadays, and we have here the first fruits of a genuine inspiration." Thomas O'Hagan described the book as one of "spiritual vision and power." The *Catholic World* wrote: "It is with many a poem and prose tale, too, that Father Blunt has brightened the pages of our magazines; and it is pleasant now to see the more permanent collection of his verses going into a second edition— Father Blunt has pierced through the simplicity of a sweet and elemental reality. Godspeed to the young soggarth's labors and to his songs."

With such success Father Blunt felt that he had a duty to Catholic literature. Not that it was his first duty. He has always maintained that he has been an author by accident. He has been an active priest, first, last and always. Even when he was a busy curate at St. Peter's, he did more writing than many a man whose sole vocation it is. It was the same when he was pastor of the

church at South Braintree, Massachusetts, where he remained
three years and where he wrote the ever popular *Great Wives and
Mothers*. He was sent then to East Cambridge to edit the *Sacred
Heart Review*, which in addition to his work as a busy pastor he
did until the paper, for lack of funds, ceased publication. He
was one of the very first writers for the *Magnificat*, which Sister
Ignatia founded and which she still edits. He has been contributing to the magazine for the past forty years, and many of his
books appeared serially in it.

He has been interested particularly in the parish school. In
East Cambridge he had every child of the parish enrolled in the
school. When he was appointed pastor of St. John's Church,
North Cambridge, where he still is, he continued the work of
making books, but always with the thought of the parish first.
Father Blunt numbers in his school eighteen hundred pupils,
with six hundred in the High School. His proudest boast is that
for the past ten years his school holds the record of being the
best contributor to the Holy Childhood of all the schools in the
world.

The University of Notre Dame honored Father Blunt with the
degree of Doctor of Laws, in 1920, for his contribution to Catholic literature. In 1919, he was awarded the Marian Poetry
Prize, by the *Queen's Work,* and in 1929 the Catholic Press
Poetry Prize.

Father Blunt is forever urging the young people to get into
the writing game. He believes that the cause of Catholic literature is a tremendous one and that if it is to continue to succeed
young Catholics must be recruited to be writers. His slogan is
that whoever can write a good letter can write a good book.
His advice always is—Keep on writing and you will find that you
have a message for some soul.

When one considers that his has been a strenuous life in the
priesthood, his literary output is amazing. Besides innumerable
articles, essays, stories, poems which have appeared in the press
but have not yet been gathered into book form (he still has
published matter that would fill a dozen volumes) he has written
the following books: (Poetry) *Poems, Songs for Sinners, Christ-*

mas Dream of Friar Celeste, My Own People, The Book of the Mother of God, Spiritual Songs, Old Nuns and other Poems, Mary Poems; (Drama) *Robert Emmett, Mother Seton, St. Francis of Assisi, St. Catherine of Siena, For Christ Crucified;* (Fiction) *Fred Carmody, A Boy Called Teddy, Through the Fires, The Boys of the Great Horn, The Dividers;* (Spiritual Works) *Great Wives and Mothers, Great Penitents, Homely Spirituals, Great Magdalens, Witnesses to the Eucharist, Give This Man Place, The Road of Pain, Seven Swords, Mary's Garden of Roses, Listen Mother of God, The New Song, Life with the Holy Ghost, Queen of Angels;* (Edited) *Readings from Cardinal O'Connell;* (Music) *Six Hymns in Honor of the Little Flower.*

REVEREND NEIL BOYTON, S.J.

Children's Stories

WHENEVER FATHER BOYTON gets the opportunity of going to the Polo Grounds to watch his favorites, The Giants, subdue The Dodgers of Brooklyntown; or, come a crisp Fall afternoon, The Rams of Fordham U. take over a visiting Eleven, he has but to look up to see the site of his birth. For there on Coogan's Bluff, overshadowing the Polo Grounds, stands the Jumel Mansion. A block north of that Revolutionary War relic, is where, on November 30, 1884, this future writer of American Catholic boys' books was born.

Naturally, Neil has not even the faintest remembrance of that first Sunday evening when he became a native New Yorker. Nor of that other important event in his life,—his Baptism in St. Elizabeth's Church, Washington Heights, N. Y. C., on December 8, 1884. Msgr. Henry A. Brann poured the sacramental waters. This same Monsignor had performed the marriage of his niece, Margaret Connolly, and Captain Paul Boyton, in Old St. Patrick's Church, Chicago, Illinois. Neil was their first born. On subsequent visits of the stork, that bird brought successively four brothers, Paul, Joseph, Claude Paul, and Francis.

While Neil was still too young to know what it was all about, his parents lived in Milwaukee, Wisconsin, and then moved to Cleveland Avenue, on Chicago's North Side. Here Neil admits his memory began to function and he remembers visits to the white buildings of the World's Fair of '93, and interminal piano lessons (that never took) at St. Vincent's Parochial School and Melrose Academy. Captain Boyton was with Barnum & Bailey Circus in those days, and there was a memorable week when Neil lived with the show. He still recalls the thrill of sitting high up with the driver of six dappled gray horses on a gay circus wagon, as it daily paraded through southern Illinois and Indiana towns; the kindness of circus folk to this visiting youngster, and the unbelievable sight of two complete shows a day! Then the reluctant return to suddenly drab Chicago and its boyhood routine. But those ancient winter months were bright, for Captain Boyton took into his home a Japanese tumbler and his son, "Six Dollars," whose mother had died on the road. Also a troop of sea lions were trained in the pool in the basement of the Cleveland Avenue house, and between the training of the sea lions and the practicing of the tumbling troupe, the Boyton basement was the mecca for the youthful neighborhood.

Neil's mother was a Sacred Heart girl and literary in taste. Early she imparted to her son a love of books. It was in *The Ave Maria* and *Our Young People,* and a well stocked Catholic home library, that Neil learned of the magic between the written pages.

An interlude to Chicago days came in 1894–1895, when Neil and his brother Paul became rather youthful Minims at Notre Dame University. Here in the great Church of the Sacred Heart, in which later, N. D.'s famous coach, Knute Rockne, would be received into the Church, Neil made his First Holy Communion on May 23, 1895.

Back in Chicago, Neil attended his first Jesuit school, St.

Ignatius on the West Side. He has a vivid recollection of a February morning in '98, when the papers were filled with the blowing up of the U.S.S. *Maine* in Havana Harbor.

Captain Boyton had invented that amusement device, Shooting the Chutes, and when he built one at Coney Island, N. Y., he moved his family back East. Thus it happened that Neil began his pleasant Coney Island boyhood, which gave him the mass of first-hand material for two of his boys' books, *On the Sands of Coney* (1925), and its sequel, *Killgloom Park* (1938).

Neil saw the new century dawn while he was spending three months amid the Boer War gloom in England and in a France that is no more.

Between summers spent working in his father's amusement park and winters schooling at St. Michael's Parochial School, Brooklyn, and, later, St. Francis Xavier High School, in Manhattan, Neil grew up. He graduated from Xavier High School that June day in '04 that the steamship *General Slocum* burnt in the East River with a loss of a thousand young lives.

That was also the year of the St. Louis World's Fair. Captain Boyton had the Chutes concession on The Midway, and Neil hastened to that city on the Mississippi to put in a hectic summer's hard work.

In the Fall, Neil resumed his educational pursuits, entering college at St. Louis University.

With the close of the World's Fair, Captain Boyton treated his family to a long-promised cruise. That was on a houseboat down the Mississippi. This *Killgloom I* made the leisurely six months' cruise from icy St. Louis to warm New Orleans. Among the adventures were a starry Christmas Eve, stranded on a sand bar in mid-Mississippi; the frozen-in months at quaint Ste. Genevieve, Mo.; near shipwreck when the ice gorge went out; hunting in Arkansas; first-hand glimpses of Mark Twain's *Life on the Mississippi;* and practical experience in boat handling in all kinds of weather.

Midsummer 1905, the Boytons had returned by steamer across the Gulf of Mexico and up the coast to New York City, where they resumed houseboat life on other *Killglooms.*

That Fall, Neil entered Holy Cross College, Worcester, Mass. An interesting commentary on those college years: Neil had the urge to write and he contributed bits to *The Purple,* but his budding journalistic style was never considered worthy of an editorship on the college paper. In retrospect, that does seem curious, as Neil has since published more thousands of words than the combined Staffs of that college paper from '05 to '08.

June '08, Neil graduated from Holy Cross College, and less than twenty-four hours later he was busy as Assistant Manager at Steeplechase Island, Bridgeport, Conn., where his father was Manager.

With the close of the season, Captain Boyton had another family cruise in prospect and he ordered Neil to take over the engineering job. In October '08, with the whole family on board, *The Water Gypsy* headed for the inside passage route down the Atlantic seaboard to Florida. Up the St. John's River to its head and then back to its mouth and down from St. Augustine to the Indian River, the *Water Gypsy* leisurely cruised the winter months. Homeward bound, tragedy saddened the pleasure cruise, as Neil's brother Paul died suddenly at Villanova College, where he was an engineering freshman.

Vocation came to Neil rather late, and December 7, 1909, he entered the Society of Jesus' Novitiate of St. Andrew-on-Hudson, Poughkeepsie, N. Y. The Jesuits, against their better judgment, decided to let Neil stay on, and he had the happiness of taking his First Vows on his Baptismal anniversary, Dec. 8, 1911.

The urge to write returned (there had been little time when Neil was in the amusement park world), and immediately after his novitiate he began publication of verse and short stories. His writings appeared in various Catholic magazines, while he was studying at Woodstock College, Md., and teaching at St. Joseph's High School, Phila., Pa. Many of these short stories later came out in book form under the titles, *In God's Country* (1923), *In Xavier Lands* (1937), and *On Hike to Heaven* (1942).

It was while happily engaged in teaching first year High at St. Joseph's that Mr. Boyton, S.J., received a sort of a valentine from his Provincial on February 14, 1916, telling him that he had been chosen to quit the City of Brotherly Love and, with another Scholastic, Mr. Henry P. McGlinchey, S.J., journey pronto to Bombay, British India. In that distant city, German Jesuits had been interned and Scholastics were badly needed. *A Yankee Xavier* (1937), which is Mr. McGlinchey's biography, describes that half way round the world journey. That period at St. Mary's High School, Bombay, where Mr. Boyton taught Anglo-Indian "babas" (boys) and did War Relief Work for the Indian Government, was colorful. Many of the experiences were subsequently incorporated in the books *Cobra Island* (1922) and *Where Monkeys Swing* (1924).

Tropical fever got Mr. Boyton, and his Superiors sent him back to America, where he was stationed at Georgetown University, Washington, D. C. Here he had the unique experience of going through the cycle of meatless and wheatless days a second time. At Georgetown he found himself an Instructor under both the War Department and the Navy Department at the same time. The Armistice of November 1918 broke up the S.A.T.C. classes and with the coming of the summer of '19, Mr. Boyton was sent to Woodstock, Md., to start his theological studies. Under a war privilege he had the happiness of being ordained at the end of his second year of Theology.

This event took place in Dahlgren Chapel, Georgetown University, on June 29, 1921. A pleasing coincidence: that date happened to be Captain Boyton's 73rd birthday. The next morning the newly ordained Father Boyton said his First Mass in the same Dahlgren Chapel, with his father and his brother, Claude Paul, as altar boys.

In the summer of '22, Father Boyton was sent to act as Chaplain at Camp Columbus, Leonardtown, Md. *Whoopee!* (1923), with its scenes set in this camp, recalls many of the events of that first of many summer camp chaplaincies.

Father Boyton was assigned in 1923 to Georgetown Preparatory School, Garrett Park, Md., where he was to teach first year High till '28. During that period he managed to write his North American Indian Missionary stories: *Mangled Hands* (1926), *Mississippi's Blackrobe* (1927), *Redrobes* (1936), and the popular pamphlet lives of the eight American Martyrs. Father Boyton was made an Honorary Corresponding Member of the Conseil Historique et Heraldique du France for these writings on the early French Missionaries in North America.

In July of '26, Father Boyton was appointed a Scout Chaplain of the Greater New York City Scout Camps. Summer after summer he worked with these Scouts, first at the Kanohwahke Lake sites, back of Bear Mountain, N. Y., and then at the Ten Mile River Reservation in Sullivan County, N. Y., the largest boys' camp in the world. During these eight seasons, Father Boyton gathered material for a long list of Scout stories. Among these are *The Mystery of St. Regis* (1937), *Paul in the Scout World* (1940), and *Saints for Scouts* (1941). This last, a series of Scout Chaplain talks on the Twelve Scout Laws, was published by the Boy Scouts of America.

Father Boyton was transferred to Regis High School, New York City, in '28, and he taught there for three years. He became active in Manhattan Scouting at this time and has since continued his interest in this kind of boy work.

His biography of St. John Bosco, under the title *The Blessed Friend of Youth,* appeared in 1929.

In '37, Father Boyton was made a member of the Gallery of Living Catholic Authors; the next year, an Honorary member of the Eugene Field Society, and in '42, the National Council of the Boy Scouts of America gave him the Silver Beaver Award for his Scout works. He is also a member of the Catholic Writers' Guild of America, the Catholic Library Association, and the Knights of Columbus.

Since 1939, Father Boyton has spent his summers as Assistant Director of Camp Gonzaga, St. Inigoes, Md. He is a Red Cross instructor in Water Safety and has been conducting Swimming and Junior Life Saving courses. Much of his water front experience is going into the making of a Catholic Scout summer camp story, on which he is now engaged.

Father Boyton has also turned his pen to boys' plays. *To Whom God's Love* (1941) has proven successful and has been staged in many places. He plans more short plays for boys.

This American Catholic boys' author has a modern journalistic style, and he confesses that he tries to make his characters
normal boys, who practice their normal Catholic life in every
day circumstances. He believes this is the most effective way
to instruct and entertain.

Since 1931, Father Boyton has been teaching at The Loyola
School, New York City. Here, year after year, he has been imparting first year High subjects to his pupils, gathering new
ghost and murder yarns for Scout Council fires, giving occasional
Retreats for boys, and trying to find time to do some more writing.

Father Boyton's books for young readers include: *Blessed Friend of Youth:*
St. John Bosco, 1932, revised edition 1934, Macmillan; *Yankee Xavier: Henry*
P. McGlinchery, S.J., 1937, Macmillan; and these Benziger publications:
Cobra Island, 1922; *In God's Country,* 1924; *In Xavier Lands,* 1930; *Killgloom*
Park, 1938; *Mangled Hands:* the story of the New York Martyrs, 1926; *Mis-*
sissippi's Blackrobe: the story of Father Marquette, 1927; *The Mystery of St.*
Regis, 1937; *On the Sands of Coney,* 1925; *Redrobes:* the story of Father
Brebeuf, 1936; *Where Monkeys Swing,* 1924; *Whoopee,* 1923.

REVEREND GERALD THOMAS BRENNAN

Children's Books

FATHER BRENNAN, popular author of children's books, entered the literary world through the back door. He met a dare. He accepted a challenge. His acceptance of that challenge marked his entrance into the field of juvenile literature. Little did he think, when he accepted that challenge, that he was entering a literary career that would not be forsaken. The appearance of his first book, *Angel Food,* won for him many friends—friends who clamored for more and more books. In response to that clamor, Father Brennan now finds himself writing one book a year, as well as carrying on the many duties of a pastor of a large city parish.

Born in Rochester, New York, on April 21, 1898, Father Brennan attended Cathedral Grammar School, Aquinas Institute, and Saint Andrew's and Saint Bernard's Seminaries of that city. He was ordained in 1923 and has a licentiate of philosophy. The year of his ordination, he was appointed assistant at Mount

Carmel Church. After nine years there he was appointed
pastor. In 1937, he was transferred to the pastorate of Saint
Bridget's where he is now stationed.

Through the years of his priesthood, Father Brennan has
been in close contact with children, teaching and instructing his
own parochial school children, as well as hundreds of public
school children. His talks at the Children's Mass on Sunday
won for him an appreciative audience. His contention has always been that the Children's Mass should be just that—a Mass
for the children, with special emphasis on a sermon for children.
The technique of his sermon consisted in telling the children a
story, and then drawing a moral or lesson from the story. After
all, was he not following the example of the Divine Teacher,
Jesus Christ?

"Why don't you spread your stories beyond the confines of
your parish? Why don't you put your stories in a book?"
These and similar questions were repeated constantly by an
insistent friend.

Father Brennan viewed the suggestion very lightly. It was
all very amusing.

Then came the dare. "I dare you to publish your stories!
I dare you to break into print!" This was the challenge from the
same insistent friend.

Father Brennan accepted the challenge quietly. He began
to write. In the same simple language that he commanded in
the pulpit, he put on paper his favorite stories,—stories loaded
with humor and gaiety, stories from which he wove his practical
lessons. Thirty-one of these stories made up his first manuscript,
which he titled *Angel Food*. This book was written for priests,
to help priests in their instruction of the little ones. The second
copy of *Angel Food* to roll off the press, was presented to the
insistent friend in answer to his challenge. *Angel Food* was an
immediate success, and is still rolling along successfully in its
fourth printing.

Father Brennan had answered his challenge. He had written
his book. His work was done. That's what Father Brennan

thought, but his publishers, The Bruce Publishing Company, thought otherwise. His publishers felt that the stories in his sermons would lend themselves to direct reading by children. They encouraged him to write for children.

Father Brennan wondered. . . . Are they trying to make an author out of me? Why, authors wear long hair, beards, and horn-rimmed glasses. Authors carry brief-cases. They live in another world, and they don't speak my language. No long hair, no beard, no horn-rimmed glasses, no brief-case, for me! No, none of that for me! I wrote one book on a dare, but that does not make me an author.

Once again the insistent friend came into the picture. His persuasive and encouraging words led Father Brennan to follow the advice of his publishers. Father Brennan did well to follow that advice. If Father Brennan had followed his own reasoning, the charming little *Angel City,* which was written for children, would never have seen the light of day.

What was the response to *Angel City?* Letters from children in all parts of the world, poured onto Father Brennan's desk. What was the message of these letters? We want more books! Father Brennan had won his way into the children's hearts through his *Angel City.* Could he refuse the children's requests? Well, hardly! Father Brennan answered every letter with the promise that there would be more books. And there have been more books. *The Ghost of Kingdom Come, The Man Who Dared a King,* and *The Good Bad Boy,* were written in response to the insistent demands of his juvenile audience.

While Father Brennan has several popular juveniles to his credit—he has written five books in four years—he still laughs when his friends refer to him as an author. He shaves every day, and visits the barber once a week. He wears no horn-rimmed glasses, and is allergic to brief-cases. He insists emphatically, that he is the Pastor of Saint Bridget's Church.

When do you find time to write? This is the question most frequently propounded to Father Brennan. His answer to that question is: "I make time. Most of my writing is done in the evening. My day is spent in the school, in the parish, and with the sick. Writing is my recreation. Is there any more profitable way to spend the long winter evenings than to allow one's imagination to run wild with thoughts of elephants, fairies, kings, and queens? I think not. Yes, writing is my recreation, but I am not an author."

In reading any of Father Brennan's books, one is immediately impressed at the simplicity of his language. There are no involved sentences, no ten dollar words. Nor does he speak down in a condescending manner. He speaks the language of children as though he were one of them. The remarkable part of it all is, that Father Brennan uses no word lists or vocabulary lists to guide him in his writing. His close associations with children for nineteen years, have helped him to master their language. He enjoys the confidence of children and listens attentively to their mode of expression. He studies the children of his school and keeps close to them. His children, he claims, are his best teachers. No wonder he talks their language!

Every comedian at some time or other, entertains the ambition to play "Hamlet." Every tragedian too, aims to play comedy. Now, you may think that Father Brennan has ambitions to write in the fields of theology, philosophy, and history. Well, Father Brennan has no such ambitions. He is having too much fun with his children's books. Where would he find a more appreciative audience? After all, children may not read the best sellers, but they do read the best books. They select good books, and they read good books. They remember what they read. This, for Father Brennan, is sufficient compensation for his efforts.

Father Brennan very often goes back in spirit to his little pulpit at Mount Carmel. Little did he think in those days that his little audience there, would one day become world-wide. As he says, "Can you imagine! Why, children in India, Africa, and Australia, are reading my books!"

As Father Brennan looks on the ever-growing row of books that he has produced, he concludes: "I began to write for children by accident. I am determined to continue writing for them out of love."

Father Brennan's advice is to accept every challenge. If you do, you too, may write a book!

Father Brennan's books for children, all published by Bruce, include: *Angel City*, 1938; *Angel Food*, 1939; *The Ghost of Kingdom Come*, 1940; *The Man Who Dared a King* (St. John of Rochester, England), 1941.

MARY JANE CARR

Children's Books

FROM THE TIME WHEN she was a very small girl, Mary Jane Carr wanted to be an author. At first, her ambition was to be a poet like her favorite poet, Longfellow, and she was about eight years old when she attempted to write her first poem. She had thought it all out. It was very beautiful and long and sad; but she had written only eight lines when she was completely over-come by her own emotion. She was sitting at the desk, pencil in hand, tears dropping on the unfinished "poem," when her father came into the room, and astonished, asked the cause of the tears.

"I've been writing a poem," the small writer said, "and it's terribly sad."

Her father, who was, himself, a writer of considerable ability, read what the child had written. "But—isn't there more to it than this?" he asked, with a puzzled expression. The lines on the paper were certainly not sad enough to have caused all that grief.

"There is lots more," the would-be poet explained, "but it is in my head, and it's the part in my head that is so sad." She went on to explain further: "That line about the kite isn't the way Longfellow would write it, but it is hard to find something that can both fly and rhyme with night."

Mary Jane Carr's father understood. He told her not to try to write any more just then, but to run out and play, and he predicted that she would write much, much more some day.

The incident of the first "poem" would have been forgotten had not someone in the family found the lines among her father's papers after his death. Mary Jane Carr was a young woman by this time and was already well known as a writer. As she read the "poem," written in a labored, babyish hand, she remembered vividly her grief over the part that was too sad to be written and her struggle with the line about the kite, the line that was not as Longfellow would have written it:

THE ANGEL'S CALL

A little child was sleeping
In its crib one summer night,
When an angel floated downward
Like a flying kite.

He looked upon the infant
Who slumbered peacefully.
I wonder if that child, he said,
Would like to come with me?

That first "poem" was followed by many others, and by many stories and plays. The young writer found an attentive audience for her literary output in her four brothers and four sisters.

"The old house in North Portland in which all nine of us were born provided ideal facilities for presenting plays," says Miss Carr, "and I made good use of the opportunity. The stage curtain was a sliding door between the two front rooms. I wrote, coached and staged the plays to which all the neighborhood children were invited. Sometimes, when suitable actors were not available, I played all the parts, and always I produced the sound effects, thunder, rain, bird calls, etc., on the piano, announcing first, "a terrific thunder storm broke," or "the sun came out and birds began to call softly"—whichever the case might be. The children always understood and accepted my efforts without question. We all enjoyed ourselves immensely."

Looking back on those young days, Mary Jane Carr recalls that there was a period in which everything she wrote was tragic. This was especially true of the plays. One day complaint came from a neighborhood mother that her little girl always had nightmares after witnessing one of Mary Jane Carr's plays. This presented difficulties for the playwright who felt that she couldn't restrict her art to accommodate one nervous child. She finally relieved herself of responsibility by making a sign to hang on the street door while the play was in progress: "Notice: People with Nightmares Not Invited."

The writer's serious work began when, after two years in St. Mary's College, Portland, now known as Marylhurst, she went to work on a weekly paper, *The Catholic Sentinel,* of Portland, of which her college history teacher, John P. O'Hara, was editor. She remained there for several years. Of those years Miss Carr says: "I can think of no better training for a young writer than that afforded me by my work on the *Sentinel* staff. John O'Hara was a writer of genuine ability and a scholar. I received practical experience in every phase of journalism from proofreading to editorial writing."

Later, Mary Jane Carr joined the staff of the *Oregonian* of Portland. What eventually became her first book, *Children of the Covered Wagon* was published serially in that paper. This book, a narrative of the Old Oregon Trail for boys and girls, has gone into many printings. Her next book *Peggy and Paul and Laddy* was published in Great Britain as well as in this country. Her third book *Young Mac of Fort Vancouver,* which deals with fur trade history, was a choice of the Junior Literary Guild for older boys and also of the Pro Parvulis Book Club for September, 1940, the month in which it was published. These three books were transcribed into Braille—*Children of the Covered Wagon* by the American Red Cross for New York Central Library; *Peggy and Paul and Laddy,* for the Wisconsin State School for the

Blind, and *Young Mac of Fort Vancouver,* by the Red Cross for the New York Institute for the Education of the Blind. Excerpts from all three books are included in anthologies and in many school readers. These books have been found especially valuable, too, for radio adaptation and for school dramatization.

Although Mary Jane Carr's work in historical fiction has won for her a place among the country leading writers for young people, history was a subject she most heartily disliked as a school girl. As presented by the text-books of the day, it seemed to her to be a tiresome procession of dry-as-dust dates and hard, cold facts, and consequently her grades in history were grades of which she wasn't proud. She thinks that it was, perhaps, her resentment of the text-books, and her belief that history could and should be made interesting for boys and girls that led her to write historical romance. She believes it to be the ideal method of presenting history, provided, of course, that the romance in no wise distorts the fact.

Mary Jane Carr is also the author of a book of verse for little ones from three to six years old, entitled *Top of the Morning.* In writing these verses Miss Carr was careful to use only ideas presented to her by children and she was amazed and delighted, she says, to discover how often she could use the very words and expressions of the children in the verses.

Miss Carr's books for young readers, all published by Crowell, include: *Children of the Covered Wagon,* 1934; *Peggy and Paul and Laddy,* 1936; *Young Mac of Fort Vancouver,* 1940; *Top of the Morning,* 1941.

REVEREND PATRICK JO-
SEPH CARROLL, C.S.C.

An Interview with H. C.

IN AN ATTEMPT TO get some personal information from Father
Carroll to serve as an introduction to his writings, I quizzed him
one morning. I had my questions set down on paper in 1, 2, 3
order, so to keep my mind anchored to what I wanted. Here is
the result in a pattern of question and answer. I would like to
say, in parenthesis, that Father Carroll is easy to interview, if
you are not obliged to ask him to repeat something in order to
check on your accuracy. If you do, he may say: "It is just as
difficult for me to repeat what I said the first time as for you
to remember it."

"But what you say, Father, is important to me."

"All the more reason for getting it right the first time."

In the order of my selection, here are the questions I put to
him: "What gave you the urge to write?"

"The urge gave it to me. I liked to write. I liked to write
and therefore wrote."

"One of the Sisters in your summer school course told me

about your first bit of verse, accepted by Father Hudson of the *Ave Maria.* Tell me about that, Father."

"Oh, that. It was in 1897. The verses were called 'The Wrecks of Departed Years.' I took the small manuscript to Father John Cavanaugh who was then associate editor of the *Ave Maria.* He was living in the Presbytery back of Sacred Heart Church at the time—in the room directly across from the room where I live now. I waited while he read the verses. 'Why this is good,' he said when he had finished. 'I think we can use it.' It was published in the issue of March 19, 1898, much to my delight."

"Did you like the poem, Father?"

"I must have, for I read it over at least fifty times. Today I find it isn't anything to brag about. It was Father Cavanaugh, not Father Hudson, who admitted me through the contributors' door to the somewhat choosey *Ave Maria.*

"Was your first group of stories in the *Ave Maria,* published later in book form as *Round About Home,* written all at one time?"

"They were written week by week, with no assurance of continuance. Every sketch was on trial. The acceptance of this week's offering gave no assurance that next week's would pass muster. It somewhat resembled a prize fight. You were scheduled for so many rounds, but you might take the count long before you reached the limit. After I had written twenty-six, I quit from exhaustion. Then Father Hudson had all the stories published in a book for which I suggested (you could only suggest to Father Hudson) the title *Round About Home.* The title was suggested by a cut in the *Dome,*—Notre Dame Yearbook. It represents May of the year. There were figures of boys swimming, playing baseball, lolling on the grass. Under it all was the caption: Round About Now. That decided me to call my West Limerick sketches *Round About Home.*"

"Somebody told me, Father, that your *Patch* was written much the same way. Was it?"

"Somewhat—with a difference. *Patch* was really written to

kill time. I was Vice President of Notre Dame in 1927 and had the business of extending student credits. In the whiles of waiting I decided to write a sketch of my school days, telling how the sudden death of an octogenarian saved me from the punishment awaiting me for skipping school. I called it 'Paddy Owen's Good Turn,' and gave it to Father Eugene Burke, then associate editor to the aging Father Hudson. Father Burke asked for more, more, more, until I had twenty sketches completed. The sketches were titled 'Memories of an Irish Boy' in the serial, but became *Patch,* after the hero, in the book. It is undoubtedly the best liked of all my ventures."

"*Smoking Flax* seems more romantic than most of your stories, Father. How did you happen to change your style of plot here?"

"If you mean by 'romance' the love element, I think you will find a love plot in *The Bog, The Mastery of Tess,* and *Many Shall Come* equally with *Smoking Flax*. The themes of *Many Shall Come* and *Smoking Flax* are more directly religious, however."

"Which of your books do you like best, Father? And which is most popular with readers?"

"Of all my books of fiction I think I like *Many Shall Come* best. I feel this story has presented the thesis I had in mind when I began it more to my satisfaction than any other fiction I have written. Of the people I have tried to create, there is no one I should like better to walk into this office any forenoon and say 'Good morning, Father,' than Helen Rice of *Many Shall Come*. But *Patch* is more or less myself—whom I see all the time. I am wondering just now if the sequel, *Patch of Askeaton Days,* to be published some time in the future, will capture as large a following as the first *Patch* written in weekly installments."

"Do you think writing is an acquired talent, or is it a born gift?"

"I suppose people write because they like to write. The liking may be what you call a 'gift.' The power to express thought

in arresting language, however, is not normally nature's dona-
tion to us. It is achieved through the novitiate of work. We
acquire commanding speech by reading examples of commanding speech, and by ourselves trying to express commanding
speech in a daily succession of attempts to express adequately the
possessions of the mind."

"Do you dictate Father, or use the typewriter when you compose?"

"I don't do either. I use a lead pencil and a scratch pad.
Then the secretary types what I have written—when she can
make it out."

"That means you make corrections?"

"Hundreds of them. Sometimes I discard not only whole
sentences, but whole paragraphs and pages. You see, one is
never satisfied that what is written may not be written better."

"Do you sometimes read the books you have written?"

"Never, after I have read them in proof. They no longer
express any joy of surprise. For the same reason I never read the
Ave Maria after it appears. I read it in manuscript, in galley
proofs and finally in page proofs. That quite satisfies me."

"As an editor, Father, have you any suggestions to offer young
writers who are ambitious to write fiction?"

"Nothing which has not been said hundreds of times. Have
a story to tell. Learn how to tell it. In order to become a good
teller it is necessary to become a good writer. The language of
a story is generally different from that of an essay; and the language of one story may be in a different pattern from that of another. But before you can modify expression to your uses it is
important that you have mastered expression. In other words,
you must have government of language before you regiment language to fit your objective. To be able to tell a story is more important than to have a story to tell. A poor craftsman will
spoil the best material; a good one will save inferior material
through good craftsmanship."

"How do you like editing the *Ave Maria?*"

"Do you see the picture of Father Hudson up there?"

"Yes, Father."

"Well, he carried on for half a century until a year or so before he died—for the Blessed Virgin. I won't have any such tenure; but I'll try to work until I'm no longer necessary or useful: for the Blessed Virgin also—as I dare hope."

EDITOR'S NOTE: Father Carroll was born in County Limerick, Ireland, in 1876. After being ordained a priest in the Congregation of the Holy Cross in 1900, he served as president of St. Edward's University, Austin, Texas, and vice-president of the University of Notre Dame, and has been editor of *Ave Maria* since 1934. His books include: *Songs of Creelabeg,* 1916, Devin-Adair; *Heart Hermitage* (poems), 1928, Scott, Foresman; *The Man-God: a Life of Jesus,* 1927, Scott, Foresman; and, all published by the Ave Maria Press, *Bog:* a novel of the Irish Rebellion of 1916 and after, 1934; *Many Shall Come,* 1937; *The Mastery of Tess,* 1935; *Memory Sketches,* 1920; *Michaeleen,* 1931; *Patch,* 1930, 1936; *Round About Home,* 1926; *Ship in the Wake* (a play), 1916; *Smoking Flax,* 1939; *Vagrant Essays,* 1936.

BURTON CONFREY

Educational Writer

BIOGRAPHICAL REFERENCE WORKS record that Burton Confrey, born at La Salle, Illinois, February 1, 1898, got his bachelor's degree at the University of Chicago in time to take part in World War I in infantry, psychological laboratory, and Chemical Warfare Service. He then returned to the University on a graduate scholarship in English and got his master's degree in 1926. After a year of teaching at the University and another at the University of Minnesota, he turned to Catholic education and taught at the University of Notre Dame for eight years.

Two years of subsequent formal study at Catholic University brought him a doctorate in education, whereupon he opened a Catholic junior college and spent the next several years helping Catholic colleges toward accreditation by secular standardizing agencies. For three years he lectured at the Catholic Summer School, Cliff Haven, on Lake Chaplain, and is now in the Graduate School of St. John's University in Brooklyn.

From Rome came the suggestion that he be made an honorary member of L'Institut Historique et Heraldique de France.

Then followed membership in the National Social Science Honor Society, Pi Gamma Mu, The Mark Twain Literary Society, and the Gallery of Living Catholic Authors.

Dr. Confrey's first book manuscript was used by the director of his graduate work, a Monsignor to whom he later dedicated the volume, to open a series of monographs sent by the University to other schools and to important libraries with whom the University exchanged publications. *Secularism in American Education: a History* was a doctoral dissertation investigating how education in our country had dropped its intimate connection with religious teaching, since all but one of the large universities east of the Alleghenies (Pennsylvania) had been founded to train youth for the ministry.

Another of his teachers was responsible for the publication of Dr. Confrey's *Faith and Youth*. This priest, an author whom Benziger published, recommended to that firm that they present these results of a rich experience in combining the functions of English classes with religious instruction. Another Monsignor, to whom Dr. Confrey later dedicated *Social Studies,* wrote an introduction, at the publisher's request and without charge. (In its issue for December, 1941, the organ of the American Association of University Professors discusses the racket of paying someone whose name is well known to write an introduction to a book which might not be worth publishing because of the author's obscurity. The famous name induces the publishers to bring out a book which they might otherwise refuse.) Although grateful for the charitable gesture of the Monsignor who introduced *Faith and Youth,* Dr. Confrey never had another book so presented.

Travel Light had a curious genesis. A Sister, a model religious, a graduate student of maturity and poise, whose only brother had been killed in France became dominated by the idea that soldiers could not live in a state of grace. The more she read about World War I, the more she feared that her brother's soul was lost. She was upset emotionally by the report that the battle in which her brother had been killed had been entered in order to boost the sale of War Bonds by lacerating the feelings and larruping the emotions of soldiers' families. Her emotional life was seriously affected and insomnia was depleting her nervous vitality when she asked Dr. Confrey, whose classes she had attended, about his experience in the War.

All his brothers and himself were of draft age; and so that each would be sure to have news of the others and of home, he had written a series of chain letters which he sent first to his home. From there, having been added to, they were sent on from one brother to another. Because he wished to prevent his mother and his sisters from visiting him in camp and being upset by what they saw, he used humorous headings for his letters—even though it meant that he never got any mail during his period of service, because no one had his exact address.

He had had in class at Notre Dame a group of seven engineers who had formed a club to study Catholic liturgy, art, and literature. One of them broke his neck making a shallow dive during the summer vacation (and sixteen years later is still completely paralyzed from the neck down—an inspiration and a marvel to all who know him). Dr. Confrey dedicated *Travel Light* to him and used a series of chain letters from seven college chums who had entered different branches of service to motivate the recording of their humorous ideas on life, Joe's reaction to suffering, and Catholic youth's keeping of womanhood on a pedestal.

Young women in a class in advanced composition read the manuscript and accepted the strictures placed on the type of girl who steps down from the pedestal; but they suggested that somewhere in the letters there be included St. Paul's statement that all men are fools.

The Sister who had lost her brother was convinced by *Travel Light* that youths could live in a state of grace even though, because of the flu epidemic, they might not have opportunity of assisting at Mass on Sunday.

Having opened a Catholic junior college for a Religious Order, Dr. Confrey saw need out of *Readings for Catholic Action*. When he discovered that there were less than a dozen copies of the book unsold, he convinced a non-Catholic publishing house that they could, at a profit, reprint *Readings for Catholic Action* under some such title as "Sermon Material." He offered to write the Introduction and tell of his discouraging experience when seeking suitable material—even though he had paid as much as ten dollars for one batch of mimeographed stuff. The Company's representative had judged the material, estimated the probable price for which the book would be sold, and so on, before Dr. Confrey was approached. He felt that a layman's book entitled "Sermon Material" would not sell and did not follow up the project.

The acknowledgment opposite the title page in *Original Readings* will suggest the variety of Catholic magazines to which Dr. Confrey has contributed. (When it was thought of advantage to the school with which he was connected to appear in non-Catholic periodicals, he wrote for such magazines, as *Education, English Journal, Junior College Journal,* and *Modern Language Notes.*) Some of the articles reprinted in *Original Readings* had appeared in a monthly put out by a Religious Order who (to encourage humility) vowed to work in a country whose language they must learn. When the first issue of their magazine appeared, Dr. Confrey sent them, as a form of charity, an article for their next number. For thirteen years since, he has supplied them with at least one article every month; at times there have been three of his contributions in an issue—a story, an article, and a poem. One issue included a page of poems (about a dozen). To help the Editor plan, Dr. Confrey keeps a dozen or more articles ahead of the printing so that any emergency in lack of material may be met.

Initiating Research in Catholic Schools resulted from Dr. Confrey's experience with Religious in Graduate Schools of Catholic universities who had to write dissertations. The idea behind it was to begin with freshmen on college level to train them to choose and limit subjects, to read economically and effectively, take notes, and so on. The book (now out of print) contained hundreds of suggestions for subjects of investigation in the fields of English and education, for controlling the resources of a library, building an outline, revising a manuscript, making an index, and even a chapter on meeting discouragement successfully.

In rapid succession a dozen books followed, all growing out of immediate needs: *Catholic Action* had included a "Digest of Skills"—methods of study in all phases of academic work; for a text in social science for those Catholic students who do not attend a Catholic college. *Social Studies* resulted (the first such text in the field) whose aim it is to inculcate a Catholic sense— the ability to see eye to eye with the Church in all matters of faith and morals. However, teachers in Catholic high schools demanded a book of readings to supplement the text because their libraries lacked the Catholic magazines and newspapers referred to in the Activities included in the text.

Next there followed a demand for a teacher's manual, which would include précis of each article in the Readings, answers to the tests on the Encyclicals which were part of the text, and additional readings and information so the teacher could enrich the course for these students who mastered what *Social Studies* and its Readings offered and wanted more. The demands for these books were met, but the three volumes were bound as one to prevent an objection to buying two texts for one course. As a result, the Teacher's Manual edition contains three sets of pagination—one for *Social Studies,* a second for the Readings (in which the page numbers began again with Arabic 1 and are followed by an asterisk), and a third (beginning again with Arabic 1) for the Manual.

After *Social Studies* appeared, there was demand for a similar text suited to college level and study clubs. *Catholic Action* resulted. Again followed the cry for readings because of the inaccessibility of current Catholic newspapers and periodicals referred to in the Activities of the text. *Original Readings for Catholic Action* included pertinent articles Dr. Confrey had written for newspapers and periodicals (he has done over five hundred); then followed *Readings for Catholic Action* (articles, particularly on the liturgy, written by Religious. Dr. Confrey felt that a layman's writing on the liturgy might be looked askance).

A reviewer of *Social Studies* wrote in the leading Catholic scholarly magazine of the time that Dr. Confrey had evidently included in the book everything he had—implying its completeness. When the tetralogy on Catholic Action (including *Social Studies*) was completed, that reviewer must have been surprised, for *Catholic Action,* and its Manual included over four hundred pages, *Original Readings* over eleven hundred, and *Readings for Catholic Action* seventeen hundred—a million and a quarter words on the subject!

For several years an able and popular preacher got two courses of Lenten sermons annually; it attracted such favorable attention that a book grew out of the idea—*Techniques for Students* (now out of print).

Method in Literature met a demand for outlines that had previously been mimeographed for graduate students to help them get an airplane view of English literature in preparation for a comprehensive examination. The laboratory method of teaching literature, the use of Catholic material as antidote for nasty plays being used in courses in the drama, the endless suggestions on decent reading, the lecture outlines, and the concrete assignments in the various types of literature impressed teachers most favorably.

The Editor of a magazine published for priests asked Dr. Confrey for an article on the moral mission of literature. There seemed, by this time, a market for a collection of Dr. Confrey's essays; and they were given the title of *The Moral Mission of Literature,* the subject of the initial paper. The rest of his books grew out of his teaching experience and the voluntary papers of students recording the enrichment of their inner lives.

Book reviews, editorials, talks before school and parish gatherings, ghost writing, and the use of six pen-names gave Dr. Confrey additional practice in writing. In his latest book, *Creative Writing for Catholics,* he presents in detail the various approaches to creative writing—not necessarily for money, rather as an apostolate. Manuscripts of books in process include: *Integration Through a Catholic Sense, The Catholic Philosophy of Literature, Better Talk, Achieving a Catholic Heritage,* and, *The Speech Apostolate.*

Among Dr. Confrey's books published by the Magnificat Press, Manchester, N. H., are *Educational and Vocational Supervision for Catholic Schools* (1939), *Following the Liturgical Year* (1940), *Initiating Research in Catholic Schools* (1938), *Method in Literature for Catholic Schools* (1938), *The Moral Mission of Literature* (1939), *Original Readings for Catholic Action* (1936), *Readings for Catholic Action* (1937), *Sensory Training for Catholic Schools* (1938), *Spiritual Conferences for College Men* (1939), *Stencilled of God* (1939), and *Techniques for Students* (1939); while Benziger published his *Catholic Action* (1935), *Faith and Youth* (1932), and *Social Studies* (1934); and the Catholic University of America Press issued his *Secularism in American Education* (1931) as one of its Education Research Monographs.

ALOYSIUS CROFT

SOME AUTHORS start to write because they feel that they have something which ought to be said. Others begin because they are talked into it, or dared to do it. Aloysius Croft claims to belong to the latter class. Two of his books were written, he says, because he criticised the similar works of others too openly—and was invited to see if *he* could do any better. Another, *Twenty One Saints,* was done because he remarked that someone ought to make the saints appealing to boys. At once he was appointed to the job himself.

Born in 1906, at Janesville, Wisconsin, Aloysius Croft attended the public and parochial schools in that city. 1921 saw him enter St. Francis Seminary, near Milwaukee, Wisconsin, to study for the priesthood. Eight years later he left that institution, convinced that his vocation lay elsewhere. In the meantime, like all seminarists, he had gone through a thorough liberal arts course, and had studied philosophy and some theology. On the way he had acquired Bachelor and Master of Arts degrees, together with a firm conviction that a great deal of fine Catholic writing was being wasted on young people, because it was not being done in terms that attracted them. This conviction was strengthened by his experiences in the editorial department of the Bruce Publishing Company, into whose employ he went immediately upon leaving the Seminary.

In 1935, when the C.Y.O. was being launched in the Archdiocese of Milwaukee, Mr. Croft was called in as one of the consultants on the program. The aims of the organization were set up, and the whole program was founded on a religious basis. It was recognized, however, that formal religious programs in themselves would not be enough to hold boys over a long period of time. There had to be some sugar coating. How could this be provided?

According to Mr. Croft's story, it was at this point that he brightly suggested that something might be done to make the boys proud of their religious ancestry; something that would bring them to point to the saints with the same pride with which they looked upon outstanding members of their families; something that would make them happy at being the younger brothers of the saints. Perhaps this would serve both as the "sugar coating" which was needed, and as a splendid end in itself. Mr. Croft also maintains that while making his suggestion he looked pointedly at one member of the committee who had already done some rather successful books for boys. The glances were ignored, however, and Mr. Croft walked from the meeting with a new job on his shoulders—the writing each month of a 2500 word sketch of a saint that would hold the attention of boys from the ages of 12 to 16.

The sketches were written each month for a period of two years, and were sent in mimeographed form to the C.Y.O. branches for use at meetings. Criticisms were sought and listened to, and suggestions were adopted. For their purpose the lives had to be brief—hence the "sketch" form was adopted, with a story-opening carrying punch and an index to the saint's character, followed by a brief resumé of the highspots of his life, the whole liberally sprinkled with dialogue. Keeping in mind the fact that boys like action, the author selected subjects whose lives would provide good examples of action. Knowing, too, that most boys are not archeologists, Mr. Croft made his saints talk the language of today. He let the stories speak for themselves, moreover, and was careful to do no moralizing, because he felt that boys are quite capable of picking out a moral for themselves if there actually is a moral to be picked. That boys agreed with the author's ideas was clearly proved, not only in the Milwaukee C.Y.O. but throughout the country when the stories were later published in book form, under the title, *Twenty One Saints.*

Since the publication of the book Mr. Croft has received letters from many places, telling of the interest in the saints which it has aroused. The one he treasures most, however, comes from the librarian in a boys' high school. Speaking of the fact that the three copies of *Twenty One Saints* in the library are always in the students' hands, the librarian wrote: "It has done a lot to develop a finer spirit among them."

Prior to the writing of *Twenty One Saints,* Mr. Croft had produced two small prayer books for young people. The first of these, *With Heart and Lips,* contains traditional prayers and some simple original prayers. The other, *The Greatest Prayer: the Mass,* was written as the result of a dare. Mr. Croft had occasion, in his work, to criticize a certain Mass book written for the use of young people. The reply of one of his employers was that if he could do a better book, it would be published. Realizing that there are no better prayers for Mass than those provided by the Church herself, Mr. Croft made a free translation and adaptation, in the simplest possible language, of the Ordinary prayers. These, together with brief explanations of the various parts of the Mass and a fine set of Mass pictures, form the book known as *The Greatest Prayer.* In eight years on the market, sales of the book have gone well into six figures, and it has outsold the book which it was written to rival.

On two books Mr. Croft acted as collaborator. *Symbols in the Church* was written with Mr. Carl Van Treeck, stained glass artist and church decorator. On this book Mr. Croft claims to have been little more than a mouthpiece. His latest work, done in collaboration with Mr. Harry Bolton, M.A., is a translation into modern English of the *Imitation of Christ*. This project represents Mr. Croft's idea that our devotional literature should be written in language that modern Catholic Americans understand. Too many of our prayer formulas and too much of our religious and spiritual writing, he feels, are cast in the language of the Middle Ages. Latin is the official language of the Western Church: there is no canonized English form. Latin, when it is translated, should be brought into the terms of today, as it can easily be. There is, Mr. Croft maintains, no reason for using terms in our conversation with God that we would not use in conversation with our fellowmen—terms of which we have only the vaguest understanding. Reverence and dignity can be maintained in modern English as well as in archaic English. There must be others who feel the same way, for the first edition (a large one) of the modern *Imitation* sold out in less than a year.

The task of translation took somewhat over three years. Working directly from a Latin version published in the last century, and using as reference another Latin text of the 15th century together with a polyglot edition of the 18th and a large number of English translations, the translators tried to present as correct and readable a version as could be produced. They feel that their work has been amply repaid by the reception which their version is receiving.

Besides his books, Mr. Croft has contributed articles to a number of magazines, articles dealing mostly with the saints or with various aspects of Catholic book publishing. *America, Ave Maria, The Catholic School Journal, The Little Missionary, The Journal of Religious Instruction,* and *The Young Catholic Messenger* have all carried material by him.

Mr. Croft feels that the fact that he has written anything at all is due, at least in part, to his chance connection with a Catholic publishing firm. Brought into close contact with the Catholic market, and seeing at first hand the needs for certain definite types of Catholic reading material, he has tried to provide some of the things which were needed. He is convinced that we must have more good Catholic juveniles that are actually juveniles, and not books written about young people for adults. He is convinced, too, that a good deal of Catholic writing is failing of its object simply because it is being produced by experts who cannot forget that they are experts. The average Catholic reader (which means almost every Catholic reader outside the ranks of the clergy and sisterhoods) needs books written on various phases of his religion in language that he can understand and in a way that will interest him; he does not need the expert's view but the view of one who is not much less "average" than himself.

Mr. Croft unlike some writers, does not feel that he is in possession of any message that the world simply must have. Writing is hard work for him, and his every sentence has to be gone over again and again before it is presentable. Like most persons who have ever written, however, once ideas do come he has no peace until they have been put down on paper. As a result his desk is full of articles that no publisher would possibly accept, and which were written simply to relieve the strain. He does write best, strangely enough, when under pressure of a deadline, and says that he might produce more if he could find someone who would force him to meet definite dates.

EDITOR'S NOTE: Besides the books mentioned above, which are all published by Bruce, Mr. Croft, in collaboration with his wife, is the author of three delightful daughters.

THOMAS AUGUSTINE DALY

Poet

T. A. DALY—born in Philadelphia, May 28, 1871—first looked into Chapman's *Homer* (vide John Keats) about 1884. At that time, his chum at Villanova College, Frank Donnelly, of Pittston, Pa.—now (1942) the Rev. Francis P. Donnelly, S.J., of the faculty of Fordham University—introduced him to the mysteries of verse-making, both boys contributing charades, anagrams and the like o' that, to the Puzzle Department of *Golden Days*, popular boys' paper of that time. Followed F. P. D. to St. John's College, Fordham, in the fall of 1887. Became a contributor to the *Fordham Monthly*, carrying on under the competent tutelage of the Rev. James V. Kelly, S.J., moderator of that journal. Started as a reporter on *The Philadelphia Record* in 1891, and contributed occasional verses to that newspaper. In 1898 became General Manager of *The Catholic Standard and Times* (Phila.) and in the following year inaugurated the column "Jests and Jingles" on its editorial page. There, in 1904, appeared the first of his Italian dialect verses *(McAroni Ballads)*; and, in 1906, under the imprint of the C.S. & T., *Canzoni*, his first book of verse was published. In 1915, left the C.S. & T. to inaugurate "Tom Daly's Column" in the *Philadelphia Evening Ledger*. In 1918, returned to his "first love," the *Philadelphia Record*, as Associate Editor. In 1929 the *Philadelphia Evening Bulletin* gave sanctuary to his column "Rhymes and Ripples," which still (1942) flourishes on the editorial page of that conservative journal.

EDITOR'S NOTE: Mr. Daly has received honorary doctorates from Fordham (1910), Notre Dame (1917), and Boston College (1921). His principal works are: *Canzoni*, 1907, Harcourt; *Carmina*, 1909, Harcourt; *Little Polly's Pomes*, 1914, Devin-Adair; *Madrigali*, 1912, Harcourt; *Songs of Wedlock*, 1917, McKay; *McAroni Ballads*, 1919, Harcourt; *Herself and Her Houseful* (telling the experiences he and Mother Daly had in raising seven children); *Selected Poems*, with an Introduction by Christopher Morley, 1936, Harcourt. Mr. Daly is also the compiler of *A Little Book of American Humorous Verse*, 1926, McKay; and *Wissahicken*, 1922.

ENID DINNIS

Novelist and Short Story Writer

SOMEONE HAS DRAWN a shrewd distinction between Catholics who write and Catholic writers. I became a Catholic and a writer— a professional writer, that is to say—somewhere about the same time. I was received into the Church at the Ursuline Convent in Thildonck, Belgium, in the year 1897, and my first printed-and-paid-for article had appeared at the beginning of that year. It dealt with the names of the streets in the old historic city of London. The City of London—the one-time walled-round mile —was my magic city until I became acquainted with "the City set upon a hill." Yet, although Catholicism presented itself to me in the glory of a high romance, it was some years before the Catholic and the writer became fused in a joint production of the pen.

I have always set this down to the fact that it is sometime before a convert from Protestantism realizes that religion is no longer a Sunday affair which can only intrude into weekday life without unseemliness in the form of good behavior implying a religious basis. My pen was at that time employed in the production of humorous verse of a topical character, turned out week by week, and articles of the informative kind. Fiction, for some reason, did not attract me. My Catholicism remained in a shy, watertight compartment. A more Catholic environment brought me to realize that Catholicism is a religion that does not merely encroach occasionally on the preserves of the six secular days, but one that sets the week-day going, as it were, with an all-the-year-round daily Mass. This new conception of religion took the shyness out of my Catholicism; and it enabled me to tap an entirely new vein in my writing.

I think it was Robert Hugh Benson's *Light Invisible,* a collection of stories of a mystical character—one might call them celestial ghost stories—that first opened this vista to me. *The Light Invisible* was not a "pious book." It was read by the ordinary novel reader. It embodied the thrills that had as yet found no outlet from my water-tight compartment. The new vista opened the view to possibilities in the writing of stories—romance—where there had previously been a solid wall. It started me on a quest which in twenty-five years adventuring has not exhausted its magic. I became a Catholic writer instead of a writer who happened to be a Catholic.

There surely need be no apology for introducing the supernatural into a story? Mystery stories are popular, and surely it is something for an author to be able to present a mystery story which keeps its Mystery after the last page has been read? Is that not going one better than the thriller? The supernatural is ever present with us. None of my stories ever really happened, but I maintain that each one of them *could* have happened. They have their parallels in the true stories that are brought to me with the invitation to use them. In no case is truth stranger than fiction than in the case of supernatural stories. Indeed, did I attempt to recount some of these authenticated stories I might well be charged with going beyond the limit permissible in a non-fairy tale. To be able to find a plot which "makes of one day adventurous Eternity," is surely no light discovery?

The older one grows the richer appears the mine to be quarried. My past out-put includes ten volumes of collected short stories, the first of the series being *God's Fairy Tales,* published in 1916; three historical novels, *Mr. Coleman, Gent., The Three Roses,* and *Bess of Cobb's Hall;* and two mediaeval novels, *The Anchorhold,* and *The Shepherd of Weepingwold.* This has ousted other kinds of writing, with the exception of an occasional frolic in verse.

But, so much for one's own line. It is not to be inferred that the Catholic writer is in any way bound to this definite introduction of Catholicism into his work. Far from it. Catholic values, the Catholic code of morality, Catholic balance,—all serve to make an ordinary secular story Catholic. That is the kind of fiction that is needed. The temptation to be drawn into the conventional line of modern fiction is ever present to the Catholic fictionist. It has to be combatted with the sword of the spirit. There may not be a word of religion in the book. It may be the lightest humour, a feast of fun,—and yet the sword may be at work preserving the standard of Catholic writing.

That is why it is not enough to be a writer who happens to be a Catholic. That is why it is not enough to write your story and forget that you are a Catholic—as one might forget it whilst one was totting up a column of figures or doing a cross-word puzzle. The pen is a sword which we may very easily find ourselves grasping by the blade instead of by the handle. It can easily wound the hand that holds it. A keen wit has a cutting power from which one needs to be protected by the bar which makes of the handle a cross. But what a weapon when rightly wielded! The world is in direful need of Catholic writers. Apologists, social students, pamphleteers, fiction writers. Writers conscious of their vocation if it only be a vocation to amuse and recreate. These last may open the little gate of Hereabouts and embark on the wider adventure. Fiction can become truth if it is touched with the supernatural.

EDITOR'S NOTE: Miss Dinnis (in private life, Mrs. William Cassell) lives in London, England. Her books include: *God's Fairy Tales, Mystics All, Once Upon Eternity, More Mystics, Travellers' Tales, Out of the Everywhere, By Fancy's Footpath, In Merlac's Mirror, The Curtain Rises, The Road to Somewhere, Meadowsweet and Thyme* (poems), *The Anchorhold, The Shepherd of Weepingwold, Mr. Coleman, Gent., The Three Roses,* all published by Herder. Bruce issued her *Bess of Cobb's Hall.*

REVEREND FRANCIS PAT-RICK DONNELLY, S.J.

A Line of Verse—Its Source and Outcome

FROM 1905 TO 1906 I was on the staff of the *Messenger of the Sacred Heart,* and one day this line popped into my mind, "Shepherd my thoughts and fold them into prayer." The future of that line as well as its origin in the past could well serve as a text to the writer's life. A short time after its appearance I wrote a four-line stanza ending with the impromptu line. The next year I was teaching, and I pulled the quatrain out of my notes and expanded it into a sonnet, which was published in the *Messenger.*

Later I received a letter from the wife of a Chicago lawyer, a graduate of St. Joseph's, Emmitsburg, and a well-educated and deeply religious woman, who met with a painful death through an accident some years ago. She had been attracted by the verse and after some time located me at Poughkeepsie. About that time Mother Machree was a popular song, and I received a letter from Chicago, asking me what Machree meant. I began first in humorous fashion to say it meant a dappled doe in the moon-lit forest and other pretended Celtic twilight mysticism. Then it occurred to me to put down in rime everything which an Irish heart would love, because *croiohe,* like *kardia* in Greek and *cor* in Latin means heart, which is the English cognate of the word. My correspondent had asked for the meaning, and I answered with "What an Irishman means by Machree." The lines were done quickly, but without knowing it I became famous.

I had seen no great merit in the lines, but my correspondent urged their publication. I was sending some verses of students to the *Irish Monthly* in Dublin, and I enclosed the interpretation. Its publication in Ireland was followed by its publication here in many places. I was quite surprised at the reception. The popularity of Mother Machree advertised my contribution. The actor Chauncey Olcott asked permission to put the lines to music and to use them as an encore to Mother Machree. The plan changed, and he had no music written as far as I knew, but many others have made songs of the words. A Miss Seargent of California gave them an operatic setting. A Jesuit, provincial of the Missouri Province, made a hymn of the lines. An organist of Dundalk, Ireland, by name Kerbosch, has printed a setting. Ernest Torrence, the moving-picture actor, wrote music which was to have been sung by John McCormack in his film, Song of My Heart, but copyright laws kept the song out of the picture. Torrence's setting has, however, been printed by Boose. The lines have been sung to several Irish airs, especially to the Dear Irish Boy. The setting composed by Mr. George Gartlan of Brooklyn and published by Leo Feist is perhaps the one best known. At any rate it is that setting which appears in the book of songs selected by Major Bowes of radio fame.

It was Chicago that urged the publishing of my verses and chose *Shepherd My Thoughts* as the first selection and title. The volume of verses barely struggled through one edition, but the line that came out of the void more than thirty-five years ago has finally won for its author a fame to which Major Bowes has added the crown.

That line of verse which grew to a sonnet and the meaning of Machree were not after all wholly spontaneous. They went back to a boy just past seven years, who wrote his first lines of prose or rather penned what a kind Sister dictated for a letter to the boy's mother, who was in a Philadelphia hospital, suffering with an illness that proved fatal. It was she, I like to believe, who brought for our slender library *The Prose and Poetry of Ireland,* and John O'Kane Murray's *History of the Catholic Church in America,* both of which books left their impress on my mind. I read and even chanted aloud the lines of Thomas Davis, Gerald Griffin, of Banin, Moore and others, and when some years later my teachers at Fordham set me writing verses, I read Tennyson from cover to cover, noting down lines that appealed to me, and I saw my taste growing from 'Blasts that blew the poplar white' to 'In the teeth of clenched antagonism to follow up worthiest till I die.' There is much Tennyson in the "Knight of Rhodes" inspired by Mother Theodoria Drane's history and in the "Glastanbury Thorn." These verses appeared in *The Fordham Monthly* in 1887–1888 and "Knights of Rhodes" won a money prize from Father Finnan, our parish priest. I became a professional and was declared the winner over the present Dean of Marywood College, Scranton, Pa. I hope she may forgive that unchivalrous act of more than fifty years ago.

The Prose and Poetry of Ireland set my thoughts to meter and rime and, with the help of all Gerald Griffin's works, fostered the Irish bent that interpreted Machree. Gerald Griffin's relatives had migrated to Susquehanna County, Pa., where my father and mother were born, and also my mother's sister, who for several years after mother's death became a second mother to the eight children, ranging from one to fifteen, who were left orphans. That aunt, a deeply religious woman, enlarged our small library with Griffin's works, and added Faber's works and the *Glories of Mary* by St. Alphonsus and Furniss's *Tracts.* The examples in the *Glories of Mary* were liked. The chapters, however, which the examples illustrated, were beyond a young boy. The fiery imagination of Furniss made him tremble on the verge of sleep. I was toying with Faber, but boasted to my Sister teacher about it. She discouraged me. "It was above me," as it was; but I do not recall any proposed substitute. Later on when, in a like boastful spirit, I told my Fordham Sophomore teacher that I was reading Balmes' *History of European Civilization,* I was again discouraged. This time I was given Jeffrey's *Essays,* reprinted from the *Edinburgh Review,* and was urged to read his review of Allison's *History of Taste,* the only essay in the book which I could not finish. I read Balmes. From these incidents I learned one lesson. Do not discourage any reader from any reading unless evil, and then begin with likes and direct to similar but better books. I asked my Boston high-school lads of thirteen what they liked. They liked war stories. Try Abbott's *Life of Napoleon.* A lad did so and then read the lives of many great generals and ended the year with Allison's *History of Europe* in four volumes, because Abbott referred to Allison.

With no home or town library, I began reading *The Boys of New York* and the like and Beadle's Library. Christmas and Fourth of July pocket-money was invested in stories which now are bound in cloth. Jack Harkaway on his horse led me down to a river and plunged me into the land of romance where I have met and forgotten thousands of heroes. In my father's furniture store was a heap of mattresses for sale. They were beside a window. I moved the upper ones out and stretched on the lowest read my stack of wild-westerns, deaf to all cries of my name for pressing chores, which my father favored for his sons. In those early days I met Robinson Crusoe, ran home from school and buried myself in the story, omitting the family supper and feeding on second table fragments.

It was that reading experience which made me coin the slogan, Readers are Leaders. At least, they show some skill of composition in the style they have devoted themselves to. In forty years of teaching I have usually been able to pick out the readers from the very first compositions handed in. I have written text-books on compositions, but if students read widely and well, all such books would be superfluous. I have learned spelling and grammar and sentence structure and build of paragraphs and longer compositions, not from grammars or rhetorics, but from reading the types of composition which I was attempting. That is why in my text books I have multiplied examples and abbreviated rules.

I am grateful to Sister Charles, my teacher at Pittston, who made me a lover of words. When I wrote "Greek Speaks for Itself," a plea composed of English words derived from the Greek, some one said that I must have spent a long time at it. The immediate writing did not take long, but the interest in words began in my first teens when I studied Butler's *Scholar's Companion* under Sister Charles. It was she, too, who taught me how to solve puzzles, a recreation still giving me daily pleasure. That solving of puzzles became the occasion of starting Tom Daly on his poetic career. At Villanova College, where we met in 1884, we both read *The Golden Days*, a boys' paper. We both avoided the Bible page, and I directed his attention to the puzzle page. His first venture into verse was a charade. He was not satisfied to solve, as I was; he went on to compose puzzles. That friendship begun at Villanova, strengthened at Fordham, has grown stronger through the succeeding scores of years.

Puzzling introduced me to Webster's big dictionary, which my father bought to help me solve puzzles. The dictionary made accurate the knowledge of words and perhaps added to a boy's vocabulary, but there are no complete sentences and no paragraphs in a dictionary. Writing is mastered by the reading and rivaling of wholes, not of separate words with multiplicity of senses.

When "Shepherd my thoughts and fold them into prayer" popped into my head, I could not flatter myself with Pope that I lisped in numbers. I did, however, sing out the lines of Davis and Moore and Griffin, and so got some of the lilt of verse into my system. It was the *Prose and Poetry of Ireland* which first tuned my ear to verse, and it was a kind father who began my training in the melody of song. One Sunday night, when I was about eleven years of age, on a visit to cousins, my father heard one of them play Irish Airs from Haverty's *Three Hundred Irish Airs*. Next morning my father brought me to a music teacher at St. John's Academy and told her: "Teach this boy to play Irish Airs." The good Sister did her best; but for the three years I took lessons, I could not stretch my fingers to an octave. The time for practice was spent in reading with one hand and pounding the piano with the other. The Sisters' library was close at hand, and there I read the *Martyrs of the Coliseum* and the *Victims of the Mamertine*. I deceived my music teacher and never became an expert performer, but her teaching has been one of the most fruitful and most pleasant experiences in my life. I gained a love of Irish music which has stayed with me all the years. My first public appearance as a musician was on St. Patrick's Day when I was about thirteen, and went out with a fife and drum corps of the Temperance Cadets to play the one and only tune we knew, Dandy Pat. Without that music training, Major Bowles would not have had "What an Irishman means by Machree" to give me a place in his Hall of Fame. That music training helped me to write the words for hundreds of songs and for a cantata, "Home," which is all in Irish music.

In my father's limited library was John O'Kane Murray's *History of the Catholic Church in America*. In it I read of the Canada missionaries who were tortured by the Indians, and I was fascinated by the bravery of the missionaries. What did S. J. after their names mean? I did not know. Turning to another page where statistics of Orders were given, I saw that one Order, having then the largest number of members in our country, was first on the list. I wanted to be of the first, and I resolved to be a Jesuit. One of our priests heard of my ambition through a pious penitent, a house-maid whom I had told. That priest, afterwards Bishop Hoban, gave me a Litany of St. Ignatius Loyola to say for my vocation. I said it daily, even when I was with the good Augustinians at Villanova, and only stopped when I was well on the way to realization at Fordham.

To my twelve years of schooling before entering the Jesuits, the Order added twelve years more. Then I entered the classroom as a teacher, where I have been for forty years. My one year on the *Messenger of the Sacred Heart* started the thoughts that have been shepherded into several books which make up the "Heart Series." Other books, too, reflect the Ignatian second Method of Prayer for the Our Father, the Hail Mary, the Anima Christi. The dozen religious books, as well as most of the others, had to be written in parts and afterwards gathered into books. *Mustard Seed* appeared as editorials in *America*. I had been

preaching to myself as well as to others when writing, and I was
amused when one of my Jesuit students, reading one of these
editorials, on irony, entitled "It has Slain its Ten Thousands,"
said to my typist, who was in the know: "Father Donnelly ought
to read that!" For him I had not succeeded in writing out of my
system the demon of sarcasm, which is still, alas, not exorcised.

It has been my good fortune to be kept teaching the art of
composition exemplified in English, Latin and Greek. Out of
that class-room experience have come books of precepts and
rhetorical commentaries on English, Latin and Greek speeches.
Teaching the same author year after year has revealed details of
the art of composition which are omitted in most editions of the
classics.

That same interest in the art of composition has prompted
various magazine articles or talks which have found their way
into other books. The spirit of controversy is easily aroused
within me, and I have fought against the dominance of history
and various other sciences which have made literature an encyclopedia of facts instead of an exemplification of style and an
inspiration to write.

It would be of interest to me and perhaps to others, if I knew
all the causes which concurred to shape in my mind unconsciously the line "Shepherd my Thoughts and Fold Them into
Prayer." The multitudinous thoughts, the Scriptural form, the
holy wish, all in regular measure, have had causes as well as
effects. The child is father to the man, is a well-worn adage, and
did I know the source of every literary habit and how I won
every permanent element of training I possess, no doubt the results would be instructive. I have had the custom of jotting
down in a day-book random thoughts under headings. When I
had a number on one subject, a short article might result. Had
I not jotted down the line above, what I should have missed!

Father Donnelly's recent books include: *The Heart of the Gospel and The
Heart of Revelation* (a combined edition of two of his earlier works), 1941,
The Apostleship of Prayer; *The Heart of the Mass,* 1940, Benziger; *The Heart
of the Rosary,* 1941, Catholic Literary Guild.

ETHEL COOK ELIOT

Writer of Novels and Children's Stories

MRS. ELIOT did not think of herself as a writer, or of writing as a profession she might think of qualifying for, until she was through high school and had an editorial job on *The Ladies' World,* a woman's magazine formerly published by McClure. Yet she had always written. She remembers no time after she started school when she wasn't avidly reading stories and perhaps even more eagerly writing them. By the time she reached high school she had filled many blankbooks with romances, fairy-stories, plays. Writing was just a way of having a good time. It came second only to playing Indians, or knights and ladies, in the wide playground of New England fields and woods that stretched right up to the house where she spent her childhood.

Landing an editorial job in New York after finishing high school is something that wouldn't happen so easily nowadays. That was in 1911 when there were fewer college women to compete with, and fewer young people with hearts set on getting to New York and into a publishing office.

The work for which the magazine editor hired young Ethel Cook consisted of cutting stories and articles to make them fit the magazine pages, and even sometimes padding them. She is appalled to remember how many authors already famous suffered by her shears and her pencil, while she struggled to fulfill her boss's orders. Another part of the job was to receive and talk with writers whom the editor didn't want to see. He seemed to want to see very few. Even when he had bought their stories or articles, and paid astonishing prices for them, the writers themselves were whenever possible eluded. But Ethel Cook loved it. It was these contacts with people who not only wrote, but sold what they wrote, that made her ask, Why didn't she?

When an editor begins to want to be an author—not only to write, for of course any editor worth his salt must like to write, but to sell his writings—he should either put the temptation firmly behind him, or quit his job. But that shouldn't mean starving in a garret while trying to write and sell, but finding another sort of job than editing—something that has nothing to do with literature—and writing on the side. A starving writer is no more likely to succeed than an editing one. Work that gives wide experience and contact with a great variety of people— preferably types of people hitherto but little known to him—is what a young author should live by, while making his first efforts to sell his scripts.

For Ethel Cook, however, romance and marriage came along, even while she was graduating out of *Ladies' World* hackwork and actually publishing, in *Story-Tellers' Magazine,* a series of original fairy-stories she had made up for a ten-year-old nephew. Housekeeping and the arrival of a daughter and a son pushed her writing very far "on the side," so that it was 1918 before her first book appeared. Like all her books, it came out under her married name, Ethel Cook Eliot. For five years she exploited the fairy world she had invented, in books called *The House on the Edge of Things, The Little House in the Fairy Wood, The House above the Trees,* and *The Wind Boy*—which made a deep impression on many people, both young and adult, and is still in print after nineteen years and still evokes enthusiastic letters from all sorts and kinds of people with a hunger for mystical experience.

Not long after writing *The Wind Boy,* with its strange, unwitting adumbrations of Christian truth, Mrs. Eliot became interested in Catholicism. And though she was received into the Church in 1925, she did not venture to put religion into her books until six years later. The make-believe of her imaginary world was no longer possible for her, but she filled the years from 1924 to 1931 with gay and exciting stories for girls of high school age: *The Vanishing Comrade, Fireweed, Waul & Dyke, Inc., Storey Manor, The Dryad and the Hired Boy,* and *The Gay Mystery.* Then, after the birth of a second daughter in 1930, she wrote her first novel, *Ariel Dances,* and followed it up with *Green Doors,* in which two of the principal characters are Catholic. The success of *Green Doors* and the recognition it received in the Catholic press, encouraged her to write a second even more Catholic novel. This book, *Her Soul to Keep,* aroused both enthusiasm and antagonism. It bewildered some non-Catholics and irritated others, and it seemed "rather strong" to many a Catholic reader of timid or conventional taste. It received a hearty commendation from Catholic publicists and lay critics, it became the subject of sermons from Protestant pulpits, and it influenced the thinking of many an open-minded reader. Somewhat less successful, probably because it was more subjective, psychological and mystical, was *Angels' Mirth* (1936), a poignant story of an adolescent girl, brought up with no religion, who comes into intimate contact with both Christian and neo-pagan *mores* and personalities.

Books from each of the three "periods" of Mrs. Eliot's authorship are still selling. Many of them have been published in England, and some have been translated, e.g., *Storey Manor* into Danish, and *Her Soul to Keep* into Italian. The continued sale of the early children's books, even the 1918 one, *The Little House in the Fairy Wood,* provides a steady income that sometimes makes their author wish she had not outgrown that pleasant field and embarked on the highly uncertain sea of novel-writing. But you can't write children's stories to order, nor just because you want to. Just because of the limitations on what you may use, you must be at infinite pains to keep the story sincere and true. The imagination must be dredged deep when you write for children. It is as grueling a form of art as writing poetry. Mrs. Eliot laughs when her friends ask her why she doesn't toss off something for children in between her novels, and not work so hard.

Writing for a Catholic audience is almost as difficult, however. One must try not to offend, while still maintaining one's artistic integrity and writing a novel of real life that non-Catholics, too, will find convincing and absorbing. A duty of the Catholic novelist is to awaken or stimulate the interest of non-Catholic readers, and present an undiluted, unsentimental, *whole* religion to people with no religion or only a vague, sentimental religiosity. If this is done in terms of life-as-it-is, without "miraculous" coincidences or rewards of piety, the Christian cause is better served than by unreal religiosity that Catholics will be the very first to resent. And non-Catholic publishers will accept such works on purely artistic grounds, and newspaper critics will review them on those grounds. It has been a particular pride of Mrs. Eliot that reviewers on leading papers, American and British, have treated her Catholic novels as works of art, not as special pleading. She wishes that young Catholic writers would aim at the big secular publishing houses and their great, heterogeneous public, and "preach the Gospel to the Gentiles" in rivalry with the un-Christian or anti-Christian best-sellers that these houses pour out. No good writer can conceal what lives at the core of his being, and an author who is thoroughly Catholic must perforce write in the Catholic spirit without disguise or compromise. Make a virtue of this necessity: write as your heart commands with all the skill and artistry your talent can acquire. Thus you will both inspire readers and please God.

Mrs. Eliot's novels include: *Angels' Mirth*, 1936, Sheed; *Ariel Dances*, 1931, Little; *Green Doors*, 1933, Little; and *Her Soul to Keep*, 1935, Macmillan; Doubleday issued these of her stories for young readers: *Gay Mystery, Storey Manor, Vanishing Comrad,* and *Wind Boy;* while Stokes published her *Little House in the Fairy Wood,* and *Little Black Coal.*

REVEREND GERALD ELLARD, S.J.

A Liturgist among the Authors

WALT DISNEY'S DUMBO, in a moment of super-exaltation, discovered himself equipped for flying, and so entered on a new and entertaining phase of his career: the Jesuit Father, Gerald Ellard, borne on the momentum of the Liturgical Movement, found himself suddenly ranked among the authors, and, to say the least, has vastly enjoyed the joke on the profession of the quill, the fountain-pen and the portable. He could no more tell you how he became an author than Dumbo could account for his being so high in the tree after the long line of pink elephants had faded from view. If there were some short reply that could serve in the embarrassing challenge as to how *he* entered the house of authorship, if he could say, for instance, "It was by osmosis," or "capillary-attraction," it would be easier to face both the writing and the reading public. As it is, he can but shuffle and say limply: "Well, he found himself wrestling with a vital idea, and did not hesitate to try any avenue, even the most hallowed, that would help to bring the idea before his fellow-men."

True, as a growing boy in Ironwood, Michigan, and particularly in all the literature courses of his high-school days at Regis in Denver, he always regarded authorship as a profession glowing in an aureola all its own. Never could he cease marvelling that words set down on paper weave themselves into soul-shaking messages in the form of biography or fiction, poetry or drama,—compositions that will live on and on as long as the world shall spin. Quite naturally, he thrilled to those stories in the manuals of how this author or that, in specific instances, produced great writing under dramatic circumstances; as when Newman wrote the deathless *Apologia* in six installments to meet a magazine's weekly deadline, while the room echoed his sobbing, and the pages glistened with the lustre of his tears. But this reverent enshrining of authorship seemed at the time only to put it all the more beyond any aspiring of his own. But, later on, he desperately wanted to put one idea before as wide a public as possible.

That dominant notion was the truth, pointed out recently by the Church, that the layman and laywoman, child, youth or adult, need not be just a spectator, but can be a player on the team; not one of the audience, but a member of the cast; not a passenger, but a rower at the oars, whenever Catholics meet in their churches for the performance of the age-old offices of worship. This idea, of course, grew on him little by little, but each increase in its apperception and appreciation made him feel the more that the notion was loaded, not with dynamite, but with dynamism very sorely needed as the old order crashes 'round us year by year.

That was the lodestar this Jesuit scholastic began to glimpse on the far horizons, as he began his theological studies in 1923. He then began to hear distant echoes of Europe's "Liturgical Movement," and long personally interested in reading about the ceremonial aspects of Catholic worship, he fancied that this "Liturgical Movement" must mean a widespread interest in this "storied pageantry" of the sanctuary. In 1925 certain students requested that they be given sermons on liturgical subjects, whereupon our scholastic sat him down and wrote his first

"Letter to the Editor" of *America*. To his measureless delight the letter was published, May 25, 1925. Should any general interest attach to the letter now, it might lie in the circumstance that this was perhaps the first public call for a liturgical movement in this country. For its writer, the letter has this interest: It records in the program it sketches how shallow an understanding of the role and scope of active lay participation in worship he then had! It had, however, two good effects: it put its writer in touch with a priest at O'Fallon, Missouri, (now) Monsignor Martin B. Hellriegel, who began Father Ellard's actual, firsthand initiation into the liturgical movement, and it brought him an invitation to collaborate on *Orate Fratres*, founded not long thereafter. This interest had grown to the extent that when the question of possible graduate studies after theology was raised, he at once suggested this field. "You can probably count on a year, on your return, in which to write of what you have learned," said his Superior in sending him abroad to study liturgy and the liturgical movement.

So began the Great Adventure! Studies begun at the University of Munich in 1928 culminated in a doctorate examination there in 1931. Two complementary lines of study had been followed: In class-rooms and libraries the monuments of early Christian worship had been examined; as an extra-curricular activity the newest modes of Catholic worship had been observed, discussed, appraised and recorded in note-books. On his return to the United States in 1931, with every turn of the propeller, so it seemed, there echoed the refrain: "You can probably count on a year in which to write of what you have learned." How best to set it out for his fellow-Americans?

First, there was a preliminary concern: Publication of the dissertation was a prerequisite to the granting of the doctorate degree. The Mediaeval Academy of America decided to sponsor the publication, and so it appeared, in the Academy's attractive style, as *Ordination Anointings in the Western Church Prior to 1000*, A.D., bearing the date of 1932.

There was thus another author in the world, but the world took no notice. The author himself took small notice of it then, for he was already immersed at all available moments in writing

"the book." This was to be the one setting out the basic idea
of the Liturgical Movement, that Catholic public worship is
that paid to God by the whole Church, or, in that phrase now
enjoying currency, by the Mystical Body of Christ, by the *Whole
Christ,* Head and members. It was the writer's conviction that
the greatest good of the greatest number over the longest time
would be served, if he could produce, on this theme, a really acceptable text-book for collegians. Writing began in October,
1932, and the completed manuscript was offered for the Religion
and Culture Series (Bruce) in April. The book appeared in late
September or October, 1933.

Perhaps it might be said that *Christian Life and Worship*
caused a mild sensation. Although offered as a text for students,
thanks to the enthusiastic and continued praise of the reviewers,
the book at once came to the notice and welcome of the general
public. From coast to coast, from week to week, the chorus of
approbation went on. Within a matter of weeks, the publisher
had decided to bring out a 'trade edition' for the general public.
The zenith of the boom was reached at year's end, and the
bounds of all verisimilitude passed, when a writer in *Commonweal* ranked it among the ten best works of the Catholic Literary
Revival available in the English language. (Quick, Watson, the
deflation-needle!) By spring the book was going into Braille, and
the American reviewers' chorus had given way to that from
England and the Continent, which was to be followed by the
press echoes from India and Australasia. The dynamism of its
idea, and the kindly support of the reviews, had carried the book
around the English-speaking world, and Dumbo among the
swifts and swallows, its writer was elected to membership in the
Gallery of Living Catholic Authors and the Institut Historique
et Heraldique de France.

Life perhaps holds for the writer no joys comparable with
those deriving from *Christian Life and Worship*. Tokens of
gratitude came from far and wide. "This book has given me a
glorious vision of what it means to be a Catholic," wrote a man
of influence, "and now I intend to do big things for Christ!"
He has done and continued to do such things. "I give this book
with success to baffled and dispirited Catholics, those in danger

of losing their Faith," wrote three Newman Club Directors on widely-separated campuses. "This is the type of book one gives gladly to a non-Catholic wife, or husband," wrote a reviewer. "I use this book with prospective converts, as the last step in their preparation for the Catholic way of life," wrote a priest years after. "I am an Anglican priest, and want to express my thanks for what this book has done for me." Among the tokens cherished most of all is the case of a man, who chanced upon the book as his daughter was studying it. Opening it at random, he found himself reading, for the first time in his life, the Rite of the Sacrament of Extreme Unction, and so moved was he by the calm faith and beautiful resignation of the prayers that he wrote out by hand that entire section. "Shortly afterwards," his daughter wrote, "Mamma died very suddenly, and Daddy kept reading over and over the prayers he had copied from my textbook."

Teachers in various parts of the country began sending the author the written reactions of students, as well as with their own reports on the book's use. These together with his own experience in using the book, convinced the author that it needed a revision badly. A thorough reworking of the whole was prepared in 1936, but very long delayed in appearance, arriving on the market only in 1939. The book ranked in 1940 as tied for third place in the list of college-adoptions in the United States.

If the reviewers "made" *Christian Life and Worship,* the absence of reviews might be one reason why *The Mystical Body and the American Bishops* has remained unknown. The little study-club manual, growing out of courses given in the Sodality Summer School of Catholic Action, was brought out, at the author's request, by *The Queen's Work* in 1939, and so fell outside the regular book-publication trade. It is a Cinderella-sister of the earlier work.

There was need, it seemed before long, of a handy manual on the origin and progress of the liturgical movement. The principles of Catholic corporate worship had been delineated as well as the author could do so, but the modern apostolate of the liturgy as manifesting itself in different countries and in our own,—

that was demanding systematic presentation and documentation. So the note-books were combed once more, and *Men at Work at Worship* came into being. Archbishop Murray of St. Paul wrote the Preface, Longmans published it, and both the Catholic Book Club and the Spiritual Book Associates made it their choice for the month of publication, May 1940. Addressed, so to speak, to "Mr. and Mrs. America," Catholic and non-Catholic alike, this book enjoyed in its turn a very good press, the most detailed appraisal being in a non-Catholic journal. One chapter of the work, suggesting the possibility of late afternoon and evening Mass, at first digested in the *Commonweal,* quickly passed into the Catholic press everywhere. Tokyo translated it into French and German for the use of the missionaries of the Orient. War conditions in many places have since brought in the afternoon and evening Mass then envisaged. Maynard's *The Story of American Catholicism* ranks this book as "the most popular treatment of the subject to appear in America."

Coincident with this sketch, the author's latest book, *The Dialog Mass,* issues from the Longmans press, with a gracious Preface by Archbishop Curley of Baltimore-Washington. This particular manifestation of the liturgical movement here receives the endorsement of His Excellency A. M. Cicognani, our Apostolic Delegate, as well as those of Their Eminences Cardinal Hinsley of Westminster and Cardinal MacRory of Armagh, and more than a score of American archbishops and bishops. It is too early yet to know how this latest comer will be welcomed.

Other books in various field of liturgy seem waiting to be written, and the social and corporate character of Catholic worship bids fair to be the unfinished business in what writing days may yet be given. A student recently wrote of Father Ellard: "He grins like a school boy." That smile is evoked by the hope of serving the generation now reaching manhood and womanhood.

Father Ellard's books include: *Christian Life and Worship,* 1933, revised and enlarged edition, 1940, Bruce; *Men at Work at Worship,* 1940, Longmans; *The Dialog Mass,* 1942, Longmans.

MARIE ST. S. ELLERKER

In Religion, Mother Mary of the Blessed Sacrament, O. Carm.

MARIE ST. S. ELLERKER, now Mother Mary of the Blessed Sacrament, Carmelite nun, and Mother General of the Corpus Christi Carmelites, is the writer of a short list of books, all done at odd moments in the midst of other duties. That may appeal to you, because many a person who would like to write is deterred from making a beginning for so many reasons centering round want of time. They have their living to earn or home duties to attend to, and have read that some distinguished author whom they admire devotes five or six hours a day to the composition of the books which have won their admiration. Mother General says she thought she had never had a clear hour for anything she has ever written. That's pretty encouraging, isn't it, for busy aspirants?

When the decree came out giving to tiny children the happiness of receiving Jesus in Holy Communion, Mother Mary of the Blessed Sacrament was a young teacher and a Dominican Tertiary, one of a small group doing educational and social work in England; for Mother is an English woman by birth, and an American citizen by choice.

It seemed to her that in the joy of this early First Communion there was a small danger of putting Holy Mass in the second place, and this led her to her first venture into the field of literature. She wanted to make people enthusiasts for the Mass. In 1912 there were only expensive religious books for children and Mother Mary of the Blessed Sacrament wanted a book which would be attractive in appearance, inexpensive in price, and written in a style which could be understood by children. This was the origin of *Behold the Lamb*. The writing of the book was a thrilling adventure bringing the writer into very intimate contact with the minds of children. Chapter by chapter it was read to a class, who proved to be extremely candid critics. They were invited to object to any word they did not like, or did not understand; and did so. They were given a choice of titles for chapters, of stories illustrating points, and of pictures. They also chose the title of the book.

The result was that when *Behold the Lamb* appeared in print it had already received its most exacting review, and a final approval from a group of those for whom it was intended. From the press it received nothing but praise. In his preface, Father Vincent McNabb says "The most childlike children are often quite old," and, as a matter of fact, the book has always been as popular with grown ups as with children.

It covers the meaning of the Holy Mass, God's lessons to His people in preparation for it, Our Lord's own lessons of preparation, and ends with its institution, Corpus Christi. There are nineteen chapters each ending with a story, and the book has five pictures.

The children even chose the colour for the cover—red by a big majority!

Simultaneously with *Behold the Lamb,* a second book was published, *A Wreath of Feasts,*—twelve of the great feasts of the liturgical year being chosen. The same technique was followed in the writing of this book; the same large type and short paragraphs being maintained. Yellow was the choice for its cover. The children voted "Flower of Babies was their King," the Christmas Feast, their favorite chapter.

The movement of lay retreats was making headway in England, and a book giving the life of a saint, which would appeal to boys in particular was called for. Mother Mary of the Blessed Sacrament responded with *The Story of Saint Dominic*, of which another writer, Mother St. Paul, wrote that she could not tell how many times she had read it to groups of retreatants and it had always met with an enthusiastic reception.

The review that has given Mother Mary the most pleasure was that of her next book *Master Where Dwellest Thou?* *The Dublin Review* gave very high praise to the book after saying that it was a departure from their usual custom to review books written for the young. This is a book which describes and gives the history of all that is found in the house where the Master dwells. It was meant to answer the "Why" which looms so largely in active minds, and it contains some very interesting illustrations of rare sacred vessels and other objects used in sacred worship.

Mother Mary of the Blessed Sacrament says the book she had most enjoyed writing was *God's Wonder Book*, her third dealing with the Holy Mass. The liturgical movement was getting under way. There were many scholarly tomes dealing with Mass and the Missal; but nothing she knew of to appeal to the ordinary busy person. She began a series of talks to some grown up girls, and also to some school children on the Missal. The result was *God's Wonder Book*. She aimed to get away from the idea of "another subject to study" and view in it the spirit of adventure; a treasure chest come into your possession from which you eagerly took out and examined one lovely gift after another.

Other books followed. *Mountains of Help* brought her more letters from those who had liked it or been helped by it than any other. It was intended to make interesting the approach to meditation.

A wish to spread devotion to Little Jesus was responsible for *God's Book of the Holy Child*.

The first book which she wrote as a Carmelite nun was *The Story of the Prophets,* dealing with those two grand and fascinating figures of the Old Testament, Elias (Elijah) and Eliseus (Elisha), who are vivid and alive in these pages.

A tiny book *When You Pray* came out to bring help and comfort to souls suffering from the terrible world war conditions. The large number of letters sent to its writer showed that it achieved its end.

In April, 1942, a booklet *For Your Safety* appeared intended primarily for service men, but not in any way limited to them.

From her book of press clippings one would gather that Mother Mary of the Blessed Sacrament has had a not too common experience. She had never had an unfavourable review. She does not write for a vague and impersonal public, but for readers who are her friends, in whom she is interested, whom she greatly cares to interest and to help. This living link is maintained by the monthly magazine published by the Carmelite sisters, *The Corpus Christi Chronicle,* which makes of her friends a close family circle.

Mother Mary of the Blessed Sacrament is at present living at Corpus Christi Carmel, Port of Spain, British West Indies, where the Sisters have two missions. The house of her Assistant and the American novitiate, is Corpus Christi Carmel, Kearney, Nebraska.

As to suggestions for the young reader aspiring to write Mother Mary advises: Live your book. Talk your book, write it, read it to others, publish it, and then enjoy the nice things the reviews will say about it. For if it is not worth while, it will have been annihilated in this process.

MABEL ADELAIDE FARNUM

Historical Novelist

ON HER FATHER'S SIDE, Mabel Adelaide Farnum is a member of an old American colonial family. One of her forebears was captain in the Continental forces at the Battle of Bunker Hill, another a member of the Boston Tea Party. Still another was a gunner on the Frigate *Constitution* and cited for heroic action in the conflict of those far-back days. Her father was a convert to the Church, having become interested in it through reading the works of Cardinal Newman.

From her maternal grandmother, who came from Ireland, Miss Farnum believes she inherited a taste for story-telling. For "Grandma" never failed to tell her one or more real "bed-time" stories when, as a child, she was tucked away for the night.

Miss Farnum wrote her first story when she was thirteen years old. It was pencilled in a blank book and kept hidden in a dark corner of the china closet in the family home, to be brought forth in secrecy, at intervals, to engage the attention of the young writer.

Miss Farnum's first published work appeared when she was fifteen. This was a serial story for boys, which ran continuously over a period of twenty weeks in *The Sunday Companion,* a magazine for Catholic children, published in New York. So enthusiastic were the editors, the teaching Sisters and priests over this story that the author was asked to contribute other stories to the paper. This she did, and for a period of several years her serials for boys and her short stories for boys and girls appeared faithfully in the pages of *The Sunday Companion.*

As a result, other magazines asked for Miss Farnum's work, among them the *Orphan's Messenger,* published by an Order of Sisters in New Jersey. Because of the finish of the stories and the maturity of thought they displayed, the Sisters believed their contributor to be much older than her actual years. When the young author accepted an invitation to visit them, and they saw at the convent door a slight girl, appearing much younger than her eighteen years, they at first could not realize that this was their "author," for whose reception they had prepared with loving anticipation. The young stranger from a small New England city was consoled with cake and milk and soon found herself at home in the atmosphere of a composing room.

The daughter of a talented musician and band leader, Miss Farnum began the study of piano at an early age, continuing it during her school days and afterward. Her professor was insistent that she go to Europe to pursue a musical career. However, the story work began to exercise a stronger appeal than ever, and his suggestion was not followed.

During her High School course Miss Farnum wrote steadily, so that at the close of the four years she had to her credit about seventy short stories and serials, with numerous articles and poems which appeared in the standard Catholic magazines. Her French teacher, a non-Catholic, became so deeply interested in these Catholic stories, etc., that she would never chide her favorite pupil for scribbling on the inside cover of her note book instead of attending to the French lesson. At graduation the young author won the literary prize in the annual essay contest of the school for the entire four years, the writer's identity being unknown to the judges; also the coveted role of essayist of the Senior Class and Class Odist. At this time she was studying music and giving lessons in her spare hours to ten children.

Of several serials published in *The Pilot,* Boston, during the early years of High School, Miss Farnum had the happiness of seeing one appear in book form. This volume was followed by two others within a short period. Both these latter books treated of the conditions of the working classes. Written in story form, they depicted these conditions as the author found them in her research work, made in the principal mill cities of Massachusetts.

Miss Farnum's sonnet, "Mary's Lament," won a place of honor in a contest sponsored by *The Queen's Work,* then a story magazine. Shortly afterward, she won first place in a national short story contest conducted by the same magazine. This story was selected out of some 3000 manuscripts, submitted by authors all over the United States. The judges were Kathleen Norris, famous novelist, and two prominent newspaper men. Several years later, our author again won first place in a national short story contest this time sponsored by *Extension Magazine.*

Still studying piano, Miss Farnum worked for a year and a half on a daily newspaper, as society editor and feaure writer. Two more books appeared at this period, one at its beginning and the other at its close. Later books, lives of two Roman Pontiffs in story form, appeared shortly afterward.

In 1938 Miss Farnum's dramatic history of the life and work of Saint Francis Xavier appeared. This book, *A Carrack Sailed Away,* marked the advent of the author into the field of Catholic research. It was followed, in 1940, by *Street of the Half-Moon,* an account of the Spanish noble, Pedro Claver. To gather data for the latter book, its author traveled to the old Colombian city of Cartagena, in South America where St. Peter Claver lived and worked forty years for the Negro slaves. A phase of this work which greatly pleased Miss Farnum was the fact that, on the voyage non-Catholics as well as Catholics, who were familiar with Colombia furnished her with many valuable details which she later incorporated into the book.

The latest literary work of our author is *The Seven Golden Cities, Fray Marcos and the Coronado Adventure,* a novelized

history of the journey of a Franciscan friar from Old Mexico to
our Southwest in search of cities which were reported to be very
rich and populous. Fray Marcos was the herald and pioneer,
commissioned to find out the facts about these cities so that the
Spanish Crown could send an army to take possession of them,
and also missionaries to convert the Indians of that country.
The dream was rudely shattered, for the cities proved only to be
poor and unpromising mud villages, inhabited by a hostile pagan
tribe.

Miss Farnum is deeply interested in bringing to light facts
either not known to the majority of readers, or forgotten, concerning great heroes of the Faith, whose sacrifices and labors are
an inspiration to everyone to at least imitate their noble spirit if
they cannot attempt such feats for God and country. She believes that no effort is too great to insure the success of this research, and that authors should, when possible, visit the scenes
where their stories are laid in order to get as close as possible to
their heroes and heroines. Also, she finds it exceedingly useful
to have at least some knowledge of the language of the foreign
countries of which an author may write. For *A Carrack Sailed
Away*, which treats of the Portuguese domination of the east
when Xavier journeyed there and of his dealings with the Portuguese sovereigns and their subjects, she made use of Portuguese
linguaphone records and text books, in order to be able to employ
simple sentences in the book, where expedient, and to gain more
of the atmosphere of the people of that country and its colonies.
For *Street of the Half-Moon* and *The Seven Golden Cities*,
Spanish records and text books were employed.

While her principal interest at present is recalling to life,
through the medium of dramatic biography or history, great
characters of the Church whose work extends to our day, such as
the apostolate to the Negroes and that to the Indians, Miss
Farnum takes time out to keep up with the children's work, especially writing for boys. At the present time a boys' book from
her pen, which ran in serial form some time ago, is soon to come
from the press.

Our author finds the study of words a fascinating pursuit. She believes that every writer should have a comprehensive vocabulary, yet in writing should make use of words that are readily understood by all readers. To aspiring young writers she would say that reading the best literature, possibly memorizing a good deal of it when time allows, is a great aid to inspiring thought and creative genius.

First and foremost, however, she thinks that Catholic writers should strive to exercise a real apostolate among all classes, including those not of the Faith. Many of the letters which she cherishes most in relation to her books, have come from non-Catholics who told of their admiration of the noble ideals of the Catholic Faith as expressed through the medium of her work.

Miss Farnum has spent several weeks of each of the past three years, doing research work in New Mexico, which is in part the locale of *The Seven Golden Cities,* and wholly that of the book on which she is at present working, a dramatic history of the pioneering days in that land where the Catholic Faith was implanted so strongly by the Spaniards upon their coming there more than three centuries ago.

Miss Farnum's later works include: *A Carrack Sailed Away,* 1938, The Society for the Propagation of the Faith, Boston; *The Street of the Half-Moon,* 1940, Bruce; *The White Knight* (a life of Pope Pius XI, for children), Catholic Library Service.

REVEREND GERALD M. C. FITZGERALD, C.S.C.

"Father Page"

As seen through a brother's eyes, by Brassil Fitzgerald

THEY CAME trooping along a country road, small boys homeward-bound from school. It took a long time to get home from school, for this was September. In the windy sunshine was a smell of wood smoke and ripening apples.

They found the apples. They were yellow, and cool and sweet to the teeth. Contently awhile then, they sat on a stone-wall, idly kicking the milkpods and the goldenrod, talking of life, what they would do when they were men. One urchin would be an explorer; and another a sailor; one a railroad engineer; and one a baseball pitcher. No one of them planned to be a poet.

There was one small lad; he had blue eyes, a wide grin, and the loudest voice. He was going to be a colonel, he announced. A roughrider like Teddy Roosevelt. "I got to be the soldier," he explained more sincerely than modestly, "cause I'm the best fighter. I can lick anyone in the sixth grade."

There was a moment of silent thought. Then the brown-haired lad with sagging stockings stepped into the road, and drew a mark with his toe in the brown dust. His grin was gay and defiant. "Step up to the line," he said. They fought all the way home, those two bad boys. The next morning at eight-fifteen, they went off to school, friends again. They would both, they agreed, be soldiers, both colonels. A small boy is a mysterious being. Neither he nor his elders can know what he will do with the years, what the years will do with him.

That lad with the brown hair, who drew the mark in the road dust, was Ralph Talbot. That same country road is now Ralph Talbot Street; and there is a United States warship named *The Talbot*. For Ralph, in the air over France, won the Congressional Medal of Honor, and died in glory.

That boy who fought Ralph, the loud-voiced fierce little fellow, his name was Gerald Fitzgerald. He was to be a soldier, too, but a soldier of Peace, and a writer of poems. So now he would say to every boy and girl, "Make your plans boldly. Dream bravely your dreams. But be certain only of this: God has work for you to do. When the time comes, He will tell you. Obey Him then, and you will find happiness."

Father Fitzgerald, from the day he obeyed, and entered St. John's Seminary at Brighton, Massachusetts, has been a happy man. That, he thinks, is what has made him a poet, just being happy, and seeking to share that happiness.

He did not plan his books. They grew out of his daily living. His *Letters of Father Page,* published in 1940 by Longmans, came to be thus: A busy priest, at first as curate in the parish of Our Lady of the Presentation at Brighton, Massachusetts, later as a priest of the Congregation of the Holy Cross, he had more friends than time for friends. He spoke with them in letters. In such letters, he sought to share with those in need his own daily happiness in Christ. Here is one of these messages, typical of many:

Dear——:

In your last letter you wrote me of your conviction that you had no vocation. Very well; but please remember this: much as I love to see a soul give itself to God in the oblation of the religious life, yet never have I failed to recognize that though everyone has a vocation, not everyone's vocation is to the religious life. Besides, I love my own vocation too deeply to desire any recruits save volunteers; volunteers who come of their own free will because of love to serve the God of Love. Our Lord, Himself, has made His consecrated service a matter of invitation. "If you will be perfect," He says to those who stand at the cross roads. If you do not feel drawn thereto by love, then by all means do not go forward. We need priests, yes, but only real priests who will be concerned about the interests of Jesus, first, last and always.

However, please do not say you have no vocation. Everybody has a vocation, every soul that comes into this world has a vocation, and all vocations are essentially one—to know, to love, and to serve God. Everybody's vocation is the loving service of God.

A Catholic editor, Myles Connolly of *Columbia,* saw one of these letters, and with the author's permission, published it in *Columbia.* The editor was pleased, and the author amazed, at the response it drew.

Father Fitzgerald learned then that many who write are needlessly concerned about the size of "their public," straining to shape their work to please a million readers. He believes that the best approach to writing is to have something worth expressing, then to express it as one would to one dear friend. If that dear friend be pleased or comforted, many others will be. Because in deepest reality we are brothers and sisters, all of us; if a writer touch one human heart, he touches many. One's public is just one friend, multiplied.

That letter which appeared in *Columbia* was the first of many. In time they became a book, *The Letters of the Late Father Page.*

"But why Father Page?," readers ask. Father Fitzgerald has been known to smile at that question, and speak of other things. But he'll tell you now.

When he was a young seminarian, he liked to think of himself as a page in the Court of our Queen Mother. Pages, as you know, are not important at courts. They come last; they stand in the background. But they are always there to do their Queen's bidding. So he prayed to do his Queen's bidding, to be a page, as it were, for our Lady Mother. The years have made that young seminarian, a priest with greying hair, a teacher in the Seminary of Our Lady of Holy Cross, North Easton, Massachusetts. Yet the years have not changed that ambition. He still prays to be always a page, an errand boy for the Blessed Virgin.

Thus, when there was a question of publishing his letters, he chose a pen-name that would have for him a secret and happy significance, "A. Page."

> "Before Life's throne he stands a page
> Holding with reverence
> His tiny flame of light
> To mark with joy
> The Presence of The King."

Father Fitzgerald's verse, too, had a similar genesis. Almost without exception his early poems were written, not for print, but to share with some friend, an hour of sorrow or a moment of joy. He liked to think of them as little notes he carried for his Royalty, for Christ the King, and Mary. Here is one such note, from *Streets in Nazareth,* published by Kenedy, in 1940.

TO AN EX-SACRISTAN

> Tenderly, wistfully you touch
> for the last time, the altar lace,
> the missal stand, the book,
> and take a last deliberate look
> at this little world
> in which you reigned
> supreme:
> And now
> when you have all these dear things left
> and kneel resigned
> at the grill invisible
> obedience has raised,
> Behold—
> The White Dove
> comes—
> The Sacristan
> of Love
> within your soul.

Father Fitzgerald, as a writer, seeks no unfading laurels. In "Paths from Bethlehem," he has judged himself.

> Mine is no flashing soldier-blade
> Drawn in the fore of the cavalcade;
> Mine is no rapier graceful and keen

To quicken the heart of a sovereign queen;
Mine is only a rimester's art,
Mine is only a minor part
In the ageless singing of faith and love,
In the timeless chorus that thrills above
The boom of guns and the cry of pain:
Yet I know one who will not disdain
The simplest thought from a love-dipt pen,—
You, sweet Mother of God and men.

He thinks, for a poet, but one thing is important; that he be constantly aware of beauty, and of its source; saying always, "Thank you, Father." There are so many beautiful things. And their meaning is one. The beauty of dawn sky, of birds in flight, of summer rains, and grass-blown shadows. The beauty of people, of an aged face at peace, of a father's work-worn hand that holds a small one. There is the beauty daily born on our altars, The Mystical Rose. To the Catholic poet, beauty is never mere color, nor sound, nor form. All things beautiful are but outward signs, but the trailing robes of our God Invisible.

Father Fitzgerald is the author of: *Paths from Bethlehem* (verse), 1938, Magnificat Press; *Juxta Crucem* (a life of Father Moreau, C.S.C., the founder of the Congregation of the Holy Cross), 1938, Kenedy; *Letters of Father Page*, 1940, Longmans Green & Co.; *Streets in Nazareth* (verse), 1940, Kenedy; *God's Rainbow*, 1939, Salve Regina; *The Holy Face in the Way of the Cross*, 1940, St. Columbans.

(ROBERT) BRASSIL
FITZGERALD

A "Father Page" Letter

MY DEAR MR. ROMIG:

You ask me to write of my brother Brassil. This will be a deep pleasure but, like most of our finer joys, involves for me the pain of inadequacy. My love for my brother and my appreciation of his character and literary gifts are too sacred for full revelation, even were I capable of that revelation. We inherit from our dear mother a reticence in our expression of affection which cannot be entirely sacrificed, even in the blessed cause of literary biography.

Brassil, Robert Brassil, is the nearest to me by birth of the seven brothers God has enriched my life with. One went on ahead into eternity in the interests of us all; I came next; then Brassil.

It would be appealing to be able to chronicle a great boyhood love between myself and the curly black-haired boy who grew up beside me. But unfortunately in the interests of truth, I must admit more scraps and differences than otherwise; and our loyalty was carefully reserved for those rare occasions when the world court of boyhood requires brother to stand up for brother. With Brassil, as with all my brothers, it has been the maturer years with their mingled joys and griefs, failures and successes that have drawn us closer to each other and tempered the steel of our brotherly oneness. In that mysterious sphere where the natural and the supernatural so intimately intermingle, this growing fraternal affection has been one of the most consoling of God's gifts. But let us return to Brassil.

Graduated from Weymouth High School in 1912, Brassil entered Boston College where his attractive personality won him the affection of his classmates (he was President of his class in Sophomore year), and perhaps saved him at times from the unsheathed edge of scholastic discipline. Everyone loved Bob and his ability to write was coming to notice. Then Villa broke loose south of the Border and the "Old Ninth" Regiment of the Massachusetts State Militia rolled down to the Rio Grande: Robert was present. The curtain was rising on World War, Number One.

But before we said our quiet good bye to Brassil, bound overseas in the 101st Infantry Regiment of the Yankee Division, he had quietly anchored his heart in what has proven the happiest of his ventures: his marriage to Mildred Ridlon of Hingham, Massachusetts.

The Armistice brought Brassil home to us, but eighteen months of active military service in France had exacted their toll. Brassil's health was undermined. Some day I hope he will sketch the story of that battle waged quietly and grimly on a battle line that ran from the old homestead in South Weymouth, Massachusetts, and the pines of New Hampshire to the sun-drenched desert of New Mexico. Thanks to God, and under God, to his wife and his little daughter, Betty, and the generosity of a grateful U. S. A. Brassil won,—perhaps I should say, we won.

Brassil's improved health made possible the completion of his college work, first at the University of Arizona, then a Master's degree at Stanford. The stage was set for his double career, so frequently the lot of writers, that of teaching and writing. Always with the handicap of limited physical power, Brassil's brilliant conceptions, penetrating analysis and rich sympathetic nature have brought him hard won recognition. First, at the University of Utah, then seven years at the University of Montana, Brassil taught English with enthusiastic penetration that was contagious. The short story was his special field, his own work appearing concomitantly in the national magazines both under his own name and that of Philip Burke, a pen name he used more especially in his frequent excursions into the highly controversial field of the educational essay.

From Montana with his ever faithful wife and daughter, now grown into brilliant womanhood, Brassil came back East to us and has given since then more and more of his time to writing.

These have been crowded years and in their passing Brassil has found time, besides his own professional writing, for the giving of two series of lectures on Short Story Writing for the Division of University Extension, Massachusetts Department of Education, occasional lectures to Catholic literary groups and a yearly series of lectures in the field of English biographical literature that has proven highly stimulating to the seminarians here at Our Lady of Holy Cross.

What are Brassil's special gifts as a writer? The same gifts that make me proud to own him as my brother: a living, rich sympathy with suffering humanity which, under God, he owes to his dad; a quiet pervading sense of humor to which his Irish blood entitled him; a sense of justice his mother gave him; and his quiet unostentatious faith, and for that we must all thank the Holy Spirit and Our Lady Mother, I am sure.

Cordially yours,

Father Page

(Rev. Gerald M. C. Fitzgerald, C.S.C.)

P.S. Brassil's book, *Democracy in Action,* is scheduled by Ginn & Co., for publication in January, 1943.

ELLA MARY ELIZABETH FLICK

Biographer

I ONCE BELIEVED THAT a Who's Who reference book, like the proverbial leopard, could not change its spots. Secretly, I likened such volumes to cook books in which the fanciest recipes called for but two popular ingredients,—hash and baloney, with a "date" here and there. In late years, intermarriage of these staid statistical puritans with Fairy Tale, Joke Book and True Story belles has brought forth some very giddy but very fascinating off-spring. So alluringly are we written up in these modern miracle workers that I find myself sneaking off to a book mart, where furtively I turn the pages to my own name, and peacock-proud ask myself "Can this be I!"

This account is supposed to be a sort of literary general confession in which the author "tells all." Only once before in my life did I attempt to relate my sins in public. The occasion was a religious upheaval along the beach front in Atlantic City and I was about ten years old. After listening to several men and women unburden themselves of their past life, I imagined it might be fun to tell something too. I scarcely got started. My big brother appearing upon the scene, in unison with the leader in charge, made me desist; in fact, invited me to go home. My first good story was thus choked off at birth.

Mrs. Gossip (or should it be Miss?) whispers that most Catholic writers are unhappy creatures until they are fifty years old, when automatically they become resigned to their fate. I am quite content with myself right now; which settles the how-old-is-she question, should anybody be interested. But there *is* some truth in the Mrs. Gossip story. Youth, alas!, recognizes only one reward for achievement—money. Being a writer always means being sensitive. Being a Catholic writer sometimes means being poor. Through impatience for advancement, the talented Catholic would-be writer oftentimes becomes a good shoemaker or a first-class seamstress long before the ripe age of fifty. It is only after success arrives that any writer looking back realizes how little money, or the lack of it, had to do with the happiness of achievement.

The process of putting together the story of how I became a writer is easy in my case, because my father was largely responsible for my downfall. He was a writer too. His keen eyes saw my inclinations, though I openly disowned them. His God-given patience coaxed and coddled my poor sickly little talent, and his generous pocket paid for my first robust brain children, —six historical sketches for *The American Catholic Historical Society Records.* He paid me twenty-five dollars apiece for those sketches; but I earned it. If anybody thinks doing research work under my father easy money, such a person did not know my father.

The three books listed under my name, *Chaplain Duffy, Bishop McDevitt,* and the little biography of my father, *Dr. Flick,* represent only the last ten years of my life. They came with success. All three books were written as request numbers. My special work, biographical sketches, pursued me like the avenging hand of fate, tracking me down no matter how fast I ran from it. In the twenty years before it caught up with me, however, I tried out love stories, one serial novel, some odd

hundred essays for Catholic magazines and as many unsigned
pieces for works of reference.

Each of my three books has a story attached:

Chaplain Duffy I was asked to write by Archbishop Mitty, a
great admirer and former pupil of the beloved World War hero
priest. As a child on vacation in Chelsea, Atlantic City, I early
became enamoured of Father Duffy, who did summer parochial
duty at Our Lady Star of the Sea. Just before Father Duffy died,
Archbishop Mitty wrote me: "I hope you will not forget to
someday write something about our mutual friend." I had
scarcely turned the idea over in my mind when Father Duffy
passed on to a better world, and the planned sketch turned, as
if by magic, into a full-sized book.

Bishop McDevitt was suggested to me by my publisher, who
himself had been requested to write the book by an archbishop
admirer of the Bishop of Harrisburg at the latter's funeral. To
me it was a congenial piece of work because Bishop McDevitt
and my father had been life-long friends. One became a priest
and the other a doctor in the same year, and for a period of fifty
years they lived almost like brothers, sharing the same literary
and historical interests. They died just three years apart, the
Bishop leaving behind him the promising beginnings of a life of
Dr. Flick.

The little *Life of Dr. Flick* (a booklet rather than a book)
was paid for and published by the White Haven Sanatorium Association as a souvenir of its founder. Someday, I hope to make
the little *Life* into a complete biography.

Writing to me has always had to be something I set my heart
upon so far as subjects go. In fact, if I want badly enough to
write a certain article or book, it makes little difference to me
who pays for it or if I get paid for it at all. The writing of it
brings its own reward.

I believe I specialized in biographical writing chiefly because
I have always been interested in character delineation. The
doings of men and women in various walks of life fascinate me.
I have always wanted to know why people did certain things,

and what happened after they did them. I have always loved, not only the humble beginnings of life, but the romantic (or tragic) endings and the aftermath. If I could peek into eternity and see how my subject was "taking it," it would suit me precisely.

The style of writing I like best to do was done for *America* and the *Catholic World* in light essay form. I am told this was my best work, and many times I have been asked to put these little essays into book form. Much of the data for these sketches was gathered in travel in England, Ireland and France, during the summer of 1924. "Brother St. Patrick," "Canon Sheehan's Garden," "Croagh Patrick," and "Lough Derg," were but a few of the titles. All of these pieces were truthful recitals—excepting "Lough Derg." With nearly twenty years behind me, it is safe to confess that my stay at Lough Derg lasted only until I gleaned the startling information that a lady was required to dispense with her shoes and stockings and walk barefooted during her sojourn on that interesting penance island. I left hastily with the return boat, and wrote my article in my very uncomfortable hotel boudoir in bed to keep warm.

It is difficult to say what leads up to the desire to write. As a family, my two sisters, four brothers and myself were brought up in a bookish atmosphere, which greatly tended towards literary endeavor. My parents were of the generation that fondly imagined a large family sufficient unto each other. When sisterly and brotherly affection waned, we were unceremoniously turned loose into the library to pick us a book companion, thus avoiding conflict with the commandment Thou Shalt Not Kill. By the time I was eleven years old I had read everything in my father's library, including guide books and cook books. I read my father's medical books with the boy who later became a doctor, and poetry with the future editor lad. When I first went to school (which hateful business was neglected in favor of tutors until I was ten), I think the Sisters were slightly surprised that I knew much of Goethe and Swinburne by heart. I read all the forbidden books on all the shelves, before I ever learned they were forbidden me.

Personally, I feel that a big family is a real education to a would-be-writer lady. Anytime in future years the earnest young author thing is looking for fight atmosphere, love situations, deep sorrow or tragedy, she needs only close her eyes and live again some special day in the long ago when life was real and life was earnest and imagination walked with her step by step.

Luckily for me, my own father and mother were very great personages in my eyes. As physician, scientist, historian and writer, my father thrilled me even in childhood. My mother, a convert to the Catholic religion, and one who gave up much in family ties to embrace the Faith, was equally thrilling. A descendant of one Lord Ellis of Wales and the Stones of England, her ancestral record reads like romance. Alas, she never allowed anyone to mention her family history during her lifetime. When fighting mad at each other, my brothers sometimes called each other Lord Ellis, but it was not a term of endearment.

Although as simple as a child in her beliefs, the various pietistic techniques of religion never became entirely familiar gestures to my mother. One of my earliest memories of her is the occasion of a visit of the newly consecrated Bishop of Cleveland, who stopped off in Philadelphia to bless her, her husband and her children. As Father Horstmann, pastor of Old St. Mary's, he had, but a few years before, received my mother into the Church. Upon this memorable visit, this modest gentleman who mostly kept his ringed hand behind his back, conspicuously held out his episcopal ring to her. "Kiss it, you little heathen!" he said in his fond way, laughing at her discomfiture.

Inspiration from persons and events has much to do with choosing biographical writing as a career. At least it had with me. Great folks walked through my home from my babyhood. Upon the pages of my memory book are to be found interesting men and women from all lands, who came calling on my father. Sitting quietly, listening to the brilliant conversations heard round our dinner table, oftentimes in childhood I said to myself "This is just like a book!" Bishop McDevitt brought us candy; Father Ganns, the priest musician, played the piano while

awaiting my father's return from his office; and Father (now
Monsignor) Henry, week by week, recited the whole of *Alice in
Wonderland,* making it so real that when, in grown up years, I
read the book for myself, the story seemed to have lost all color.
From the distance of the years, the great ones who filled my
father's little study loom so gigantically that it makes me feel
humble even to write about them.

The Dolphin Press issued Miss Flick's *Chaplain Duffy,* in 1934, and Dorrance
published her *Life of Bishop McDevitt,* in 1940.

REVEREND PAUL HANLY FURFEY

Sociologist

NEVER SHALL I FORGET my first published piece, a story which appeared in our paper at Boston College. I was a sophomore then, and for years I had been yearning to write for publication; but it seemed a hopeless ambition. Once my high-school English teacher had criticized a composition of mine in class and had announced publicly that I could never become a writer. I took this offhand judgment very seriously. I secretly envied my classmates who appeared in print in the school paper. To me it seemed hopeless even to try. I couldn't face the humiliation of submitting a story and having it rejected. Never would I become a writer! Others had some secret gift, some marvelous inborn ability, which I lacked. Still, my hopeless ambition made me feel unhappy.

Sophomore year in college changed all that. The faculty advisor of our Boston college paper happened to be our English teacher. Without saying anything to me, he took one of my regular weekly compositions and published it! As I look back now, I realize that the story which he published was incredibly bad. The poor man must have been desperate for copy! But at last I saw myself in print. I gained confidence and when I submitted further articles they were accepted. In spite of myself, I had learned that I could write.

Gradually an important truth dawned on me. The ability to write is not a rare gift, reserved for occasional geniuses. Anyone can learn to write—anyone, that is, with normal intelligence and enough ambition to train himself. Writing is not a gift of the gods. It is a trade, like carpentry or tailoring or automobile repairing. To learn to be a good workman, you have to undergo a hard, tiresome period of intensive training. I began to serve my apprenticeship.

First of all, I learned that it is hopeless to try to write unless one has something to say. That sounds pretty obvious; but it isn't. Many people make the mistake of writing precisely because they wish to appear in print. Such an attitude represents a wrong emphasis. The deepest motive which drives a man to write must always be his desire to put before the reading public something which he feels intensely, something so vital to him that it almost seems a crime to let it remain unsaid. Does this difference of emphasis seem like a subtle distinction? I learned by experience that it is not. After all, the people who make up the reading public don't care particularly whether you fulfill your ambition of becoming a writer or not. But if you have something worth saying, they want to hear it. And remember, if there is something that seems vital and interesting to you personally, it will probably interest the reading public as well.

Every apprentice must learn to use his tools. A writer's tool is language. So during my apprenticeship I began to learn slowly a few of the rich possibilities of the English language. When I read a paragraph which impressed me, I asked myself how the writer had obtained his effect. Then I used to reread it two or three times and generally I could discover the special device which he had employed. It isn't particularly hard to do. But if you can make an analysis a habit, you will gradually build up a repertory of techniques. Then when you are in the midst of an article and are struggling to put across an idea, one of these tricks pops automatically into your mind and you suddenly find that you have written an effective paragraph.

During my apprenticeship I succeeded in unlearning a lot of mistaken ideas which I had picked up in English classes. Above all, I learned to forget about style. When a young writer has ceased to worry about style, he is beginning to make progress. Style is not something you consciously set out to learn. Style is something which just happens to you. Some students cram themselves with a lot of artificial rules and think that if they follow them mechanically, they will acquire a good style. That is stuff and nonsense. The thing to do is to forget the rules and say what you want to say in the clearest and most forceful way you possibly can. When you succeed in doing that, you have already acquired a style.

Before I had finished college in 1917, I had published my first paid article in a general magazine. That taught me something else. There is a vast difference between writing for your high school or college paper and writing for the general periodical press. It is precisely the difference between amateur and professional work in any line of endeavor. A man who is handy with tools may succeed in building a pretty good back porch on his home if he has enough patience. But a trained carpenter will probably do a better job in half the time. So too, many a good article appears in college magazines; but put one of them beside the job of a professional writer and you will note the difference.

Perhaps the biggest difference between amateur and professional writing can be summed up in the word *system*. The amateur writes now and then as the spirit moves him, while the professional has disciplined himself. The professional is a trained workman. He knows his tools. He knows how to go about a task systematically. He may not always be at his best, but he can always turn out a workmanlike job.

One thing the professional writer must learn is to work with editors. A conventional jest represents editors as hard-hearted individuals who take delight in dashing the hopes of aspiring writers. Nothing could be further from the truth. Every editor enjoys the thrill of discovering a promising new writer. Whenever he can discover one such, it gives him prestige among his fellow editors. But an editor's big job is to know what his public wants. No matter how intrinsically good an article may be, if it is not suited to his particular public, an editor has no choice but to reject it. Amateur writers often fail to realize this. When an editor returns a manuscript with the comment that it is good but he can't use it, such writers often feel that he is not being quite frank. Professionals know better. They know that editors are expert judges of the public demand. They try to work *with* editors instead of *against* them. To the professional, a good editor is an invaluable friend and guide.

Another thing that professionals learn is the necessity of hard work. When I say hard, I mean *hard*. It is twenty-seven years now since I first appeared in print and in all that time I have never acquired any facility. I mean, I have never learned to write without an enormous amount of hard work. Better writers than myself with whom I have compared notes have told me that they have had the same experience. Just last week I completed a long book. For the fun of it I kept track of my time. I found that on the average it took between four and five hours to write each double-spaced typewritten page. Perhaps that was slow going. It was a rather technical book and required special care. But writers agree that a man who turns out a thousand words a day, about three typewritten pages is writing pretty rapidly. At that rate he could turn out a couple of average-sized books a year and a good many articles to boot. How many professional writers do that? Newspaper men may do even more; but admittedly they have to sacrifice quality for speed. A thousand words a day is about the maximum for the man who wants to maintain his best standard.

In 1926 I published my first book, *The Gang Age,* a study of the preadolescent boy and his recreational needs. I never would have had the courage to write it except that it happened to be my doctoral dissertation at the Catholic University of America. I had to write a dissertation anyway to get my Ph.D. degree, so I thought it would be no harm to send the manuscript to a publisher. In fact, I sent two manuscripts of the same book to two publishers and to my great embarrassment, they both accepted it! Perhaps it wasn't very ethical to do that; but it had seemed to me that there was only the slimmest possible chance that either would accept. As it was, I had to make an open confession to one of them and withdraw my manuscript. Fortunately, he was very kind about it, much kinder than I deserved.

When I first saw my name neatly lettered on the back of a book, I felt that I had at last learned my trade. That was a mistake. Really no one ever learns the writer's craft thoroughly. No matter how much you write, there always remains infinitely more to be learned. Indeed, that is one of the fascinating features of authorship. Authorship is the constant pursuit of an unattainable ideal. You feel certain things strongly. You know you must express them. You burn to express them in all their clarity, with all the overwhelming force with which you yourself feel them. And so you sweat and toil and use every ounce of ingenuity you can command to put yourself on paper. But the result always somehow falls short of your ideal. It is enough if you do your best. Perhaps some sympathetic readers will guess that inexpressible something which you cannot quite put on paper. And perhaps you will succeed better next time. Anyway, this quest to express the inexpressible is a fascinating quest.

Since 1925 (save for a year's leave of absence spent at the Universities of Berlin and Frankfort, in Germany, in 1931–1932), I have been teaching sociology at the Catholic University of America, becoming head of the department in 1940. This has furnished an ample opportunity to write. For, making due allowance for my professional prejudice, I still claim that sociology is a fascinating subject. It makes one understand the society in which one lives. It brings one face to face with social problems. When the sociologist realizes the sufferings of the poor, imposed on them by an unjust economic system, when he learns how the Negro is deprived of the elemental rights which democracy and Christianity should guarantee him, when he studies the other forms of social injustice which disfigure the American scene, then, if he has any idealism at all, he wants to do something about these problems. Something can be done through classroom teaching. Something can be done through public speaking. But a wider and more permanent audience can be reached through writing.

That is why I have never regretted the toil and hardships and disappointments which learning to write involved. Writing has always been, will always be, the hardest of hard work. Every production must be paid for by long and painful travail. But when the manuscript is finished, there is always a deep sense of satisfaction. No one realizes better than the conscientious author the defects of his work. Always something remains in his mind which he has struggled unsuccessfully to express. But if he has worked hard and done his best to produce a workmanlike job, then he experiences a satisfying sense of accomplishment. Somehow he has reproduced his intellectual self. He has experienced the exaltation of a creative task. He has contributed something, however small, to the literature of the race. That is reward enough for any man.

Father Furfey numbers among his books the following: *Fire on the Earth*, 1936, Macmillan; *Gang Age*, 1926, Macmillan; *The Growing Boy*, 1930, Macmillan; *New Lights on Pastoral Problems*, 1931, Bruce; *Parish and Play*, 1928, Dolphin Press; *Social Problems of Childhood*, 1929, Macmillan; *This Way to Heaven*, 1939, Preservation Press; *Three Theories of Society*, 1937, Macmillan; *You and Your Children*, 1929, Benziger.

REVEREND GILBERT J. GARRAGHAN, S.J.

Historian

FATHER GARRAGHAN's earliest recollection of a printed book is that of Washington Irving's *Conquest of Granada,* which he chanced upon one day at his grandmother's home. The book was symptomatic of the particular study he was to be drawn to in after years. At college (St. Ignatius, Chicago, 1882–1889) he served, however unknowingly, an apprenticeship to Clio. In his graduating year occurred the centennial (April 30, 1889) of the inauguration of George Washington to the presidency. Students everywhere were set writing papers and delivering orations to commemorate the historic occasion. In a prize essay young Garraghan started off with a quotation from Emerson, "This is an age of retrospection," and then proceeded to sketch out the hundred years of American achievement that lay behind. Already his look was turned towards the stories past. The prize essay appeared in the local Catholic paper, the first product of his pen to arrive at the dignity of print.

Father Garraghan is Chicago-born (1871), as his mother had been before him (1843). His interest in the stirring past of the

dynamic metropolis has been life-long. At his birth it counted
a population only about one-twelfth of what it counts today. At
his mother's birth, St. Mary's Church, in which she was baptized,
was the only Catholic house of worship in the place; today there
are some two hundred and fifty. Bedelia Kehoe Garraghan, resident of Chicago for eighty-eight years, put on record her recollections of its amazing growth in a sprightly memoir, *Reminis-
cences of Early Chicago* (Chicago, 1924). Father Garraghan, on
his part, has told the story of Catholicism in his native city in a
volume woven of many interesting and previously unknown
documents, *The Catholic Church in Chicago, 1673–1871* (Chicago, 1921).

A member of the Society of Jesus since September 1, 1890,
Father Garraghan has filled various teaching assignments, as in
Cincinnati, Omaha, St. Louis. Through a decade, 1911–1921,
he was Assistant Provincial of the Missouri Province, which included in its jurisdiction all the Jesuit houses of the Middle
West. Curiously enough, the classroom subject that engaged
him most was not history, but English. For several years
(1907–1911), he directed the English studies of the young Jesuits
of the normal school at Florissant, Missouri, an experience much
to his liking, and resulting in the publication by him of two
texts for school use, an annotated edition of Cardinal Newman's
Literature (1912) and *Prose Types in Newman* (1916).

About 1910 he was requested by his superior to compile an
historical sketch of the Jesuit province of Missouri to appear
on occasion of the approaching contennial, 1914, of the restora-
tion of the Society of Jesus by Pius VII. His actual interest in
history was in other fields of the subject, the medieval in particular. Here was an entirely new field, American Jesuit history,
which he had to make the acquaintance of. Moreover, the task
now taken in hand had to be handled while other duties were in-
cumbent upon him, first in the classroom, afterwards in administration. But the subject had attractions for him, and he gave it
all the attention his leisure moments allowed. The sketch
scheduled to appear in 1914 did not materialize. In fact, the
project as originally conceived was recast and it was now planned

to attempt a large-scale and fully documented history of the middle-western Jesuits. In all historical writing the obvious first step is to gather one's material. Bricks cannot be made without straw, nor can a history of any proportions be compiled without the necessary documents. "No documents, no history," is one of the sign-posts set up for the guidance of such as hope to do worthwhile work in the writing of history.

Father Garraghan had before him the task of telling in detail the multiple, the almost kaleidoscopic activities of a group of Catholic missionaries and educators, whose field of operations ran from the Alleghanies to the Rockies and beyond. Evidently, to come by the data on such a complex movement, one would have to search in this direction and that, which in the concrete meant visiting and making use of the many scattered libraries and archives that contained the source-material needed. Printed sources would of course furnish some of the facts to go into the story, but the bulk of the required data would have to be extracted from letters, reports, diaries and other similar still unpublished manuscript material. Father Garraghan had accordingly as a matter of necessity to travel much in preparation for his task. Archives were searched in the United States, Canada, Europe. Documents of importance were turned up in such widely separated localities as Topeka, New Orleans, St. Louis, Washington, Baltimore, Montreal, Quebec, Rome. The last named center yielded particularly rich returns. Here were the general archives of the Society of Jesus, containing thousands of letters and reports from Jesuits in the United States, a mass of material which had to be sifted, translated (most of the items being in Latin or French), summarized and otherwise made use of for the writer's purpose.

It had been Father Garraghan's plan all along to incorporate in his history a considerable quota of his material by direct quotation. Nothing lends more freshness, vividness, reality to a historical narrative than the actual words of its participants. The editor of a prominent American review once expressed the opinion that the ideal history is one largely pieced together of extracts from letters, journals, diaries, reports and other such like contemporary sources. That is the pattern on which Father Garraghan sought to construct his history, which, after years spent in the labors of research and composition, he was happy to be able to bring out in 1938 through the medium of the America Press, New York. It bore the title *The Jesuits of the Middle United States,* filled out three volumes in red buckram and was copiously supplemented with illustrations, maps and facsimiles of documents.

The work on its appearance met with cordial commendation from the reviewers, most of them professional historians. Milo M. Quaife wrote in the *New York Tribune Books:* "The work immediately becomes indispensable to all libraries and all students who are concerned with the history of the region to which it is devoted." Eugene Morrow Violette thought there was "not a dull page in the entire work," while Bishop Schlarman of Peoria gave the caption, "The Jesuit Epic in Mid-America" to the twenty-seven-page review article which he devoted to it. To Louise Phelps Kellogg it appeared that "the work will remain like the *Jesuit Relations* a standard work of reference for all future studies of religious progress in the Middle United States." This was a point of criticism especially agreeable to the author, as it had been his hope that the work would in some measure do for the midwestern American Jesuits of the nineteenth century what the classic *Jesuit Relations* had done for those of earlier centuries.

Two features marking *The Jesuits of the Middle United States* seem particularly significant. First, it tells the story of a group of men who grew up with the western country. The physical scene in which their activities were carried on was in part the Old Frontier, "the most American thing in all America." Emerson Hough waxes eloquent in one of his western books as he pursues the thought that the word "frontier" carries with it more inspirational content than any other of the specific words of American history. Here are gathered up into eight letters all the romance and glamor of the great American adventure into the West. That adventure gave us the Westward Movement, and the Westward Movement, so a whole school of historians will have it, is the only adequate key to American history. Now the pioneer Jesuits who figure in Father Garraghan's narrative moved west with the frontier. They came to know, to have personal relations with, many of the great frontiersmen of the day, as William Clark of the Lewis and Clark Expedition, America's greatest epic of exploration, John McLoughlin, "Father of Oregon," Thomas Hart Benton, father of the Pacific Railroad. So it is that into this Jesuit record of missionary adventure and zeal enters not a little of the glamor and inspiration that gather thick around the chronicle of the Old Frontier.

Another feature of *The Jesuits of the Middle United States* to be pointed out is that it is an illustration in the concrete and on a major scale of the capital truth that other factors besides economic ones went into the making of the West. Frederick Jackson Turner's famous thesis, "the existence of free land in the West explains American history," falls short of the actual truth. Admittedly it explains much in American history; it does not, it cannot explain everything. Other lures besides that of free land drew on the westward-moving pioneers. Missionaries and teachers traveled in numbers in the direction of the setting sun; but what they coveted was not free land but the opportunity for spiritual or social endeavor on behalf of their fellows, red or white. Father De Smet and his Jesuit associates pierced the wilderness of the trans-Mississippi West that they might save souls to Christ, that they might throw out even farther the boundaries of the Kingdom of God. Here is a primal truth to bear in mind, for one will meet in print the contrary thesis, now explicitly, now implicitly expressed, that the development of the West is to be explained in economic terms alone.

Father Garraghan's researches have not all been centered on his *magnum opus*. He has managed all along to carry on side lines of investigation. These have resulted in numerous original contributions illustrating the general theme of American Catholicism in its earlier growth. Thus appeared *Catholic Beginnings in Kansas City, Missouri* (1920), *The Catholic Church in Chicago* (1921), *St. Ferdinand de Florissant* (1923), *Chapters in*

Frontier History (1934). The fascinating figure of Jacques Marquette, the contribution he made to the shaping of the American scene, have always intrigued our author. The autograph letters of the famed missionary-explorer which he turned up in the Jesuit archives in Rome are the only ones known to exist. Those, with other previously unknown Marquettiana, he embodied in a brief biography, *Marquette: Ardent Missionary, Daring Explorer* (1937).

Father Garraghan's historical work has been done mainly in what may be called Jesuit institutional history. This suggests the importance of the opportunity offered to aspiring historians by institutional history in general. Some years ago a speaker at a meeting of the American Historical Association made a plea for the writing of history of this sort,—the story of your school, college, parish, religious community. The advantage here is that you are breaking new ground, not threshing out old straw. Further, you will generally have good material for the purpose in old records, reports, letters and similar private unpublished material. The claims of institutional history on the student who is looking for a subject for his researches and pen should not be overlooked.

Finally, the first capacity for anyone hoping to do something worthwhile in historical research and writing is a capacity for work. This of course is a truth holding also for the earnest student of any subject. But it seems peculiarly applicable to the worker in history. Father Garraghan has had it brought home to him by his own long experience. He likes to cite the words of the British historian, Sir Charles Oman: "It seems to me that the one counsel that can be given to the man who wishes to set sail into the ocean of research is simply to work and work and work again." There is comfort and no little truth in the old saw that "genius is a talent for taking infinite pains."

EDITOR'S NOTE: Father Garraghan died in Chicago on June 6, 1942.

DAVID GOLDSTEIN, LL.D.

Apologist

IT IS EASY to tell the story of one's own writings, but it is not always conducive to being highly regarded. For, as the brilliant Disraeli said, "The author who speaks about his own books is almost as bad as a mother who talks about her own children."

My books are myself, therefore they will be found to be propagandistic in quality. Being a propagandist by nature and avocation, and not a litterateur, I have to be careful not to blow my blast too loudly while heralding forth the story of my writings. Hence, if I use the first person singular, remember, please, that it is due not merely to my conceit, but also to having been long on the defensive against Socialists, sons of Israel, and other non-Catholics, who resented the idea of a person having so commonplace and unchristian a name as I have been blest with, joining the "Irish Church," and having the audacity to defend its principles, history and practices by word of mouth as well as with my pen. With this apology as a prologue, I confess to having adorned six books with my Hebraic cognomen. Three of them were written in collaboration with Mrs. Martha Moore Avery, to whom two-thirds of whatever credit they deserve is due. They are: *Socialism: the Nation of Fatherless Children; Bolshevism: Its Cure; Campaigning for Christ; Campaigners for Christ Handbook; Autobiography of a Campaigner for Christ;* ~d *Jewish Panorama.*

Socialism: the Nation of Fatherless Children was written at the climax of a three year battle, which Mrs. Moore Avery and I led within the Socialist movement, before we became converts from Marx to Christ. It took us all of those years to realize the impossibility of getting the Socialists of America to repudiate the unsound economics, irreligious philosophy, and treasonable political propaganda tactics of the international Socialist doctrinaires. Upon refusal of the Socialists to cease circulating the irreligious and immoral writings of Marx, Engels, Bebel, Kautsky, Loria, and other international leaders, we both resigned from the Socialist Party. My resignation ended with a threat to write an exposé of the false teachings and inner workings of the movement. Thus began my book-writing career.

At that time, books on Socialism were almost entirely of a theoretical nature. Some of them were written by men who had more literary ability than practical knowledge of the Marxists. *Socialism: the Nation of Fatherless Children* was written to fill the need of a book that would do more than tell what the materialistic conception of history, economic determinism, and the Marxian theory of value are. We held that a proper understanding of Socialism necessitated a knowledge of its tactics, its personnel, its connection with international Socialism, and its underlying objective. *Socialism: the Nation of Fatherless Children* exposed these unsavory things in Socialism that the world has since witnessed in the Union of Socialist Soviet Republics. For instance, what is known as the "zigzag tactics" of Lenin, Trotsky and Stalin, were shown to be bone of Socialism's bone and flesh of its flesh. We designated them as the now-you-see-it-and-now-you-don't tactics fifteen years before the world heard the names of the three men who led in afflicting the world with the Socialist totalitarianism that bred Fascism and Nazism. The following sentences give the character of the indictment the book brought against Socialism and its propaganda, which were backed by data and arguments to sustain their severity:

"Socialism is an intellectual disease! The minds it afflicts become gangrene, there is no vitality left in them for a wholesome understanding of life. Abnormal things become the commonplace in their view; irrational principles are the ground floor of their 'sciences'; while blasphemy takes the seat that should be occupied by faith. Proceeding with an animal-humanism, that is indeed drawn from an atheistic premise, they pile up minutiae mountains high to smother the breadth of right reason."

It was a source-book of American Socialism, and its relation to international Marxism, which was used by hundreds of writers and speakers. From it President Samuel Gompers, of the A.F. of L., shaped the severest attack on Socialism that had ever been heard in a labor convention. It took place in Faneuil Hall, Boston. Its dramatic, often quoted, ending, was: "I am entirely at variance with your philosophy; I know what you have up your sleeve. Economically, you are unsound; socially, you are wrong; industrially, you are an impossibility."

The use of the book by President Theodore Roosevelt aroused the ire of the Socialists throughout the country. They insultingly charged "Cockroach Teddy" with "stooping down into the gutter to pick up, dripping with filth, *Socialism: the Nation of Fatherless Children,* to bespatter the once-clean pages of the *Outlook* with its loathsome slime." The assaults made upon the book, and us personally, were vicious. They were not a surprise, for we had forecasted and expected it, knowing full well the way the "Comrades" deal with opponents.

Bolshevism: Its Cure came next. It was published shortly after Lenin and Trotsky led the revolt that overthrew the Democratic Constituent Assembly of Russia, that had peacefully forced the Czar and his autocratic government to abdicate. It was sent forth in the hope that Americans who love Old Glory better than the Red Flag of Revolution would heed the essential difference between those who work the will of the Marxian disrupters, and those who would give to our dearly beloved America what is due her under God.

Bolshevism: Its Cure was published at a time when Americans knew not that Bolshevism is but another name for Socialism applied on a national scale; the same kind of Socialism in principle that Pope Leo XIII warned the world of in his famous Encyclical, Rerum Novarum, in 1891; the same kind of Socialism we fought against for three long years within the ranks of the Marxists.

We were intensely hostile to Socialism, but not to Socialists, save those who lived the Socialist life, despite their vicious attacks upon us. We knew the ardent zeal with which they worked in a false cause for world betterment. We prayed that some day Catholics would be inspired with the same zeal to do public work for the understanding of Christ in His Church as Socialists work to rally "wage slaves" for the "expropriation of the expropriators," and the institution of a Communist society.

We entered the Catholic Church, Mrs. Avery in 1903 and I in 1905, filled with the propaganda spirit, and its technique, with which Socialism had imbued us. We wanted to go out into the highways and byways, to spread the good news that the Catholic Church has within her keeping the grace by which each soul may perfect its human nature, and thus bring into being the era of social justice for which a multitude of non-Catholics yearn. The opportunity came, thanks to His Eminence William Cardinal O'Connell. His confidence in our sincerity and ability permitted the inauguration, under his patronage, of the first Catholic laymen's outdoor educational campaign. This was in 1916, and on Independence Day 1917, on historic Boston Common, we, with others of the laity, began the campaign for Christ, which celebrates its silver jubilee in 1942. After demonstrating the practicability and timeliness of carrying the Catholic message to the man in the street in hundreds of cities between Boston and San Francisco, we published our third book, *Campaigning for Christ*. Its purpose was to encourage others to take up the work of spreading the knowledge of things Catholic among the people assembled in the streets, squares and parks of America.

Campaigning for Christ told the story of seven years work that we, and associated speakers, had done for God and country. It

related the method of boldly, yet courteously, appealing to our
fellow-Americans of other faiths, and of no faith, to give ear to
the claims of the Catholic Church, that they might share in the
joy that had been ours since the day when we were regenerated
in the holy water of Baptism.

The death of Mrs. Martha Moore Avery, in 1929, prompted me
to put my full time into carrying on the work to which she had
been ardently devoted; outdoor speaking in behalf of the Church
that has within her keeping the principles and practices that
alone will solve the grave problems that she and I had mistakenly
thought could be remedied by the collective ownership of the
means of production and distribution.

The need arose for a compilation of doctrinal, historical and
statistical data and arguments fitted for the various classes of
persons who assemble around the Campaigners for Christ lecture
broadcasting van. It had to be a book that would answer the
principal queries and objections propounded at open air meetings. For that purpose *The Campaigners for Christ Handbook*
was written. It was made up in part of the data in *Campaigning
for Christ*. Being a layman's apologetic product, based upon
years of experience with outdoor audiences, rather than the
work of an erudite theologian and philosopher, it proved to be
better suited for Catholic campaign work than any other books
sold from the five successive "perambulating rostrums" used in
seventy-five dioceses where meetings were held.

The continual inquiry regarding my conversion; the requests
that the story be told of battling for the Church against the
Socialist assault, under the direction of the Central Bureau of the
Central Verein and the Supreme Office of the Knights of Columbus; the experiences at outdoor meetings; the record of con-
versions, etc., were warded off as too much of an I, I, I, nature,
until the request came from Boston's Cardinal-Archbishop. The
result was *The Autobiography of a Campaigner for Christ*.

Its human interest stories, exciting debates, and "scraps," as
well as explanation of the psychology of listening crowds, and
how they are handled, caused the book to be called an "arsenal
of practical apologetics." Having continually in mind my in-

debtedness to Mrs. Martha Moore Avery for the understanding
of the principles that led me, by God's grace, into the Catholic
Church, as well as the training for the work I still continue to
do, made it a pleasure to tell the story in my *Autobiography* of
the kind of woman she was; as well as the story of our years of
association together in the Socialist movement and the Catholic
Church. It also offered an opportunity to tell the story of her
daughter, Katherine, who preceded her mother into the Church,
becoming Sister St. Mary Martha, C.N.D., now Superior of the
Sisters of the Congregation of Notre Dame, in Toronto, Canada.

There seemed to be an urgent need of a book that would give
Catholics a balanced view of present-day Jewry, and Jews a view
of Catholic teachings, from the pen of one who had passed from
the Synagogue to the Church. That thought was suggested
partly by the departure of Jews from synagogal affiliation; their
entrance into radical movements, due very often to searching to
fill the void in their lives that the synagogue is unable to fill; and
the confidence that the underlying cause of Jewish affliction lies
in their denial of Jesus as their Messiah. Yet I hesitated to
write such a book, partly on account of the bitterness of spirit
manifested by Jews towards Hebraic converts to the Catholic
Church. I had dealt with Jews only incidentally in my writings
and addresses, and then largely during quiz periods, when asked
"How can a Jew become a Catholic?, Do you favor Zionism?,
What do you think about Rabbi Wise's statement about Jesus?,
etc." I had turned down an invitation to conduct a layman's
mission to Jews in a Cleveland auditorium; and only on three
occasions did I consent to devote whole evenings to addresses on
Jewish problems, and then only in my home city, Boston.

But the realization that about one-third of the Jews in the
world reside within the confines of the U. S. A.; that the influence they exercise, politically and otherwise, which far exceeds
their numerical part of the total population, was very likely to
intensify the latent anti-semitic spirit; and the fear that some of
my fellow-Catholics were likely to be engulfed into the unchristian maelstrom of the threatening anti-semitic psychology,
prompted me to depart from my former policy and to send

The Jewish Panorama on its educational and good-will mission.

Being Catholic, that is charitable in spirit, *The Jewish Panorama* avoids being an indictment against Jews, yet it takes them to task at points; while not a defense of Jews, it does defend them at points against some of those misrepresentations that make life hard for them. It is an attempt to give Catholics a well-balanced view of present-day Jewry, in the U. S. A. in particular. It presents arguments to prove that the Catholic Church is the Jewish theocracy universalized; that when a Jew enters the Church he does not deny the faith of his fathers of old in Israel; what he does is to pass from the caterpillar to the butterfly stage of Judaism.

To try to estimate the degree of success my books have achieved, after having related their history and purpose, would be "as bad" as the mother who boasts about her offspring. I hope my writings have been of service to the cause I endeavor to serve. If not, I apologize for deigning to pass from filling show-cases with cigars to cluttering shelves with books.

EDITOR'S NOTE: Niagara University conferred the honorary LL.D. upon our author in 1939. His first three books are out of print; the second three (*Campaigners for Christ Handbook, Autobiography of a Campaigner for Christ,* and *Jewish Panorama*) are published by the Catholic Campaigners for Christ (of which Dr. Goldstein is Director), Astor P.O. Station, Boston, Massachusetts.

REVEREND HAROLD JEROME HEAGNEY

Novelist

A PROLIFIC AND VERSATILE author is Father Heagney of Stuttgart, Arkansas, who has written fully a thousand short stories as well as novels, essays and editorials. His first story was published while he was a high school student at Rockville Center, N. Y. He writes for both adult and juvenile readers and contributes to most of our popular Catholic magazines.

Living in Stuttgart, a place apparently uncongenial to the growth of literary talent, far from publishing centers and literary circles, Father Heagney has shown how much can be done in hours and seasons snatched from the pursuit of priestly duties. Self-prompted, without friends or connections in the magazine or book business, he has worked his solitary but invincible way through countless obstacles. In building his own career he has awakened an interest in the great men and women of the Church whose lives he has transmuted from the sterile pages of history *to* vital, glowing personalities.

Among his biographical novels are *Victory* and *The Blockade Runner*. The former is based on the life of John Baptist Jordan, founder of the Society of the Divine Savior, a life as modern as today's roaring printing presses whose mighty power he so clearly foresaw. "To me it was a labor of love," said Father Heagney. "To see this work in print gives me greater satisfaction than anything else I have done. I realize that it is an odd statement, but at times I have felt that I was being inspired in the writing of it by Father Jordan himself, though he had left this world, he was still more alive, more active, more keen for God's kingdom than when present. His spirit will march down the centuries like the great saints of the past." The title of the book is significant, expressing the victory of the spiritual over the worldly, the personal victory of Father Jordan in establishing the Salvatorians.

Blockade Runner, based on the boyhood adventures of John Bannister Tabb, famous poet-priest of Virginia, enjoys the distinction of being the only book of its type in the Vatican Library. It was placed there by Dr. Inigo Giordani, who is keenly interested in the American movement for better literature for juvenile readers. The book was rated one of the ten best Catholic books of the year it was published, and was selected by the Pro Parvulis Book Club. Though written for the young reader, all who have known Father Tabb or his work welcome it, not only for the interest of its story, but also for the new facts it presents about the Civil War experiences of the beloved priest.

Another famous poet-priest of the Old South furnishes the theme for "Recollections of Father Ryan," which appeared in *The Catholic World* of January, 1928.

In his short stories for both adult and juvenile readers Father Heagney uses facts as the basis for fiction. And his subjects are chosen from the entire history of the Church. For example, some of the chapters in his latest collection for young readers, *My Silent Partner,* are Little Antelope and the Black Robe (a story of Father Isaac Jogues), Juan's Lady of Guadalupe, St. George and the Dragon, The First Christmas Tree, The Martyr of Molokai, The Story of the Holy Cross, and, A Boy Martyr of Long Ago. His historical stories for older readers show a similar variety, and he often selects subjects and situations that are obscure or unusual, such as: The Best Lawyer in Naples, When Saxons were Saints, Desert Magdalen, A Message to Lepanto, and, The Black Cross of Scotland.

Father Heagney is equally at home in the mystery and adventure fields. His earlier novels, the Bascomb Boys series, are examples. The scenes, laid largely in southeast Oklahoma, are drawn to nature and written with the realism and accuracy that can only be attained by first-hand knowledge. For, although born and reared in New York, Father Heagney spent his earlier days as a missionary priest in western Arkansas. After his ordination in December, 1913, he was appointed pastor of St. Michael's Church, Van Buren, a border town, where he was called upon to attend the scattered families in the neighboring state to the west. Among his other book-length stories of the cow country are "Wings over Secret Valley," "In the Glory Hole Country," and "Paradise Valley." The beauties of the Ozark region form the background for such mystery and adventure tales as "The Cabin in the Ozarks," "The Strange Mystery of Glenn Ferguson," and "In the Devil's Bowl." Other Arkansas settings are depicted in "Spanish Hill Treasure," "John of the Ricefields," and "The Lodge of Adventure."

In the non-fiction field Father Heagney has served as associate editor of well-known Catholic weeklies and is a former editor of *The Guardian,* official weekly of the Little Rock diocese. He has been a member of the faculty of St. John's Seminary and Little Rock College. The latter institution conferred upon him the honorary degree of Doctor of Literature, in 1928, for his contribution to Catholic letters. He has served as pastor of various Arkansas parishes. Since 1939 he has devoted all his time to writing.

Writing is a natural impulse with this teller of many tales. "I don't remember the time when I was too young to love a story," he says. "After I learned how to read I found as much delight in reading as in listening to them. Then I wanted to write stories of my own. One day I scrawled on my copy paper:

A green crocodile on the golden sand. I stopped and looked at the words I had written, and I said them aloud; for I liked the look and the sound of them. I had discovered color and form, and it thrilled me. I look back upon that first dawning of literary awareness as my call to the vocation of story telling.

"I believe in the easy approach to writing. If I found the actual writing a painful task, I would not make it my life work. Back in the days when I was mastering the rudiments of spelling, first-graders used to write on slates. One day the teacher told us to write Cat on our slates. Those pupils who filled their slates with the word, correctly spelled, would receive a red ticket. In an amazingly short time, my slate went up on my head in token that the job was done. Incredulous stares and a buzz of surprised whispers went around the class room. Such speed bordered on magic; for most of the pupils were just getting started, some laboriously drawing lines on their slates with which to accurately guide their sharp slate pencils.

"The teacher hurried to my desk and picked the slate from my head, wondering if she had discovered a child prodigy in her room. Then a smile broke over the good Nun's face. The word Cat was written three times in scrawls so large they covered the entire slate! The rest of the class snickered and glanced at the perpetrator of this deed with amused contempt for such careless conduct. But Sister dropped a red ticket on my slate. Does this prove anything? I relate it only to illustrate an early example of my attitude toward accomplishment as something to be attacked with ease and completed by the most direct method and with the utmost speed. That is the way I write.

"You wouldn't approach a high dive by crawling painfully up onto the board, slowly lifting one arm, then the other, gingerly bending your knees. You'd lose your balance, if you did, and topple into the water to drown, unless rescued. It takes speed, confidence, coordination to dive or swim or perform any athletic feat, doesn't it? You'll never make progress unless you jump in and tackle the job. And the more ease you display, the more naturalness, the greater will be your success. Mental goals are attained in the same way; so don't let inhibitions hold you back. If you want to be a writer,—*write!* But be sure you have something to write about.

"All too often, the beginning writer fails to grasp the necessity of plotting his story before attempting to write it. The writer should have a definite, logical sequence of events worked out in his mind before putting a single sentence on paper. His plot must build up to a well-devised climax, it must have suspense, drama, and interest. Plotting your story takes more study, concentration and original thought than actually writing it. Once the young writer realizes this most important step, he is well on his way."

Father Heagney's books include: *Ted Bascomb in the Cow Country*, 1928, Benziger; *The Testing of Al Bascomb*, 1929, Benziger; *The Bascomb Boys on the Gridiron*, 1930, Benziger; *Blockade Runner*, 1939, Longmans; *Victory*, 1941, Catholic Literary Guild; *My Silent Partner*, 1942, Salvatorian Press, St. Nazianz, Wisconsin.

REVEREND WINFRID HERBST, S.D.S.

Spiritual Writer

TO ME IT IS rather amusing to be called a "famous author" and all that. And to be asked to write a sketch of my life as a writer is even more amusing—"it is to laugh," as the phrase has it. However, always being willing to oblige, I herewith submit the following sketchy account.

First, then, by way of introduction, I submit a few personal details. I was born in Poygan, Wisconsin, not far from the famous city of Oshkosh, on the shores of that equally famous duck-hunters' delight, Lake Poygan, August 13, 1891, in the good old horse-and-buggy days. It was there that I received my elementary education, being one of the first graduates turned out from the school after the difficult no-credit-for-regular-class-work, county-superintendent final examinations of those early days. I recall with some little pride how I used to win out in the old-fashioned spelling bees in our school and how I was the triumphant prize winner in that unique and, I am sure, since unheard-of quotation bee, which consisted in reciting quotations like "Slow and steady wins the race" until all were eliminated and I was still on the floor with some few quotations yet to spare. It was not long after my graduation that I, who was a voluminous reader, got the notion that I could also write. Whereupon I composed a short story and sent it to one of the big popular magazines, receiving in return a very courteous rejection card. How I wish I had that first story now! What a relic it would be. How heartily I could laugh over it! But it seems it was never even returned. I suppose I forgot to enclose the return postage or was too poor to enclose any.

But I must get back to my *personalia*. I had a splendid father and a wonderful mother, both sterling Catholics. Then the day came when I said to my father, "Pa, I would like to become a priest." After some delay, during which I had to run our 250-acre farm while I read and studied, matters were finally arranged and I entered the Salvatorian Seminary at St. Nazianz, Wisconsin, on Sept. 13, 1910. It was there I made all my studies for the priesthood. There I made my religious profession in the Society of the Divine Savior on Oct. 26, 1915; there I was ordained to the priesthood by His Excellency Paul P. Rhode, Bishop of Green Bay, on Aug. 28, 1921; and there I began that extremely busy life as home missionary, retreat master, editor, and author that I have been leading ever since. (This is written in 1942, same dear old place.)

During my studies for the priesthood English and English literature were my forte, the subject in which I led my class without a single exception. From the beginning Webster's dictionary was a constant companion with which I became rather well acquainted in the course of the years. I made a study of all of Shakespeare's works, and of Dante's *Divine Comedy* and of Milton's *Paradise Lost* and *Paradise Regained,* and of Tennyson's poems, of the works of Washington Irving and of Cardinal Newman and of other similar high class works. It was my principle when studying such works never to pass over a word without knowing its meaning and its correct pronunciation and its every shade of thought. I followed Ruskin's advice literally and looked hard and long at every word and let it sink deep into my consciousness. That's the way I read for years and years and am still reading today, unpardonably old-fashioned and out-of-date and behind-the-times though it may be. (Reading time: 3 minutes, 26 seconds!)

Then, in 1915, upon request of one of my tutors I wrote my first booklet, a brochure called *Is the Divine Savior Calling You?* It was a little treatise on vocation, so good that it has since been incorporated with changes in other writings of mine. My name was modestly withheld from the publication and I recall how my confreres marvelled at its excellence and wondered what learned man might have written it! Shortly afterwards I became associate editor of *Manna,* the Society's magazine for children, and of *Manna Almanac,* an annual that was issued from 1917 to 1929. I wrote much for these publications. In 1923 I was made editor of those publications and also editor of *The Savior's Call,* a magazine for adults which was begun in that year. I am still the editor, strange to say. My greatest fault as editor was that for long years I not only edited those magazines but also wrote too much of the material that entered into their pages.

Then, somehow or other, the books began to appear. They rolled off the presses rather rapidly, though, strange to say, not one of them but was in the course of preparation for some years. Some were little books, some were bigger books; some were less good books from a literary point of view, others were better books; but all were spiritual books conducive to the glory of God and the sanctification and salvation of souls.

I have said that each one of my books was in the course of preparation for a number of years. How could that be, since there are over thirty now? Well, you see, often a number of them were being prepared simultaneously, or almost so. Someone wrote to me recently, by the way, saying: "I am publishing a book and it has had me worried and working for such a long, long time. You seem to get out one after the other just as if there's nothing to it. How in the world do you do it?" Get out one after the other as if there's nothing to it indeed! It has meant endless work and worry. Take my 800-page book *Questions of Catholics Answered,* for instance. I worked at it off and on for about twelve years, writing, rewriting, adding, eliminating. Then when I thought it was about perfect I submitted the whole manuscript to a learned and prudent theologian. When he returned it I again revised it according to his corrections and suggestions. Thereupon I submitted the whole to my Provincial, as the law requires of a religious before submission to the Bishop. Again the whole was discussed for hours and hours and days and days. Then the manuscript was sent to my Bishop for the official *Imprimatur.* The Bishop sent it to his diocesan *Censor Librorum.* The latter spent three hard weeks in a careful reading of the work. Thereupon I got the official permission to print. Then came 800 pages of proofs from the printer—all had to be carefully gone through and corrected. Then the pages were duly numbered. That having been done, I went through the whole subject matter and composed that alphabetical analytical index which makes the book so handy as a reference work also. Finally, after twelve years, I sat back with a sigh of relief and turned the pages of the finished book, thinking with some trepidation of what the critics would say. That was one which we published ourselves. In the case of those published by others, Pustet, Benziger, Bruce, the manuscript had first to be carefully prepared, then sent out to one publisher after the other only to be often rejected and then finally accepted, then perhaps submitted by the publisher to some learned and critical reader, then revised according to that learned and critical reader's suggestions, then proof read, and so forth and so on! And when a man has done all this he may fall back exhausted into a chair and get the praise and the blame of a critical world. And, verily, sometimes it's like beating a cripple with his crutches.

Especially in my case; for, as regards my literary ability, I for one wouldn't give a fig for it. (I had one original thought once, but before I could write it down it escaped me. But perhaps it was not original after all. Anyhow, as one of my publishers once said: "Bah! Books are made from books!" I think he meant there aren't any original thoughts left in the world. I wouldn't be surprised. Consider the huge public libraries. . . .) The way I have to slave at the little I write and rewrite and the way I have to search for the few trite thoughts I try to give the public

is something I would not tell even in this confidential sketch.
And, as Cardinal Newman used to say (with tears, I believe, and
after thirty years of writing), I don't seem to get any better with
practice.

To make a long story short, I have in the course of the years,
up to the present time (June, 1942) written and published the
following books: *Boyhood's Highest Ideal* (on the priesthood),
1924; *Girlhood's Highest Ideal* (on the sisterhood), 1924; *Chats
and stories about the Blessed Sacrament,* 1926; *Little Nellie of
Holy God,* 1927; *Just stories* (for children), 1929; *Tell Us Another*
(for children), 1929; *Eucharistic Whisperings* (eight volumes),
1923–1940; *Vocation letters,* 1931; *Talks to Boys and Girls* (Benziger), 1931; *Holy Mass* (Benziger), 1932; *The Divine Savior*
(Benziger), 1932; *My Retreat Master, an Eight Day Retreat for
Religious* (Bruce), 1932; *Follow the Saints, Lives of Saints and
Reflections* (Benziger), 1934; *The Life of Father Jordan, Founder
of the Society of the Divine Savior,* 1935; *Jesus and His Mother*
(Pustet), 1936; *Saintly Children* (Benziger), 1936; *Spotlights on
Matters Spiritual* (Pustet), 1937; *Readings and Reflections on the
Gospels* (Pustet), 1937; *Christ's Little Ones,* 1937; *Questions of
Catholics Answered,* 1939; *Ready Replies on Religion* (Pustet),
1939; *Exhortations and Admonitions of Father Francis Jordan,*
1939; *Courageous Children,* 1941; *The Savior of the World,*
1942. In addition to these I prepared a number of books proper
to the Society of the Divine Savior. I have likewise prepared
Priest's Saturday pamphlets and leaflets and pamphlets and
brochures of various kinds. I have also written a book of poetry,
which, however is as yet unpublished—and will probably remain
so. Other books are in preparation.

When in January, 1939, I went to the trouble to figure out
how many copies of my magazines and books and pamphlets had
rolled off the press and gone out into the world on their errand
of doing good and promoting goodness I arrived at the following
figures: Magazines (*Manna* and *The Savior's Call*): 7,560,451;
books and pamphlets sold: 571,113 (close to 300,000 books);
gratis literature: 1,360,500. Grand total: 9,492,064. What the
number would be now, in 1942, I cannot guess. Moreover, I

never did have any great liking for mathematics. I was much disappointed at the figures. So small, after all the labor involved! But such is the experience of most Catholic authors, I am sure. Catholics simply don't read as much Catholic literature as they ought to. And that's that.

But then, as I mentioned when I began this sketch, I'm no real writer anyway. I have always been acutely conscious of my lack of talent in this field. I have no right to be in the Gallery of Living Authors at all. But at least I've been doing the best I could under the circumstances; for, when all is said, I'm a religious and priest first of all. The rest is only between times, you know.

JOSEPH HUSSLEIN, S.J.

The Story of a Literary Pioneer

HOW I APPARENTLY DEVELOPED a decidedly literary inclination I do not recall, except that I still remember avidly reading Cooper's *Deerslayer* during class hour in the grade school. Some boy had given it to me in a German translation, but English and German were entirely the same to me.

Our grade school education then consisted of a six year curriculum, with just one month of vacation in the summer. I was beginning my twelfth year when I entered what is now Marquette University, and at once found my true element in literature and writing. As the saying goes, I took to it as a fish to water, and the success achieved encouraged my efforts. Particularly helpful was the spirit of literary competition existing there. Other studies, however, interested me no less.

Marquette had not as yet sent forth its first graduates, and I myself was to be in the third graduating class. Our "Academics," which corresponded to the present high school, then consisted of two years only, and were followed by the four years of college, known as Humanities, Poetry, Rhetoric and Philosophy.

It was my good fortune to be taught in the Poetry and Rhetoric years by that genial personality whom every Catholic boy and girl must love, Father Francis J. Finn, S.J., whose boy stories have done so much to foster ideals of loyalty and religion, and to develop Catholic character.

While I wrote abundantly in those days, both prose and verse, my keenest interest was centered in poetry. It was not choice but a sense of duty that later switched me into a different avocation, but the old love was never lost. My years of teaching were mostly devoted to Latin, Greek and English poetry. Even during theological studies I taught the Greek drama at St. Louis University.

Familiarity with the poets is of course one of the best preparations for a literary career, and it should naturally stimulate the writing of poetry on the part of those sufficiently qualified. Prose itself has its own music, its own rhythm, and to be of high literary quality it must possess imagination and inspiration. For all these ends poetry is an excellent discipline. It refines the sense of beauty and touches with its magic the wells of emotion.

During my years of study in the Society of Jesus my private efforts at writing were largely confined to poetry, as the opportunity allowed. Though some of this work appeared in print, my purpose was not to publish at the time. Later my blank verse drama, *Athol, or Near the Throne,* was given in Cleveland on five successive nights, as a large-scale production, and elsewhere was successfully staged. But it has never been recast for publication, and so was withdrawn by me from circulation.

All this may be of interest, not so much for its own sake, as to indicate how the whole trend of a man's literary work can change almost over night. That is what happened to me.

It so came about that during the period from 1908 to 1911 I was requested to give stylistic aid in the publication of two important books dealing with Socialism in its relation to religion and morality. This brought me into contact with a well-selected library of the most authoritative books written by Socialist leaders throughout the world. Everything reliably to be known about their doctrines, methods and principles was here set down by their own hands. I could not possibly therefore, be mistaken in the complete grasp I was gaining of this subject. I realized no less the thorough, inveterate and inextinguishable hatred of Christian faith, Christian culture and of all religion that underlay the doctrines of Socialism. But worst of all was the systematic deception practised upon the masses, upon individuals and organized bodies under the guise of innocence and public-mindedness.

On the other hand, I realized no less how little informed both Catholic clergy and people were on this subject at the time. I therefore considered it a sacred duty to give what light and counsel I could in this critical situation. In the meanwhile I was also getting constantly closer to trade unionism, against which Socialists were diligently practising their tactics of "boring from within." Moreover I had behind me the strength of all the positive doctrine of the *Rerum Novarum* of Pope Leo XIII.

At the same time it was equally important to indicate those abuses of Capitalism which were the very root from which Socialism had grown and on which it was still thriving. This placed me in the position of being more or less suspected both ways at the same time. Even a conscientious Catholic editor hammered at my "capitalistic" tendencies, while from the extreme opposite camp came the letter of a double-dyed Red who delightedly approved of my radicalism, no doubt after reading an attack by me on capitalistic abuses. He earnestly urged me, however, not to be too finicky about shedding human blood, since the loss of some millions of American lives really amounted to nothing in comparison with the good to be realized in the revolution. He was an I.W.W. It was at the time of the First World War, and his envelope showed two gold stars, as if from a gold-star mother. But the police apparently were on his track, for I noticed the envelope had been opened and sealed again.

Such were the amenities of advance fighting in the social field, when there were but few writers to champion the Catholic side against extreme conservatism on the one hand and irrational radicalism on the other. You felt you were in the saddle, swinging your sword for the triumph of Truth, Justice and Charity, and it did not matter what happened to you.

These developments took place during the opening years of my journalistic career, which began in 1911, when I was summoned to New York as an associate editor of *America*. Particularly effective was a lecture given by me at this time to a progressive body of priests one of whom financed my resultant pamphlet, *The Pastor and Socialism,* which was mailed to every pastor in the United States and Canada. It served as an initial blast, and the success of it was all I could have hoped for.

This was quickly followed by my first book, *The Church and the Social Problem,* making a more positive approach, while at the same time revealing the materialist philosophy of Socialism.

A book, however, which exercised a very wide influence at a period of social crisis was the volume published by me immediately at the close of the first World War. People were asking, "What next?" Here then was at least a directive answer in *The World Problem,* with its subtitle "Capital, Labor and the Church." It was followed in successive years by *Democratic Industry,* and by *Evolution and Social Progress.*

All these books succeeded in reaching particularly those interested in the social question as seen in its Catholic aspect. They were influential not only in the United States, but in other countries also. Thus a translation of *The World Problem* promptly appeared in South America.

Particularly encouraging, however, was the request from Mr. Eyre, President of the Confederation of Catholic Societies of Great Britain and Wales, to write for them *A Catholic Social Platform,* which in due course of time was adopted by them and printed in England.

"The Catholic Social Guild has been working very hard at the distribution of the *Platform,*" the great social missionary, Father Charles Plater, S.J., wrote me from England. "It has gone to all the M.P.'s, the clergy, etc. We have a great number of letters of approval of the *Platform.*"

Naturally a Social Platform drawn up at the present moment for the United States or England would include many things not then stressed by me. But the essential Catholic social doctrine was applied within the limits proper to the time. "Your *Platform*," wrote Father Plater again from Campion Hall, Oxford, under date of March 10, 1930, "is likely to make a real impression on the country, the first 10,000 copies were speedily exhausted. It will form the theme of an important meeting in London shortly, at which the Bishop of Northampton will speak on the *Platform*."

In the meantime, in editorials and popular articles, I was doing my utmost to promote Catholic social ideas and stem the menacing evil of Socialism, in common with the comparatively few who then vigorously devoted themselves to this task. The Catholic press widely reprinted the articles.

Naturally, literature of this kind is gradually supplemented, more or less, by new books that can take into account later developments, but its message has been absorbed and continues to be spread by silent pens and eloquent lips through future years. In classrooms and libraries it is used and consulted.

Without relinquishing my social interests, I now started on a new apostolate; one of the most gratifying I have undertaken. I began a series of pamphlets, everyone of which is in circulation today after a quarter of a century. My purpose was to bring home to Catholics in a doctrinal, cultural and historical way the beauty and power of their great devotions. Laboriously I gathered my material and presented it in a popular style. Here, for instance, are some of the titles: *The Poor Souls, Christ the King, The Sacred Heart, The Blessed Virgin, Your own St. Joseph, The Heart of the Little Flower*. It was in connection with the Eucharistic Congress in Chicago that I published the booklet *The Little Flower and the Blessed Sacrament*.

What touched me was to learn that among the tiny literary collection of Matt Talbot was found my pamphlet *Your Own St. Joseph*, which this saintly man had apparently treasured. So, too, on happening upon a blind lady in a home for the aged, I saw her fingers gliding over a volume in Braille. What was she reading? I asked, and learned it was my pamphlet on the Sacred Heart. Several of these pamphlets were transcribed into Braille.

About this time, too, in order to reach large numbers, I wrote each week for three years a long editorial for *Our Sunday Visitor,* then the only widely distributed Catholic paper of its kind. To this Catholic Action period belongs my volume *The Catholic's Work in the World,* which was serially translated into German. A book on Luther written in conjunction with Father Reville was translated into Portuguese. So the good seed scatters and no one knows where it may spring up and bear fruit, perhaps a hundred fold. There is a Providence that directs it all.

During the period of my journalistic work for *America* I also wrote, for the space of three years, a monthly social article for the *Homiletic and Pastoral Review.*

After closing my editorial labors at New York I still remained for two years at Fordham University as Professor in the School of Sociology and Social Work, at the same time collaborating with an enterprise known as the National Film Corporation. This brought me into touch with motion-picture efforts on the part of Catholics throughout the world. Besides some motion-picture writings, the literary fruit of this period consisted in the two volumes: *The Reign of Christ* and *The Mass of the Apostles.*

September, 1929, saw me in charge of the social science courses at St. Louis University. The next year, then, I started a school along these lines, the former undergraduate section of this has now been embodied in the School of Education and Social Science, while the graduate part is the present St. Louis University School of Social Service, over which I presided as Dean or Director until 1940. The books published by me during this period have been *The Christian Social Manifesto,* now in its fifth and revised edition, the *Spirit World About Us,* and *Social Wellsprings I,* the last-named volume containing fourteen social Encyclicals of Pope Leo XIII, with a preface for each and additional notes. The translations themselves of the documents have been revised and popularized. A further volume, *Social*

Encyclicals II, containing eighteen social Encyclicals by Pope Pius XI, presented in the same manner, is being issued in 1942.

A final word, then, about the Science and Culture Series, begun in December, 1931.

This was my contribution to the Catholic Literary Revival throughout the world. It consists of a series of original volumes, written at my request or voluntarily submitted by competent literary men or authorities in their various fields, thus carrying on the Catholic tradition in letters and in the various scientific and cultural areas. Its object is to present to the world this tradition in its best and highest modern interpretation. The series is strictly international and no pains have been spared in securing the proper writers from all parts of the English-speaking world.

"A University in Print" is the description significantly given it, a university not confined to the four walls of classrooms, but intended for the world at large. Without sacrifice of scholarship, it is written in a popular style that makes it acceptable to the intelligent reader everywhere, Catholic or non-Catholic.

In the production of these books the Bruce Publishing Company has achieved a notable success, both in the accuracy of its work, and in the dignity and attractiveness of the volumes as they issue from the press. In the first ten years about 120 books appeared in The Science and Culture Series and about half that many are under way at the present writing.

While strictly international, the series was naturally greeted abroad as an American production, though many of its authors are leading literary men of England, Ireland, Australia, and other lands. Thus, broadcasting from Dublin no later than September 28, 1934, Aodth de Blacam said:

"I recommend this remarkable series for more than one reason. The first is that it will appeal particularly to most Irish readers as being almost the only series of its kind appearing in English that is written from what most of us regard as the orthodox point of view. . . . The Science and Culture Series should serve our purpose if we were asked to point to a really trustworthy example of American culture—of American scholarship,

deep and sound. Here we find that long range of interest, that
freshness of point of view, and yet that reverent attitude towards
tradition which together make up the characteristics of American culture."

The Religion and Culture Series and the Science and Culture
Texts may be grouped as later developments of this same series
and embraced within it. They are generally so accepted. Out
of this series, too, has developed the Science and Culture Foundation on the part of the publisher as a Catholic Book-of-the-
Month movement.

MARY KIELY

Children's Books

IN BOSTON, on a Sunday one February nineteenth, I was born into a family whose house was always, upstairs and down, overflowing with books. I believe my attraction to biography developed in the hours I spent as a child poring over picture biographies the *Mentor Magazine* then carried of the world's great musicians, composers, painters and writers.

We lived several years among the Berkshires in a house with an upstairs window-seat looking across Mount Greylock. My mother would read to us children there afternoons from Robert Louis Stevenson, and Adelaide Proctor and her beloved Longfellow. And she used also to read from a little French book the story of Tarcisius and the Catacombs. As we listened we would be watching all the while the shadows and the changing colors out on the hillsides opposite; and mountains still draw me with a profound influence. Like all children we romped around acting our story-books and poems—I remember well how we too built "A ship upon the stairs" but those afternoons at the window-seat held an enchanted quality. And the blue Irish hills the reviewers liked so well in *O'Donel of Destiny* are created from those memories still living in my heart.

Later, when we went to the New England sea-coast town of Providence, Rhode Island, I was reading everything on which I could get my hands, particularly a dog-eared Bible History. For me then the Bible came alive and I read it, literally, to tatters, with a love that has stayed with me ever since. My grandparents down in Portland, Maine, had been charter subscribers to the *Ave Maria* when Father Hudson commenced publishing it in the early 1870's. As our attic was full of old copies I would settle happily on slippery blue and age-yellowed piles of *Ave Marias,* reading from other piles of them by the hour. I read my way, in fact, down through the years from 1875 or thereabouts, acquiring familiar friendship with early American Catholics. Many I have included in *New Worlds to Live,* the catalog of youth books I first compiled in 1935, because I value their unique contribution to Catholic Americana for our modern boys and girls.

Providence was a nice city in which to grow. We must have had motion-picture houses but I only recall two movies, one of which was (I think) "the Snow Queen," starring Marguerite Clarke, lovely as a dream in a fairy boat that glided down a fairy stream. The boat was drawn by beautiful white swans and I was in a state of blissful trance when the picture ended. I also saw "Little Lord Fauntleroy." Who played in that movie I cannot now remember, but my brother and I must scarcely have breathed, so intense was our rapture as this favorite storybook came alive before our eyes. I know indeed how truly Father Francis X. Downey, S.J., the late founder of Pro Parvulis Book Club spoke when he insisted that "Children do not merely read a book. They *live* a book!" For two winters, when I was ten and eleven, we were taken regularly to a children's lecture-series on Saturday mornings at the Rhode Island School of Design. We would watch still, color-pictures on a screen and hear of many wonders. One Saturday morning the talk would be of Venetian glass and the glass-blowers. Another Saturday morn-

ing it would be about old violins and how they were made. Another Saturday morning, I remember, the talk was on Italian
Primitives. They must have been excellent programs, for we
enjoyed those mornings far more than we ever enjoyed dancing-
school in the afternoon. At home my mother would carefully
point out to us that what had been shown to us in the morning
was a beauty that had been nurtured by Mother Church and
was our Christian heritage. I believe such childhood impressions are deeply absorbing and we have concentrated in Pro
Parvulis Book Club on providing through many of our book-
selections this same important heritage for today's children of
the Faith.

Providence had a Keith Stock Company! It played summers
only, at least in Providence. The actors were hardly renowned
but when I saw the Stock play "Little Women," "Rebecca of
Sunnybrook Farm," "Huck Finn" and "Uncle Tom's Cabin,"
I fear that not even the Divine Sarah could have cast a greater
spell on me. I know indeed what first-hand experience of legitimate theatre can mean to a child and I have tried to stress in
my book *Traffic Lights* what glowing possibilities a Catholic
Theatre for our young people contains if only we can develop
one.

When I was about eight years old I was taken to hear Seumas
MacManus. I can still see the tall, angular, dark-haired gentleman standing quietly before the audience telling a laughable
Irish fairy tale in mellow brogue. My father with others went
up and spoke a word to him after the lecture while I looked on
breathlessly. That wonderful storyteller turned and smiled
down at me and I fell in love then and there with all things Irish.
It was, too, the stories of leprechauns and fairies my Irish father
used to tell me that led me, I think, to make my first book an
Irish biography. Everyone knew, of course, that someone other
than the "little people" must have once built the ruined stone
castles in Ireland, and have lived in them! But who? Where
were the family records and the blood-stocks of the individual
families? The mystery of it stayed with me and I recall talking

it over, unsuccessfully, with my history teacher in Providence
Classical High School. We were mapping the Barbarian In-
vasions of Europe and it seemed an opportune time to learn
something of the Celtic land of Erin. But the hope was vain.
Benedict Fitzpatrick had probably not then written his scholarly
books. At any rate I was making queries of the wind. After
I graduated from the Library School of the Rhode Island College
of Education I was trying one day to help a boy in the Children's
Room of the Providence Public Library find a story of Irish
knights and castles. And there was none! So for four years I
searched old manuscripts, to satisfy my curiosity. Then I wrote
O'Donel of Destiny. It is the biography of Red Hugh O'Donel,
the last Irish king before Elizabethan Cromwell destroyed Ireland and its records. The Oxford University Press published it
in September 1939. It is rewarding now to receive letters from
boys and girls all over America telling me how glad they are
to know of Red Hugh O'Donel. Shortly after *O'Donel of
Destiny* was published Mr. Hugh O'Donnell, the retired business
manager of *The New York Times* invited me to tea. He had
read my book, he wrote, and he had something he wished to
show me. It was a pencilled portrait-head, a beautifully executed etching of the last descendant of Red Hugh O'Donel who
now lives in Spain and whom Mr. O'Donnell knew and had
visited. An electric switch beside the etching lighted it and I
saw with keen pleasure the fine, aristocratic head and forehead,
the determined chin, and the name signed in one corner.

In 1937 I found myself transferring from a calm, children's
library to the humming, Empire State Building offices in New
York of the then newly organized Pro Parvulis Book Club. At
times I am still astonished to find myself a New Yorker. I enjoy
living in New York. My apartment is high above Manhattan
and when I look out and see the unearthly, soft blue haze
peculiar to Manhattan twilights filling all the sky, drifting above
the many, glowing lights, I know I would not wish to live elsewhere. New York is a city of magic. Nowhere else can one
have the stage, the legitimate theatre so easily and richly available. Nowhere I think is there a more friendly place in which

to work and live and play than the New York publishing world. And the churches of this city are jewels, liturgical, beautiful, omnipresent.

We need brave and spiritual stories today for our youth in our confused, unspiritual world. In 1940 I was persuaded by Father Downey to draft a working-plan toward this ideal, a charter as it were, and put it into a book. The book was published by Pro Parvulis Book Club in 1941 under the title *Traffic Lights.* As a practical working-out of this ideal we added also a senior high school age-group to our Book Club in 1941, calling it The Talbot Club.

I believe few things today are more important and needed than the writing of fine and inspirational books for our boys and girls, or the finding for them books written by those who have given ability and hard work, sincerity and Faith to so high an ideal. Handling these two thrilling tasks is my happy privilege.

EDITOR'S NOTE: Miss Kiely, who is editorial secretary of Pro Parvulis Book Club and editor of *Pro Parvulis Herald,* is the author of: *O'Donel of Destiny* (Oxford University Press, 1939), a story of Elizabethan Ireland and Red Hugh O'Donel, the last king of the land; *Traffic Lights* (Pro Parvulis Book Club, 1941), a series of twenty illustrated chapters on the philosophy of book-selection for boys and girls; *New Worlds to Live* (Pro Parvulis Book Club, 1935), an annotated, selected, graded list of 1,000 books for boys and girls.

REVEREND THOMAS A. LAHEY, C.S.C.

Writer for Children

HELLO, MY YOUNG FRIENDS, and particularly those of you still in school, every single one of you right down to the last little fellow down there in the last seat of the last row! As I sit here at my typewriter, I see all of you in imagination before me—fat, thin, tall, short, a scattering of red-heads, some colored youngsters, a few Chinese lads and lassies, yes, even some blind and crippled boys and girls whom I would like to pat on the back for the brave little smiles that I see on their faces.

How different you all are in appearance—yet how alike in your ambitions and in the hopes and ideals of your fresh young souls! This writer, too, had those same ambitions when he was young—without the talents with which God has gifted so many of you. And because he feels that all of us have so much in common, he is going to tell you as well as he can how he got along and what many of you can do to make yourselves into future successful writers.

To begin with, my young friends, the writer was not what you would call a "Quiz Kid" when he went to school. But he did want to write, and because he wanted to write, he wrote and wrote and wrote—first for a little memeographed sheet at St. Mary's High School in Michigan City, Indiana, and then for the Notre Dame *Scholastic* during his four years at the home of the Fighting Irish. And when he uses that word "wrote," he really means it; for during those high school and college years he turned out literally wagon loads of poems and essays and stories, most of it junk, but with an occasional line or two a little above the average.

Well, you can't keep on writing year after year, my young friends, without something happening; so the miracle happened when this writer won the English medal in his senior year at the University of Notre Dame against talent which was really away out of his league. That's when he found out for the first time that even a little talent and a great deal of work will get you farther in the long run than lots of talent and not so much work. And most of you have a great deal more talent than you suspect. Don't forget that!

Well, for four years after graduation the writer was so busy with his theological studies at the Catholic University in Washington that he did not have much time for writing. Then came that wonderful event in every priest's life, ordination; and after that more studying at Columbia and New York Universities and at the University of Notre Dame.

These activities resulted in the writer's first book, *The Morals of Newspaper Making,* written and published as a part requirement for his Doctor's degree in the field of Journalism. After that came several years of teaching Advertising and Selling to the young men of Notre Dame University and later on to the young ladies of Notre Dame's sister college at St. Mary's. Then he was asked to serve as an Associate Editor of the *Ave Maria,* that fine Catholic home magazine which has been going out of Notre Dame almost since the foundation of the University.

That, of course, meant a lot of writing in addition to such other duties as correcting manuscripts, reading proofs, etc. Much of that writing was in the way of editorials, and therefore unsigned. But there was an occasional story or essay and a regular weekly page of interesting items which have been running for several years now under the title, "Bits Out of Life."

In addition, there were a couple of novels for young readers; one in book form, one printed in the *Ave Maria,* and one still in the manuscript stage. The one in book form is entitled *Twisted Trails.* It tells the adventures of a red-blooded Catholic boy who ran away from school to rescue his kidnapped sister—something he really accomplished after living with tramps, traveling with a carnival, etc. The story which was published serially under the title, *King of the Pygmies,* but is not yet in book form, relates the experiences of a young boy who was wrecked off the shores of Africa and captured by the Pygmies who later made him their king in addition to helping him rescue his father who, in the meanwhile, had been captured by cannibals. The story still in manuscript is too far from completion to say much about it.

But the author's writings which have been most successful are in the form of several series of pamphlets upon which he has been engaged in recent years. They came about in this way. One day he was asked to review a book for children on the *Lives of the Saints.* After falling asleep over the first fifty pages, he said to himself: "No wonder children are not better acquainted with the saints. They have never been shown how human and interesting those friends of God really were."

So the writer set out to read all he could about the saints. And what do you suppose happened? Before he got through he found so many interesting things that he had all he could do to squeeze them between the covers of twenty separate pamphlets. And did the children enjoy them? Within a very short time they have ordered in the neighborhood of a quarter of a million of these pamphlets, with the demand still going on. The set is entitled *God's Heroes.*

Encouraged by that success, the author produced a second series of pamphlets about the wonders around us. The circulation of this series, entitled *God's Wonderworld,* will soon reach the hundred thousand mark. Next year, with the help of the good Lord, another series will come out on the various vocations of life, and, after that, so long as the children continue their enthusiastic support, still other pamphlets of interest to our young readers.

And now for a final word as to just what you young people can do in the matter of learning now to express yourselves well. The very first thing, it seems to me, is to have faith in yourselves. The Hall of Fame is filled with the names of men and women in every field who believed in themselves when everyone else doubted. Secondly, learn to make use of your eyes, so that you can pick out those million and one interesting things which most people miss in their passage through life. Thirdly, develop the ability to see the relationship of things, instead of just looking at objects by themselves. Thus will be opened up to you an entirely new world,—the real world as it was originally designed by God, although generally unseen by most men and women. Finally, keep trying to express what you see and think in the best possible manner until your words begin to carry the light and color of your own personality: that is the secret of what we call a good style.

If you keep these four objectives continually before you, I think I can promise you that some day you will become an excellent writer, and probably an excellent speaker into the bargain. Mind you, I did not say a *great* writer or speaker. Only a few have the touch of genius that arrives at real greatness. But to be a really good writer or a really good speaker is something that all of us can achieve if we will only have faith enough to work at it day after day in the manner I have indicated.

Above all, do not allow yourselves to get the idea that you lack the talents necessary to arrive at such a goal. God was not stingy in the distribution of His talents. You can be certain of that! But God does want us to show ourselves worthy of His more important gifts, so He generally buries those talents rather deep in our nature, so that we will really have to work to bring them out. Remember that Goldsmith, Dryden, Sir Walter Scott, James Russell Lowell, Emerson, Gladstone, and Thackeray didn't show much promise in their youths. Yet they kept on trying; and look where *they* got in the field of literature!

You may not climb quite so high as they did in their literary efforts; but I can assure you that if you have faith in yourselves, if you make use of the eyes and ears which God gave you, if you learn to see the relationship between things, and finally, if you follow these efforts by continually trying to express what you see and think in the best possible manner,—well, I can't say just how high you will climb; but I can promise you that it will be miles higher than most people around you. And upon that achievement, let me congratulate you, for I know that most of you are going to make the effort.

EMMET LAVERY

Dramatist

I BELIEVE VERY MUCH in this assembling of biographic material
on Catholic authors which is somewhat more personalized than
the data usually available.   But in the midst of jotting down a
few notes, I can't help recalling the old warning: if you really
want to find out about authors, the things to read are their
stories or their plays, *not* their autobiographies.

Well, it's the truth! Writers can hardly help revealing themselves in the stories they write. They can hardly avoid conceal-
ing themselves in the material they choose to assemble about
themselves. A posed picture is a posed picture. So, if you want
to catch any of us off guard, don't spend too much time on these
notes.   Read the basic material instead.

The vital statistics show that I was born in Poughkeepsie,
N. Y., Nov. 8, 1902, the son of James A. Lavery and Katherine
Gilmartin Lavery. My father was a newspaper editor, labor
leader (first President of the New York State Federation of
Labor), and New York State Civil Service Commissioner from
1914 to 1916. My mother was a woman who loved music as much

as my father loved politics. She was as quiet as he was talkative; as careful and cautious as he was reckless and daring. They were both born in Poughkeepsie, but they both felt close kinship with everything Irish, my mother in a quiet way, my father with a ready speech whenever the occasion demanded (or even if it didn't!). Their parents had come to this country about 1861 from Ireland, and I can recall my Grandmother Gilmartin telling us stories of how her brother and her sisters had much to do with food distribution during the famine in Ireland.

I never intended to write for a living. My earliest ambitions had to do with becoming a good lawyer. Principally, I suppose, because my father was a good talker and I liked to talk too. I lived around the corner from the Marists who were teaching St. Peter's Boys' Grade School and I graduated there in 1914. In 1918 I graduated from Poughkeepsie High School at the age of 15, but had to change my plans about going to college. Family finances, unpredictably up one year and down the next, were on the decline. So my mother, with an eye to the practical realities, sent me to Eastman Business School in Poughkeepsie.

I think now that this early exposure to the rules of shorthand and typing may explain many things. If the unexpected delivery of a typewriter at the door made a playwright out of the lady in *You Can't Take It with You,* then my early training on the typewriter must be all that got me a job at the ripe age of 16 as sporting editor on a daily morning newspaper in Poughkeepsie, the *Eagle-News.* I know now that I could not have been very good. But I could spell and I could operate any machine in the office, factors not to be overlooked by any city editor whose eyesight was being ruined by horrible typing and atrocious spelling.

My early newspaper career was of short duration. After a year or two, I switched to the Poughkeepsie Chamber of Commerce, where I filled in as a stenographer for a year. From there I moved across the street and became secretary to County Judge Arnold. In the fall of 1921 I returned to the staff of the Poughkeepsie *Eagle-News* as a court reporter and, with the blessing of an understanding managing editor, I began a three-year

commuting trek to Fordham University Law School. Up at
6 A.M. to catch a local for New York, then to morning classes in
the Woolworth Building, back on a noon express to Poughkeepsie, reporting to the paper about 2:30 P.M., continuing on
duty until 10:30 o'clock at night. I seemed to thrive on it, and
graduated from Fordham with an LL.B. in 1924.

My father died when I was in my junior year at Law School.
He had wanted very much when a boy to be a lawyer, and he
probably would have been very happy to be on hand when I
was sworn in as a member of the Bar of the State of New York
in 1925. But my mother was there and I have her to thank for
the patience and understanding which made so much of my
work in Law School possible. And, appropriately enough, I had
not heard the last of my father. I was to cross and recross his
trail many times, in politics as well as in the theatre.

In 1925 I married Genevieve Drislane, who had graduated
from Vassar in 1922, and who had been with me in the class that
graduated from Poughkeepsie High School in 1918. My wife
and I were both born in Poughkeepsie, and there is a tradition
in the family that she established some kind of priority by calling
on me when I was not more than a year old,—she being one
year my senior. However that may be, the fact is that we did
get married in 1925, and I promptly returned to newspaper
work. The practice of law in Poughkeepsie at that time did not
offer much of a budget for a young married couple, and I gladly
became city editor of the Poughkeepsie *Sunday-Courier,* a post I
held until 1935.

I didn't know it, but life was as nearly idyllic then as it has
ever been. For money, I edited a Sunday newspaper on a nicely
casual basis: reporting for work on Tuesday and having a leisurely week with the exception of a long trick on Saturday.
For fun, I acted in the Poughkeepsie Community Theatre and
with the men's acting company in the Experimental Theatre of
Vassar, under the direction of Hallie Flanagan. Somewhere
along the line, I got stage-struck in no uncertain fashion, especially after playing *Merton of the Movies* for the Community
Theatre. I remember I even went so far as to ask Theresa Hel-

burn of the Theatre Guild for a job, and she wisely advised me to stay in Poughkeepsie, where I could have the law, journalism, the theatre, *and* a home,—with none of the disappointments of infrequent employment on Broadway.

If I had only known it, this was the point at which my father's past was beginning to catch up with me. He too, I learned, had wanted to go on the stage as a boy. He had discovered an Irish cornetist in a Polish band who was able to hypnotize people as a special interlude during a concert of a Sunday afternoon. And father apparently saw a great future for them both "on the road." My grandmother thought otherwise, and the stage lost what certainly would have been one of its most determined managers.

About 1927, I began to work intensively at play writing. The New York theatre was only 75 miles away; so there was the chance to see good plays. And there was always an opportunity to observe the work of Hallie Flanagan's classes at Vassar. My enthusiasm developed more rapidly than anything else, with nearly disastrous results. Since the Poughkeepsie Community Theatre had been founded originally by Professor Gertrude Buck of Vassar College to encourage the writing and testing of new plays, I decided to live up to tradition. I offered the theatre my first play, *Crusade*. Well, offered is hardly the word. I forced it on them in a none too delicate way. It was a newspaper play, which stemmed a little from local history. The papers roasted us and the executive committee of the theatre voted never to do a new play again. I am happy to report that the motion lost by one vote—mine.

In between the writing of plays on every theme imaginable, there was the much more important business of living. Our oldest child, Emmet Jr., was born in 1927. In 1928 I was elected as a Republican to the Board of Aldermen, where my father had sat for many years before me, and where an uncle, Charles I. Lavery, now sat as minority leader on the Democratic side. In 1930 our Deborah was born; and by that time I was serving as President of the Board of Aldermen. Those were the days when we Laverys —accidentally but effectively—rather dominated the political scene in Poughkeepsie. Another uncle, Thomas A. Lavery, a

Georgetown graduate, was serving as a (Republican) Assistant District Attorney.

Deborah died in 1932. Elizabeth, our red head, was born in 1934, and the same year Bert Lytell produced *The First Legion* on Broadway. It ran for three months in New York, six months on the road; and thereafter was translated and produced in ten languages. Through it I discovered many fine things: many rare and enduring friendships in the theatre the world over, among non-Catholics as well as Catholics; best of all, I discovered the Catholic tradition of which the play was unconsciously a part. As for the play, I wish I could do a book about it. Or rather about the people whom it brought together in and out of the theatre. For there isn't so much to say about the play. It was number eight or nine in the family series; a sincere effort to study the problems of men in the Church, prompted in part by our pleasant experiences at home in a community production of Sierra's *Cradle Song* at Christmas time. We came together from all parishes to do this play for the Monsignor who later became the Monsignor of *First Legion*. We never found another play we liked so well, and I began to wonder if there was a play in the men of the Church. *The First Legion* was the result, but only a book could do justice to the men and women the world over who, sometimes Catholic and sometimes not, have fought and lived for this play. I owe more than I can report to the early encouragement and steadfast faith of Father Francis X. Talbot, S.J., in the whole enterprise. He was then the crusading Literary Editor of *America,* and long before production he gave unreservedly his professional opinion that the play would be good for the theatre and good for the Church. Now it seems surprising that anyone ever questioned the fact. But back in 1934 he was a lone voice speaking out when few were ready to hazard any opinion in public at all.

Our John was born in 1935, and died the same year. That fall we went to Hollywood, where I remained as a scenario writer until the spring of 1937. On the way East, we stopped off at Chicago and there we organized the first session of the Catholic Theatre Conference. From 1937 to 1939 I served as Director of the National Service Bureau of Federal Theatre. In the spring of 1939, my wife and I had the good fortune to make a quick trip to Europe. In Paris I saw the 200th performance of *First Legion* at the Vieux Colombier; in England we met the author of *Brother Petroc's Return,* which I had adapted for the stage, and Father Henry Tristram of the Oratorians, who had helped me so much with the manuscript of the Newman play, *Second Spring.* In the fall of 1939, I became visiting lecturer in drama at Fordham University. The major output of our play writing seminar at Fordham was the student play on Edmund Campion, entitled *Who Ride on White Horses* (included in the Longmans' publication, *Theatre for Tomorrow*).

We spent the year 1940 at Vassar, where I served as Assistant Director of the Bureau of Theatre Research on a grant from the Rockefeller Foundation, assisting Professor Hallie Flanagan in the preparation of *Arena,* the history of Federal Theatre. While at Vassar, I collaborated with Ernst Krenek, composer of *Jonny Spielt Auf,* on a new form of modern opera, *Tarquin,* which we tested in a special demonstration reading for the Experimental Theatre.

In 1941, we came back to Hollywood to work at RKO, where I still am in the summer of 1942. I am continuing as chairman of the Catholic Theatre Conference and, needless to say, I believe more intensely than ever before in the survival of the theatre. Pictures are one thing. The stage is another. Both mediums will endure so long as both have the necessary vitality. It is not a question of either supplanting the other.

I haven't any advice to offer writers. The rules are seldom the same for any two people. For myself, all I can say is: writing for the sake of writing is pretty empty stuff. Life comes first. If you have something to write about, the chances are that the honest saying of it will create its own form. Consequently, it's much more important to determine what you're going to *live,* rather than spend so much time deciding what you're going to write. No wonder doctors, for example, have been writing so many good books in recent years: the life came first, the writing later.

I believe in the visualizing power of good theatre to make real the enduring fact of Christianity; I believe especially in the power of sound historical drama "to make the great ones live again;" I believe in the non-professional theatre as much as I do in the professional theatre, hoping and working constantly for the wise interchange of values between both these fields of theatre; I believe, above all, in the power of a theatre with a philosophy of intensely human experience so constant and so clear, that we can face frankly the issue: are we living what we think, and if not, why not?

Dramas by Mr. Lavery include: *First Legion*, 1934, French; *Second Spring*, 1937, Longmans; *Brief Music*, 1940, French; *Brother Petroc's Return* (adapted from the novel of that title by S.M.C.), 1940, French; *Monsignor's Hour*, 1937, French; and, in collaboration with Miss Grace Murphy, *Kamiano*, one of the three plays in *Theatre for Tomorrow*, published by Longmans.

**REVEREND DANIEL
ALOYSIUS LORD, S.J.**

*Novelist, Dramatist and Writer
of Religious Works*

I SUPPOSE that every writer, be he important or occasional, of the eternal or the purely topical breed, must pay his respects to heredity and environment.

My own bow to heredity is deep and grateful. There was in my remote past a grandfather who left me his love of writing and his unspeakable penmanship. He was a Presbyterian Minister who wrote the most charming letters to my Father, which my Father turned over to my Mother for the simple reason that he couldn't possibly make out the awful scrawl. But I sat enthralled at the wit and charm of those letters, and their influence was considerable.

Then there was that dear Mother, who should have been a literary woman, if the death of her father and the genteel poverty of her mother had not sent her out to work when most youngsters are entering sixth grade. But how she loved books! How delightfully she could read aloud to that little family circle over which she presided! How carefully she inducted me into the

great writings from the fairy tales to Shakespeare, from Mother
Goose to Thackeray! And how charming were her letters until
the end of her days.

Then there is my debt to environment. From infancy, I find
myself living in an atmosphere of books. We never were well
to do, our family; but we were well enough off to indulge a
taste for a good library. And I can remember books all over
the house when I can remember almost nothing else. From the
first Christmas I can recall, my Mother was teaching me to accumulate my own library, into which came, when my Grandfather died, a large stock of the books he had loved and gathered
around him.

Then in the apartment below us moved young Doctor Bailey,
a physician who practiced medicine skillfully and loved books
devotedly. So he turned me loose among his shelves, and I
read and read and read—books which to these days stick to the
ribs of my soul and have been a lifelong influence.

Sister Mary Blanche got me interested in the splendid Sodality
Library she built up for us at old Holy Angels. And when I
reached the end of my high school days, Claude J. Pernin, S.J.,
crossed my lucky path, and I sat at his feet in his smoke filled
room while he talked of books and authors and writers and writing with a persuasive eloquence I've never felt in any other man.
He'd been a newspaper man before he became a Jesuit. To the
end of his useful days as lecturer and teacher, he inducted two
generations into the joys of reading and the skills of writing.

So you see, with that sort of start the wonder is that I didn't
become a good writer, instead of merely a writer. For I can't
recall a time when I wasn't trying my hand at literature. As a
little kid, I tried to write plays for boys and girls of the block.
Mathematics might bore me; I never failed to enjoy the task of
turning out an English theme. I can recall plotting out a novel
in my first year high—and getting as far as the middle of the first
chapter.

In first year high, by the way, I had the good luck to meet both
Brother Paschal, my teacher, and Brother Baldwin, my principal,
at De La Salle in Chicago; and both of them could teach English

most delightfully and persuasively. They found me a willing
pupil, and though I never got first place in English Comp., nobody handed in longer themes or had more fun doing them
than I did.

At St. Ignatius in Chicago, I first ran into the possibilities of
school journalism. Because of what it did for me, I spend a lot
of time telling young people to be sure to write for their school
papers. Father Pernin was our journalism moderator; around
him he had assembled the finest crowd of young fellows, all keen
on reading and all determined to be writers. Roche today is a
very important advertising man; Royce has long edited the *In-
land Catholic* in Spokane; Quinn is Jesuit Dean of Detroit University, and I made up the fourth of our aspiring writers.

But we wrote all we could. We thought we ran the school
paper, and did our share of it. We experimented with all sorts
of literary forms—short stories, verse, criticism, drama. Bert
Leston Taylor had just invented the art of columning; we imi-
tated him faithfully. We discovered the nonsense verse of the
Ingoldsby Legends and the great Gilbert, and tried to duplicate
it. We even wrote our own musical comedy, with Quinn and
myself doing all the music, Royce and myself the lyrics, and
Roche the book. And Father Pernin turned upon our stuff a
critical eye that was like a blue pencil rampant. Great training,
and I loved it.

Then I jointed the Jesuits. There I found a tradition of
writing as old as the Order itself. Jesuits began their work when
the printing press was still a novelty, and they had used it to its
limit.

So from the start, I was fired with the desire to write. I put
aside about four hours a week, and spent that much time writing,
come high water or the call of the ballfield. Writing, I had
already learned from Father Pernin, is not a matter of inspiration; it's a trade and must be mastered like a trade—with work
and more work, with experience, practice, and effort. For that
information, I am most grateful.

During my Juniorate, I started a paper for my fellow Jesuits,
and after a time found that I was not merely editing but actually

writing most of it. Then with a small group, I formed the WWWWW Club, called usually the Five W's. That meant "We Will Write, Won't We?" and on holidays we read one another our productions, took criticism gamely, and dished it out lavishly. Of the six who belonged, five have since done professional writing.

A lucky illness brought me professionally into the writing field. At the end of my fourth year as a Jesuit, I had an attack of typhoid which kept me from going on with the regular course of studies. Instead I was deflected to St. Louis to help Father Garesche found *The Queen's Work*. So for a year I was more or less free to try to write and edit. It was a great experience, and set me finally in the line that I've never quite forsaken. But, for your encouragement, of the first nine productions I submitted for publication, eight were turned down flat, sent home repeatedly with curt rejections. (That was bad; for my very first attempt at professional writing, a short story written in my college Sophomore days, was bought by *The Black Cat,* and my first verse sent off was bought when I was a Junior by *The Lady's Home Companion.)*

During my philosophical studies, I wondered if I could write Scholastic Philosophy in a style anyone could understand. So I tried my hand at it, first in some short bits for *America* and then in the series which afterwards came out as *Armchair Philosophy*. Simultaneously Frank Quinn, now a fellow Jesuit, and I, turned our hands to musical comedy, and did "Full Steam Ahead," "Rouge and Rapid Fire," and "Over and Back," all varsity shows for St. Louis University students.

By this time, thanks to the kind interest of Father Tierney, I was a regular contributor to *America.. Extension* had taken a story or two, and *The Queen's Work* found me often in its pages. Then a great piece of luck happened. I often tell young writers: "If you want to write, get a strong like or a powerful hate. The hate may prove more effective." I ran across George Bernard Shaw's *Androcles and the Lion,* grew perfectly furious at his treatment of Catholic martyrs, wrote furiously and for the first time fluently, and found Father John Burke of *The Catholic*

World accepting it, and asking for another on Shaw. Which he eventually got.

At the same time, because I loved the theater, I was trying out varied play forms, chiefly short plays and things to be put on by youngsters in grammar school. A number of them have since appeared in print. They led, by the way, eventually to my writing a series of pageants, "Alma Mater," "The Dreamer Awakes," "Mother of Youth," and so on; and much later to our series of Catholic Follies, an experiment that gave a lot of young actors a chance to do their stuff for Catholic truth and art.

In 1925 I was reassigned to *The Queen's Work,* this time as its editor; and to the Sodality, which meant that henceforth I should work largely among young people.

That is how the pamphlets happened. I had done one on the Little Flower at the request of Benzigers. Now I wanted pamphlets that would answer the questions asked by young people and that would tackle the problems they constantly find. Those pamphlets still continue at the rate of about ten a year. They are always the result of suggestions or questions young people ask me. They have a circulation of something under a million a year.

When the Mother died who had so profoundly influenced my life, I wanted people to meet her. That is why I did *My Mother.* When I found out that the teachers and moderators were often puzzled by their young people, I wrote *Some notes on the Guidance of Youth.*

A trip to Europe resulted in a series of letters home, which eventually appeared in *My European Diary.* And a series of lectures at one of our Summer Schools of Catholic Action later appeared as *Our Lady in the Modern World.*

Writing is by no means the most important job assigned me. My real work is for the Sodality of Our Lady. Writing must be incidental to that, and largely directed to help the young men and women with whom pleasant association throws me. For them I edit *The Queen's Work,* writing a fair share of it, including a serial novel each year. Out of the pleasant things that happen to me in my travels I write a syndicated weekly column called "Along the Way." For a time I did "Hi, Gang!" for *Our Sunday Visitor* the first part of which is now published in a book.

But to anyone with any slightest inclination toward writing, I should say, "Gratify it to the full!" It's hard work. You have to be willing to slave at your trade. You have to launch an article and have no slightest response. You send out your book not knowing whether it will be liked, ignored, or torn to pieces. People will read your stuff and write you unintelligent, insulting letters. Critics will miss your whole point and abuse you for what you never said.

But you don't much care. You have the constant sense of achievement. You come into contact with the most delightful people. The fact that you are looking constantly for material, keeps your eyes open, your ears sharp, and your sense keen. You read more avidly because you want to see how others do what you would like to do. You find the whole world acutely interesting, for out of it you may find grist for your mill.

If you happen to be a genius, you won't need any of my advice or counsel. If you are just a plain person like myself, who writes because he enjoys it, because it is a sort of continued correspondence he keeps up with a clearly perceived audience, just remember that it's work but grand fun.

With the enemies of God using writing so effectively against truth and decency, even someone with quite ordinary abilities and not great literary style, someone, in other words like myself and maybe yourself, can do a little for the glorious truth that is Christ's, the splendid beauty that fills the world, and the advancement of the Kingdom of God in the hearts of men.

The Guide to Catholic Literature, 1888–1940, includes seventy-eight of Father Lord's works. Since its publication he has written *Hi Gang* (1941), *Murder in a Sacristy* (1940), *Our Lady in the Modern World* (1940), *That Made Me Smile* (1941), and a number of pamphlets. All are published by The Queen's Work Press, in St. Louis.

ANNA SHANNON McALLISTER

(Mrs. Earl S. McAllister)

MY PATERNAL GRANDPARENTS came to America from Athlone, Ireland, in the 1840's, staying for a time in Maryland where my father, Frank Shannon, was born, and later migrating to Ohio. My mother, Ella Stewart, was descended from Patrick Stewart, who emigrated from Perthshire, Scotland, to Salisbury, North Carolina, in 1739. After the Revolution, mother's branch of the Stewarts went to Pennsylvania, settling Stewartown, now Etna.

I was the sixth of eight children, and was born in Cincinnati, Ohio, in 1888. For two years I attended Court Street Academy taught by the Sisters of Notre Dame de Namur. Our family moved to Columbus, Ohio, in 1896, and I had the same excellent teachers at St. Joseph's Academy. In 1905 I graduated from the Columbus School for Girls. I was president of my class as a senior and presided over the alumnae for ten years. I received a B.A. degree from Ohio State University in 1909, presumably majoring in History and English; but, being a sociable person, I really majored in campus activities. The summer after graduation I spent abroad with my parents and sisters.

In November 1911, I married Earl Sadler McAllister, of
Columbus, a graduate of Arts and Law at Ohio State University.
My husband did not practice his profession, but went into busi-
ness, retiring in 1933. Among our many mutual interests was a
love of reading. Together we read the lives of great Americans.
Sometimes I wrote reviews and an occasional magazine article.

But I never wrote formally until I read Lloyd Lewis' *Sherman:
Fighting Prophet,* in 1933. I closed the book wishing fervently
that I knew more about General Sherman's wife, Ellen Ewing,
and her delightful mother, Maria Boyle Ewing. Then I decided
to write a sketch of their lives myself. I found no material on
either woman on our libraries, and thus I had to rely on family
letters. My first problem was to locate relatives. I prepared a
list of questions to ask each one, believing that if I checked their
answers, I could not be far wrong in my conclusions. Ellen
Sherman's niece, Mrs. Charles Montgomery, of Newark, loaned
me hundreds of family letters; but she doubted if anyone had
any of her Aunt Ellen's letters. She told me, however, the
Shermans had a son, Mr. P. Tecumseh Sherman, living in New
York City, who might have some. My letter to Mr. Sherman
must have caught his fancy, though his reply was cautious. Most
of his parents' letters had been destroyed by fire, so he wrote;
but he added that his niece, Miss Eleanor Fitch (who was then in
Rome) had much data on her grandmother's life and might be
able to help me. Then to my surprise, a few days later Mr.
Sherman wrote that he "had dug out an old chest" and found his
mother's and grandparents' correspondence and would send it
to me as soon as he had it filed.

At my dictation my husband had been typing the letters we
already had. We had barely finished them when a huge package
of letters arrived, giving me my first glimpse of Ellen Sherman.
Before me lay the history of her life up to the Civil War. From
then on there were only six letters to show her attitude during
those soul-trying years. And still I had not seen one line of hers
to her husband! Then one day in July 1934, Miss Fitch expressed two heavily-insured boxes containing a thousand of
Ellen's letters to General Sherman. Fascinating epistles they

were, sparkling with the charm that kept Sherman captivated
through long years of separation. Far from destroying his
wife's correspondence, as he had been accused of doing in gruff
indifference, the General had saved it all. Carefully he marked
her name at the top of each letter with the date he answered it.

By now I had nearly three thousand letters. Day after day I
dictated and studied them until I was saturated with my subject.
In October I went to New York for a personal interview with
Mr. Sherman and his niece. The experiences of that visit would
seem incredible to me if I had not kept a diary. I shall never forget my first dinner with Mr. Sherman. I needed no note-book
to ingrave on my mind the slim, soldierly figure, nor the huski-
ness of his voice as he spoke of his tenderly loved mother.

Each morning I worked at the New York Historical Society
going through old newspaper files. I had luncheon and tea
with Miss Fitch. One noon she asked Father John A. Toomey,
S.J., associate editor of *America,* to luncheon. On leaving, Father
Toomey invited me to *America* the next afternoon. I was
promptness itself for so unique an appointment. I remember
vividly the editor-in-chief, Father Francis X. Talbot, S.J. He
seemed genuinely interested in my proposed book.

Proof of how naive I was, I strolled into the *Commonweal*
offices one morning and asked to see the editor, Mr. Michael
Williams. By merest chance I struck a leisure moment. Inviting
me into his private office, Mr. Williams listened attentively to
my tale. When I finished I asked him what he thought of a
book on Ellen Ewing; and he too, like Father Talbot answered:
"I think it is a Catholic literary scoop."

I came home quite worn out after two weeks research in New
York and a week in Washington, D. C., visiting the family of
General Charles Ewing. But a few days' rest with the memory
of all the encouragement I had received, revived me. For eight
months I wrote steadily, ten and twelve hours a day. Then my
long-suffering husband typed and retyped the pages until chapter
by chapter was completed, and I had reconstructed the life-story
of *Ellen Ewing, Wife of General Sherman.*

After its publication by Benziger Brothers in June 1936, I

began almost at once to look for another subject. For many years I had kept a journal of the books I read and the people I should like to know more about. Turning its pages I found the name of Sarah Worthington Peter. Born in Chillicothe, Ohio, in 1800, and dying in Cincinnati in 1877, she was an attractive and important personage. Contrary to my experience with Ellen Ewing, I discovered considerable published material on Sarah Peter. Every encyclopedia had articles about her. The newspapers of the day headlined her. Highly educated, a fluent linguist, and a world traveler, Sarah Peter knew everyone of prominence in her time. Pope Pius IX held her in esteem. The cardinal-princes of Rome vied with each other in granting her favors. The royal families of Austria, Saxony, and Bavaria received her time and again in audience.

I managed to secure the two-volume *Memoir of Mrs. Peter,* written by her daughter-in-law. Told in rambling fashion and with total disregard to chronology, the *Memoir* nevertheless supplied many leads. A biographer is somewhat of a literary detective. Really, more than half the fun comes from discovering and running down clues. For instance, I wrote to Mrs. Margaret Chanler, author of *A Roman Spring,* whose mother, Mrs. Thomas Crawford, was a warm friend of Mrs. Peter. Mrs. Chanler suggested that I appeal to Mrs. Lancelot Wood, residing in Rome. In turn, Mrs. Wood referred me to Mr. Frank Spearman, noted author and convert, living in Hollywood, California. Thus it happened times without number that I sent inquiry across the ocean, only to be shuttled back to our own continent, gathering crumbs of information along the way that must all be sorted out and appraised in value.

Perhaps my most interesting experience was in Cambridge, Massachusetts, where my husband and I spent a day at historic Craigie House, long the home of Henry Longfellow. I was eager to see if I could find any information about Sarah's association with Longfellow when he was a young professor at Harvard and taught her two sons. Mr. Henry Dana, a grandson, graciously showed us through the beautiful old mansion, even unlocking a corner cupboard containing his grandfather's diaries and class-

books, and telling me I might copy whatever was of interest to
me. Left alone with these priceless records, I could scarcely
confine my attention to the pages referring to Sarah and her
sons. The richly-furnished library, together with the intimate
glimpses into the poet's heart, distracted me. Nonetheless, I
contrived to fill many pages with valuable notes.

Arranging the abundant data was no slight task. A grand-
nephew, Mr. James Worthington, of Chevy Chase, sent me a
drawing of the famliy crest. Its motto, "In Winter We
Flourish," I thought an appropriate title for a biography of
Sarah Peter, whose winter of life was so fruitful. Longmans
published this, my second book, in October 1939.

To complete a trilogy of notable Ohio women, I did extensive
research on Madeleine Vinton Dahlgren, who was born in the
fascinating old French settlement of Gallipolis, Ohio, in 1835.
The impossibility of obtaining necessary data from abroad, com-
pelled me to lay my manuscript aside. I hope only "for the
duration."

I am now engaged in the agreeable occupation of writing the
life of Ellen Ewing's cousin, Eliza Gillespie. Known in religion
as Mother Angela, she was the American Foundress of the Sisters
of the Holy Cross. Her story is set against a background rich in
historic and spiritual adventure.

I use the words "agreeable occupation" in their full meaning.
I like to read biography,—and I like to write it. Not that the
writing is always easy. Some days I sit at my typewriter for
hours at a stretch, and then have nothing to show for my labor.
But the next day I reap the reward. My mind soars on wings.
The sentences flow smoothly, the paragraphs have their proper
sequence, the story takes on reality. Thus, while some authors
set themselves a daily quota of *words,* I find a daily quota of
hours at my desk a more effective discipline in composition.

A beginner may choose whichever method of work best suits
his temperament. He will do well to cultivate a graceful style
of narrative. Whether he writes history, biography, or fiction, a
felicitous selection of words and material is essential. Even what
is called Catholic fiction should not be read like a pietistic

homily, no matter how cleverly disguised. Catholic fiction
should tell the incidents of every day life, lived according to
Christian principles, but narrated as naturally and unconsciously
as the characters breathe God's air. Religion colors and spices
our thoughts and actions. A spiritual implication dramatizes
them in fiction as well. Every one loves a happy ending to a
story. Today, more than ever, we must believe that there will
be a happy ending to our troubled old world. We can do our bit
towards that inevitable culmination by lighting the fires of faith
and optimism along the road.

Biography of the right sort does just that. And that is why I
have chosen for my special literary field the re-discovery of our
great Catholic women, whose notable achievements in a past
generation are virtually unknown today.

REVEREND JAMES F. McELHONE, C.S.C.

Spiritual Writer

SOME YEARS AGO—between 1896 and 1903—it used to be quite a thrill watching the steamboats go up or down the Allegheny River. That was before the lock was built near Highland Park. Of course the boats had to stay clear of shallow waters and keep in the channel in such places as necessary.

Coming down the river with their heavy loads of sand or gravel, the boats proceeded with more caution than when going up travelling light. But, whether the water was low or not unusually high, the pilots expertly guided their cargoes down stream past sand bars and gravel bars to sure and safe deepness.

Up the river, where the Five Mile Bridge once stood, there was one particularly dangerous spot. Seemingly the sand or the gravel in the river drifted, and in spite of expert caution, or what we believed to be expert caution, occasionally a boat or a barge would go aground. Then came our thrill! Word would run along and we would hasten with all speed to the river, watching from the shore, listening to the bells, wondering what they

meant. Awed we were, no doubt, as the crew tried this maneuver
and that to get their boat or barge into deep water.

Excitedly we looked on, our imagination at work then and,
save for the main fact, now. Still, at that time, there could be no
prophetic foresight telling us that the day should come—well,
bit by bit, the boat or the barge would be worked into navigable
waters by the crew; and bit by bit books have been written.

To emphasize and also to explain in a fuller way. From the
window of his room this author can look across the east corner
of one of the lakes at the University of Notre Dame. The cross
on the church steeple rises high; and so does the American flag
on the flagstaff. Nowadays sometimes near twilight a mist comes
drifting and mingles with the evening shadows. Then it is easy
to recall that a century ago Indians lived here, that the pioneer
missionary, Father Badin, is buried here, that members of the
Congregation from France founded a school which has been
blessed. Fire visited it, but new beginnings were made, and
progress continued. Spirit grew more strong. Many buildings
and a wide campus give testimony. The message of the Church
and the glory of patriotism were sincerely regarded as the important measures of development.

This, then my tribute. Many are the items which deserve
praise. Selection is required. So my tribute is to my grade
school instructor who made winning the memorization of poetry;
to my high school instructor who aptly used class periods for the
public and inspiring reading of short stories; to the priest who
labored that we, his students, might learn to write with at least
some distinction; to the varied elements of education (debates,
oratorical and elocution contests, musicals, lectures, dramas,
distinguished visitors and speakers, worth-while sermons), for
these, somewhat singly and certainly altogether, fostered in their
continued and appropriate manner an appreciation of the
cultural.

The joys gathered from reading cannot be estimated; nor the
instruction. Would that the authors could know that! Valued
were the books of younger years. Naturally the appreciation of
them notably and noticeably, deeply and sincerely increased.

Furthermore, the reading was accompanied by class assignments in writing. Several things of this author were printed before his graduation from Notre Dame in 1911, the year he joined the Congregation of the Holy Cross. The verse, just commonplace verse; the prose, without real quality, save for an essay or two.

After his ordination to the priesthood in 1916, among other classes at Notre Dame he taught English, and really learned a lot. That statement is justly and charitably accurate. A few years later came the realization that a meditation book was needed for seminarians and young religious. He began to write—maybe five or six meditations a week (perhaps three or four pages). A book took shape—possibly over a period of five years. In 1926, it was published under the title: *Following Our Divine Model.* Later, bit by bit, other work being taken care of, a second book was written, and published in 1929. It was called *Particular Examen,* the name of a religious exercise at which a particular, not a general, examination of conscience is made. A juvenile, *Tim,* was written gradually, printed in serial form, and in 1934 in book form. And in 1935, the material of a serial was printed: *Feasts of Our Lady,* thirty-one meditations for May or October or the days on which the feasts occur.

Slow and steady and persevering was the writing. The material was gathered. The effort was to be practical; and the hope, helpful. Reviewers and critics have been kind.

EDITOR'S NOTE: Father McElhone, now Associate Editor of *Ave Maria,* is the author of: *Following Our Divine Model* (Herder, 1926, 2d edition 1929), *Particular Examen* (Herder, 1929), *Tim* (Benziger, 1934), and *Feasts of Our Lady* (Bruce, 1935).

SISTER MARY MADELEVA,
C.S.C.

(Mary Evaline Wolff)
Poet

PETER ARNTZ was a scholar and a frontiersman. At thirty he had acquired five languages, travelled two continents, and come back home to Essen on the Rhine to marry nineteen-year-old Bernadine Schmidt. Immediately they sailed for America and settled on a mill site at the dells of the Wisconsin River. Mr. Arntz was a lumberman. His mill supplied the lumber for the first buildings at the Dominican convent and academy at Sinsinawa, Wisconsin.

During the first seven months in her new Wisconsin home, the lady wife from the Old World saw no woman but Indian squaws. She acquired of necessity a heritage of courage for her thirteen children.

Lucy was the third eldest and the self-appointed mother of these. Her sense of responsibility developed from childhood. She finished country school and later through high school qualified to teach her own district school. Summers she clerked in the big general store in Mauston, Wisconsin.

Years before, a little peasant boy in a Pomeranian village of Prussia hopped home on the flagstones from the brook where he had washed his bare feet. Home was a thatched cottage with a big fireplace and a crane for cooking. He was August Wolff. His father was dead. His brother and sister, twins, and his sturdy little mother were all the family. They were leaving for America.

Nine weeks in a sailing vessel and a long overland journey brought them to Richwood, Wisconsin, where they began life anew on a small farm.

August supported himself and in part the little family from this, his ninth, year. A Lutheran Sunday school supplied most of his education. He learned the harness trade in Watertown, Wisconsin, worked in the harness shop of August Ringling of Baraboo with the brothers of circus fame, then went to Mauston to take charge of the harness shop in the big general store.

Here he met Lucy Arntz. They were married New Year's Day, 1884, and went to Cumberland, Wisconsin, to begin life together in a northern Wisconsin lumber town.

There were three children, Fred, Eva, Vern. The only daughter, baptized Mary Evaline, was born May 24, 1887. Childhood for all three children was filled with the wild, rich beauty of northern woods and lakes, the rigor of severe winters, the disciplines of simple living. Even as a small girl Eva knew wild life with accurate intimacy, skated and swam with intrepidity, and longed to live on a farm. Sundays in summer were spent on long drives, walks, boat rides, picnics. During the fall they hunted. Winters the small girl climbed on her father's knee and together they read poetry, humor, cartoons, but mostly poetry.

At eighteen she had graduated and postgraduated from the public high school. Fred was a junior engineer at the University of Wisconsin, so she matriculated there. The two were part of the group of Catholic students to found the Newman Club at the university, the first Newman Club to be established at any state university.

One evening during the summer vacation she sat on the porch

reading a current magazine. She had been persistently per-
turbed with the question of God's purpose in creating her. The
magazine carried the usual summer advertisements for schools.
Among them she found a small notice of Saint Mary's College,
Notre Dame, Indiana. She read it over with peculiar excitement. She put it beside her growing anxiety as to why God had
made her. The next day with characteristic decision and independence, she announced to her parents that she was not returning to the university in the fall; she was going to Saint Mary's.
She did what she decided to do.

Adjustment from public school and coeducation to the almost
French discipline of boarding school were as much a problem for
her prefects as for Eva Wolff. The transition involved multiplied penances, but no casualties.

She shared the proverbial aversion for Freshman English and
expected to major in mathematics. Sister Rita had just returned
to Saint Mary's from a trip abroad in a party of which Elizabeth
Jordan was a member. She taught English. She transfigured
life for Eva Wolff.

There was the discovery of an ability to write, to write verse,
of a love of words and of their obedience to one, of Beauty beyond
beauty. The English class and Sister Rita became the great inspiration in life.

There was still the question of why God had made her. On
Memorial Day, 1908, one of her teachers said casually, "I suppose
if you thought you had a vocation you would be furious." The
girl answered without hesitation, "No, I would be the happiest
girl in the world."

She entered the novitiate at Saint Mary's September fourteenth
of that year. On December tenth she received the habit of the
Sisters of the Holy Cross and became Sister Mary Madeleva.

For the next eleven years she taught in the high school and
the college there. At the sudden death of Sister Rita in 1910, the
mantle of the beloved teacher fell on her young shoulders and
her work of teaching college English began in profound earnest.

While teaching, she had the opportunity to complete her work
for a master's degree at the University of Notre Dame. Summer

school brought her the inspiring direction and friendship of
Father Charles O'Donnell and her first experience in writing
for publication. The *Ave Maria, The Bookman, The Catholic
World,* printed her verse.

In 1919 she left Saint Mary's for the West, its inspiration and
grandeur. As principal and English teacher at Sacred Heart
Academy, Ogden, Utah, she found herself under the fortunate
necessity to continue writing. In 1921 she entered the summer
session of the University of California at Berkeley and the classes
of Professors John Livingston Lowes and Benjamin H. Lehman.
As a result of her work with them she was admitted to candidacy
for a doctor's degree. She was sent to Holy Rosary Academy,
Woodland, California, to facilitate her studies, to teach, and to
act as principal of the academy. When her work was completed
in 1925, she was the first Sister to qualify for a doctor's degree at
the University of California.

During these four years she did critical writing under the
direction of Henry Seidel Canby and published her first three
books, *Knights Errant, Chaucer's Nuns, Pearl.* The two prose
volumes were done as seminar papers and dissertation. The following year she returned to Utah.

The Sisters of the Holy Cross began the building of a college
in Salt Lake City in 1925. Sister Madeleva went up to the new
building, high up on the Wasatch Mountains, with the first load
of furniture to open the college in 1926. Here she was first dean,
then president.

The next seven years were times of robust pioneering and sub-
stantial academic adventure. Mountains, horizons, deserts became a part of a very wonderful education for teachers as for
students. And another book, *Penelope,* had come into existence.

New horizons opened in 1933, when Sister Madeleva was sent
by her mother general to Europe for a year of study and travel.
The study was essentially Oxford. The travel took her as far
as the Holy Land. Europe meant people as well as places to her:
Charles DuBos in Paris, Edith Wharton in Hyères, Johannes
Jorgensen at Assisi, Helen Robins at Siena, the Meynells in London, Yeats in Dublin, Seumas MacManus in Donegal. From all

she returned to Saint Mary's in August, 1934, to find herself the president of the college to whose rules she had found such difficulty in adjusting twenty-eight years before.

Here she has met the challenge and the opportunity that youth always presents. Her greatest ambition for her students is to make them lovers of truth; for her faculty, to make them lovers of wisdom. To that end the text has been engraved at the entrance of the college, "You shall know the truth and the truth shall make you free."

A Williamsburg house set in an English garden has been added during her administration to the department of home economics, and a beautiful library, the realization of an ambition of years. During her unimaginable leisure she has contrived numbers of lectures, has got together a half dozen small volumes of verse, has become the president of the Catholic Poetry Society of America. She has likewise been included among the first in the Gallery of Living Catholic Authors.

If you go into Sister Madeleva's office you will find an old world on the walls, pictures from Chartres and Florence, triptychs from Greece. Somewhere in the files are parchments and academic hoods testifying to degrees of doctor of letters from Manhattan College and Mount Mary College. Her inner office is her treasure house, rich in manuscripts, old books, the mystics, Chaucer, quaint walking sticks, bird and flower books.

If you look for her you may find her on the campus rhapsodizing to some student on the wonder of the unfolding leaves of a copper beach, or you may discover her down the avenue sharing with the exclusive thrashers the secrets of building a nest.

Sister Madeleva is the author of *Chaucer's Nuns, and Other Essays*, 1925, Appleton; *Pearl: a Study in Spiritual Dryness*, 1925, Appleton; and (poems) *Christmas Eve*, 1938, St. Anthony Guild; *Gates*, 1938, Macmillan; *Happy Christmas Wind*, 1936, St. Anthony Guild; *Knights Errant*, 1923, Appleton; *Penelope*, 1927, Appleton; *Question of Lovers*, 1935, St. Anthony Guild; *Selected Poems*, 1939, Macmillan; *Four Girls*, 1941, St. Anthony Guild.

HELENE MAGARET

Three Discoveries

WHATEVER A BOY or girl may become in time—a writer, a farmer, a politician, a housewife—in the journey from childhood to maturity he or she will make three discoveries: the discovery of the world, the discovery of self, and the discovery of a significant relationship between them. Every individual must use the wisdom gained from these discoveries, but only the author will keep a written record of them.

It is in childhood that we first discover the world—the fragrance of earth after spring plowing, the whorls of russet hair on the chest of a pet dog, the plunge of an elevator down a long dark shaft, the impatient clang of trolley cars, the odor of monoxide gas, lights flashing at night along a rain-swept highway. The growing child may form these images into a pattern of words, and the result will not be prose, but poetry. I have an early memory of myself as a thin, weedy child of seven or eight, trying awkwardly to make a permanent record of such transient sensations. I was not to realize the meaning of these efforts until many years later.

Only with the second discovery, that of self, does the imagination create dreams of personal success. Then the child says
boldly, "I shall be a writer." His elders, if they are wise, will
hold their peace. Sometime the discovery of self comes suddenly
with the first sharp grief or the first joy of young love burning
its way into the adolescent heart; sometimes it comes in a sense
of tremendous power. Now word-pictures of lakes and wind-
blown trees take on new life. The images become less important.
They are only the means by which the young writer expresses his
grief or joy or wonder. Here lyric poetry begins. Such were the
half-finished verses which the weedy child, grown taller, more
shy and furtive, hid in bureau drawers or scrawled on the back
pages of school notebooks, always half-hopeful, yet afraid, that
someone might find them. This may also be called the discovery of the soul.

The child became a girl, and with two helter-skelter years of
college behind her, she found herself in an office in her home-
town, Omaha, Nebraska. Sigrid Undset once wrote that she
was for some years an "office-rat." I have wanted to reply that
it makes no difference what one does or where one lives, so long
as the interplay between the world and the self gathers richness
and meaning, and so long as one battles against the world's effort
to bend the self to its own will. While the young woman grew
to hate the click of typewriters and stamp machines, the ill-humor
of business men incoherently mumbling dictation behind the fog
of cigar smoke, the bickering among stenographers, and the
dreary monotony of identical days, all these experiences seeped
into her subconscious mind, giving her knowledge, maturity, in-
sight into human nature and understanding of one small corner
of a complex civilization. If the days were unpleasant, so much
sweeter were the evenings kept free for writing.

These, I think, are the most important years of a writer's life,
when the only faith one knows is faith in oneself. Then the
sheets that tumble into the wastebasket, the unwanted manuscripts that again and again return in the mail, the novels
planned but never written are like Czerny Exercises. In later life
the writer may not work with such confident hope, with such

dogged determination, or with such apparent waste of human strength. Later, although the writing may come harder and less pleasure be gained from the labour, the work will have more substance and form and purpose.

During these years in an office the girl learned a number of things: that no persons, however distasteful, coarse or ignorant they may be, are unworthy of the heart's affection; that intellect has value only when it is properly directed; that some writers like Whitman may "loaf and invite the soul," while others, forced by circumstance, can end a long workday with a cold shower, a walk in the twilight and a four-hour tussle with the English language. The last lesson she learned during those years was that one who intends to write for publication must prepare himself in many ways. This was the prelude to the third discovery—the significant relationship between the world and the self.

So the young woman returned to school, this time to Barnard College in New York City, hoping to learn something about the meaning of life she had seen and about the great literary traditions which must condition her own creative work. For a while her verses appeared frequently in current magazines. Then a long period of artistic sterility came upon her. No matter how hard she labored, no matter how many hours she bent over her desk, the same dead rhymes recurred, the flat thoughts repeated themselves. At last she said to herself, "I shall have to find a new medium; perhaps I could write a long narrative poem."

Money was not plentiful in 1932. After the glamor of commencement had passed, the girl found herself once more in an office. This time she had to work harder than before, often until nine or ten o'clock at night and frequently on Sundays and holidays. Quite by accident she read something in a magazine which suggested a lyric to her, and the lyric suggested the subject for a narrative poem. In this way she began her first book. Many parts of it sagged, because she still had much to learn about the art of telling stories. Yet it marked a new stage in the girl's development. Her private emotions grew less absorbing; her ideas about others grew a little taller. When a contract came for

the publication of *The Trumpeting Crane* she was so excited
that she suffered an attack of lumbago. Nevertheless, she managed to get to the office each morning. If she kept the contract
out of her thoughts, she could take dictation and write letters
very well; but when now and then she thought, "I am going to
have a book published," her heart would beat so violently that
she could not work at all. At last a package arrived containing
the first copies. Such blotches came before her eyes that she
could not even see the jacket design.

Her second book, *The Great Horse,* caused no such upset. It
too was a narrative poem written during the short evenings after
work at the office. Long before it was finished she had made
plans for a prose work, the life of Father Pierre Jean De Smet, a
Jesuit missionary who had worked among the Indians of Montana during the middle of the nineteenth century. One day,
browsing in the local library, she had read some of Father De
Smet's letters.

As soon as *The Great Horse* was finished, she began to gather
historical material for a narrative biography of the priest. Although it had not been difficult to scribble a few lines of poetry
between dinner and bedtime, she soon discovered that a prose
narrative cannot be written in so casual a fashion.

Since graduating from college she had spent some years in
office work. Now she applied for a research assistantship at the
State University of Iowa and began to work for a master's degree.
At the end of her first year at the university, the American Association of University Women granted her a fellowship for the
purpose of writing a life of Father De Smet. Never before had
she written a prose narrative. All the manuscript produced during a summer at an artist's colony went into the wastebasket. For
nine months she toiled over the first fifty pages of the book, but
nothing came of her labor. The characters were stiff, the conversation mechanical, the situations clumsy. Had she not already accepted and spent much of the fellowship money, she
would surely have given up the task in despair. A year passed
before the book began to grow; two years later it was done.
Much more lay behind it than a struggle with language, ideas,

incidents and characters; a tremendous amount of reading in historical and religious background had been necessary. It was at this time that the writer really came to understand the third discovery—the relationship between the self and the world. Even before *Father De Smet* was off the press she knew that the writing of the book was less important than the knowledge she had gained. That winter she was received into the Catholic Church.

At last the young woman knew what life was for and she understood that the talents given to one are not to be used for pleasure or for personal success alone, but also for pointing out the pattern which lies behind the confused fragments of life. All kinds of books are written today; many of them are written well, but without wisdom. Only when the self grows very small in the awareness of humanity and when it disappears in the awareness of God has the artist learned the great lesson of his life. Thenceforth he has a new responsibility.

With the completion of *Father De Smet* the young woman received her doctor's degree. She is now a professor of English at the College of Saint Teresa in Winona, Minnesota. The lyrics which she wrote so long ago have been gathered into a little volume called *Change of Season*. It is a good title, since the writer herself has known a "change of season."

In Genesis we are told that after the Fall the whole earth was of one language and one speech. Then the people built the Tower of Babel. God saw their work and He said, ". . . let us go down, and there confound their tongue that they may not understand one another's speech." And suddenly the people were confused, for they spoke in strange and different tongues. Men and women are still speaking in a confusion of tongues, and they suffer because they cannot understand one another or the world or God. When the terrible wars of this generation are over, men will have small taste for those books which offer them nothing but a record of this confusion. Then, as never before, we shall all be hungry for pattern, for an increase of that spiritual light which for many years has burned so dimly. Then, I think, many more people will know the meaning of the third discovery.

They will see literature not merely as a series of word-pictures of the world around them, or as the expression of personal emotion, but as an art which can resolve order out of chaos and find meaning in that which appears to be meaningless.

Miss Magaret is best known for her *Father De Smet* (1940), and *Change of Season* (1941), both published by Farrar & Rinehart.

THEODORE MAYNARD

Poet and Historian

I THINK I AM almost completely devoid of what is usually understood by literary ambition and certainly I drifted into writing
almost unawares. Most of my books have been written almost
by accident. To give instances: my early *Our Best Poets* was the
outcome of a lecture at which a publisher happened to be present. My anthology *The Book of Modern Catholic Verse* was put
together because I was asked to revise Joyce Kilmer's *Dreams and
Images* by bringing it up to date, but as I found so much to add
(and so much to omit) the idea came into my mind of making an
entirely new compilation. Nor had I so much as thought of
writing a biography until Henry Longan Stuart, running into me
on the street in New York one morning, said he was going to
edit a series of lives of Catholic explorers for Longmans, and
would I write one. That is how I came to do my *De Soto and the
Conquistadores*. As for my *Story of American Catholicism*, it
would probably have never been written at all had not Dr.
Guilday made the surprising suggestion that I undertake it.
Yet, with all this varied work, I continue to look upon myself

as primarily a poet, and it is my poetry that I value most of all my work.

The first of my twenty-two books appeared (with an introduction by G. K. Chesterton) in 1915, when I was twenty-five. But I had no idea of becoming an author, and by the time the little collection of poems appeared I was a Dominican novice in England. I left after seven months, however, and then began to write busily—articles and poems for various magazines, but mostly for Chesterton's *New Witness*. Though I hardly guessed at the awful truth, my somewhat strenuous career as a writer had begun.

Another career soon began—and this also was a mere accident. In 1920 I came to the United States for a lecture tour, and while in California I was invited to become a college professor. This was all the more astonishing because of the fact that I not only had never taught but did not have any degree. It was while I was professor at Fordham that I somehow found time to complete what was necessary for the B.A., and while I was at Georgetown that I obtained my M.A. and Ph.D., being all the time enormously busy with my classes and outside lectures and the production of articles and poems and books. Looking back upon it all, I still wonder a little how it was done.

Perhaps the explanation is that I have wasted very little time. Though I was famous for my laziness at school, I have since made up for this. My unfailing recipe for writing a book is: first, to know before I begin exactly what I am going to say; secondly, to stick at my typewriter, holding a whip over myself, and demanding the steady production of 4,000 words a day. In my case I may say that the book is virtually written before I write a single word. For this reason I begin at the beginning and go on to the last page, never looking over what I have done until the whole thing is complete. Then of course, I revise and after that make a second draft. I don't say that this is the best way to write, but it is the only way I can write. However, this applies only to prose. My poems are painfully produced as a rule, and I am as likely as not to begin with the end or the middle instead of the beginning. But even in the case of poetry, I always have the feeling that the poem really is composed before it is set down; the only difficulty is to extract it from my system.

What a writer writes always depends upon his private life. Mine has been related in my autobiography, *The World I Saw*. The three most important things that have happened to me are that I was brought up in India as a boy (where my parents were Protestant missionaries); that I was received into the Catholic Church, in 1912; and that I married, in 1918. India inflamed my imagination, the Faith gave me something to write about (and also whatever balance I possess); and as for the marriage and the seven children that resulted, there is probably some connection between that fact and the industriousness which is the only virtue I can be perfectly sure I have.

I have done a great many different things in my time in addition to those things mentioned here—from working in an office in London to working in a mill in the United States, when I was here for the first time from 1908 to 1911. During the same period I was for a few weeks a minister, until my congregation fired me, and after my return to England, I preached a number of times, almost up to the moment of my reception into the Catholic Church. I have peddled books and sewing-machines; I have been a journalist; but I have done practically no work with my hands; which has been bad for me. And I have never fulfilled my ambition of editing a paper; which is perhaps good for everybody else.

For the rest, I have lived in California, New England, the New York area, Washington, and am now in a small country town, Westminster, Maryland. Though two-thirds of my adult life have been spent in the United States, it was not until early in 1941 that I was naturalized as a citizen. But it is evident that my work lies in America. So here I intend to live and die.

Dr. Maynard's more recent books include: *Apostle of Charity* (St. Vincent de Paul), 1939, Dial Press; *The Odyssey of Francis Xavier*, 1936, Longmans; *The World I Saw*, 1938, Bruce; *Not Even Death* (poems), 1941, St. Anthony Guild; *Queen Elizabeth*, 1940, Bruce; *The Story of American Catholicism*, 1941, Macmillan; and *The Reed and the Rock:* portrait of Simon Bruté, first bishop of Vincennes, Indiana, 1834–1839, 1942, Longmans.

J. CORSON MILLER

Poet

I WAS BORN in Buffalo, and educated at St. Agnes School in that city, and Canisius College. Never attended any schools but those operated under the aegis of the Church, for which I am truly grateful. Centuries before the modern educators were ever thought of, the Church was busy with scholastic administration. As to religion in education, well, Dante and Milton, probably the two greatest poets that ever lived, were religious poets, and their work is thoroughly permeated by their philosophy, and strengthened by a spiritual intensity.

I think what led me to try my hand at verse-writing, was the inspiration gained from the very able work of my English teacher at Canisius College, Father Nelles. This man, in addition to being a keen interpreter of the classics, was, by nature, a student of the drama, and a musician. He had the knack of "putting an author across" to his class.

Of course, my mother was an inveterate reader all her life, deeply emotional, and gifted with a sense of literary values and the beauties of the imagination. My father, by the way, could, on occasion, rhyme extemporaneously, and, added to this, my maternal grandfather wrote verse privately, and was a lover of Goethe, Schiller and Heine. If heredity plays any part in the germination of a poet, I suppose I come under the law.

After my English initiation at Canisius, where, I must confess, I took the English prizes each year, I read most all of the worthwhile works in English literature, especially the poets; never lost my admiration for Tennyson, Keats, Francis Thompson and Poe. I also read translations of foreign-language authors—the masters.

The first poem I ever wrote was taken by the Lady Editor of an obscure woman's magazine, and I received for it the munificent amount of $1.00, and it was in stamps, and came by registered mail. This gave me quite a thrill, and was the spark that set me off. Upon sending other manuscripts to this lady, she promptly rejected them all. However, she was good enough to suggest that, inasmuch as I seemed to possess a knack of rhyming, combined with a flair for feeling and imaginative conception, I should study the technique of the art. Then I bought some books on the mechanics of verse, and went to work. I started to sell verse to a Sunday Magazine Syndicate, and this was all that I needed to keep me going. The sight of my name, in conspicuous letters, with certain well-known names in the National Sunday Magazines was worth more to me than the checks I received for my contributions.

One of the most powerful influences in the life and work of any artist, I believe, is an acquaintance with music. I have always been interested in music, from the lightest to the heaviest, and have experienced many "moments" from grand opera, where the superb singers of all time give of their best, in stories and themes that are heart-and-mind-shaking. I think music is a real factor in the development of the spirit, in the stirring of the esthetic sensibilities. I have, incidentally, wrapped myself in the spell of church-music, the music and ritual of the Mass, works of the great sacred composers. Having been a member of our parish choir for years, I have, consequently, been in close contact with the mammoth themes of music and prayer, as evidenced in the pomp and ceremonial of the Church. Not for nothing is one present in the choir on the great feast days and holy days of the Church, to help in honoring the Lord, His Blessed Mother and the Saints. In church, after all, is where the real verities of life are placed before one. There is where one hears of the highest exemplars in song and story, the tales of sainthood and sacrifice. There is where one hears exalted the glories of human and divine love, the merits of spiritual achievement, the golden tale of the God-Man, the Protagonist of Pain, the Son of God Himself.

Then, again, in my boyhood, I was a lover of the out-doors, living close to the soil, being one of the common people, mixing in with them, and sharing their joys and sorrows. Life was more simple then, but harder than it is today, yet it had its compensations in that it taught the stern but valuable character-building lessons of reality.

While I have always had to go to the office and do a daily stint, and poetry has been rather an avocation with me, still I have always found time to read and dream. The joys of the mind, in my opinion, far outweigh the joys of the physical—the routine, materialistic, sometimes very monotonous pleasures of the modern world. To be sure, to be a real poet, one will never have time to accumulate much money. A poet would be too busy working on the dream—the Great Dream, if you will—that will never materialize, but which every poet, big or little, clasps to his heart in the joy of creation.

It is true that poets should be born with the inborn talent, but they can be, and are, developed through scholastic training. One can take special poetry courses in high school or college these days, which are the day of the specialists. Perhaps, one can be under the tutelage of critics of literature or under teachers who are well-known themselves. This is as it should be, because would-be doctors study under medicos, and embryo barristers under good lawyers.

As to suggestions to the beginning writer, I would say that if one can sell a single poem to a reputable publication, it is a criterion of additional successes in the future. Of course, one has to have the never-say-die spirit; the will to sweat and work in the face of discouraging rejections—the decision, against all odds, to battle on. One should be grounded in the literature that has stood the test of time; how the masters did it, is a good thing to study. Furthermore, one should always write on subjects with which he is familiar. It is much better to handle a simple theme with power, than to write on a grandiose matter and bungle it. Over and above all, the budding poet *must* have real inspiration, the inner fire; the uncontrollable urge to "put it on paper." The next thing is to let somebody see it, either the teacher, a friend, or an editor.

Yes, I have had all kinds of experiences in trying to sell verse to editors. Some editors published my work, and when I asked them for the usual check, they said they were sorry, but they thought I knew they did not pay for contributions. Some editors when written to months afterward about manuscripts, replied they could not find them; they were lost. Other editors clipped a stanza or two out of a poem, and used it that way, without permission. Some editors returned poems that were afterwards accepted and included in important anthologies. One certain poem of mine was definitely belittled by a teacher of English literature, and later, after being used by a very reputable publication, was included in a representative anthology, edited by a well known poet and critic. It has happened that I have been able to sell verse to a magazine for years, but when the editor changed, it was all off—no more sales. I have had composers set my poems to music, and never hear from them again. Of course I realize, it is as hard sometimes to sell a song to a musical publisher, as it is to sell a poem to a literary editor. Certain pieces of mine have been set to music and sung at recitals and concerts, yes, on national tours, with work of other American poets, and I never received a penny therefor. Friends of mine, well known poets, with whom I discussed the matter, told me the composer was a genius and we had to support him. It was the same as if they had said "he has to live, too." My poem "Epicedium" has been read on the radio, on a national hook-up for years on Armistice Day. My verse has also been presented at the Tomb of the Unknown Soldier in Arlington.

Have done some public readings and lecturing, but, on the whole, think a poet should stay at home, and write new poems, —and keep improving if possible, every day of his life.

It has been a pleasant experience to meet the poets and editors through the years. Most of them, when you meet them personally, turn out to be entirely different than you had imagined them to be. All in all, I should say that writing verse and trying to sell it, is an exciting business, if you get what I mean.

Have not been doing as much work recently as in past years for the reason that in 1936 I accumulated a wife, and a daughter whose name is Jean Corson Miller. I consider Jean a poem herself, and through the play of smile and tear and various changes from storm to sunshine in her temperament, I can see the beauties of life and the great meaning of existence.

It may be worth while to digress here and say that I write all my first drafts in shorthand. This enables me to save time, and to get my thoughts on paper much more quickly than in the stereotyped way. Of course, it could be done on the typewriter, but I never work that way. I don't think there are many poets who write their verses in shorthand; at least I never ran across any.

What little success I have had in the field of poetry, I feel I owe to the influence of, first, my mother; second, my teachers in early life; and third, the great spiritual and cultural influence of Holy Mother Church.

EDITOR'S NOTE: Mr. Miller, who is employed by the City of Buffalo, is an Academy member of the Catholic Poetry Society of America and a member of The Gallery of Living Catholic Authors. He is the author of the following volumes of poetry: *Veils of Samite,* 1922, Small; *Horns from Caerleon,* 1928, Vinal; *Cup of the Years,* 1934, Bruce Humphries.

REVEREND JOHN E. MOFFATT, S.J.

Religious Writer

IF YOU WOULD MEET Father Moffatt, whose contributions to Catholic devotional literature have, during the past twenty years, amounted to some twenty-five titles, you must journey to the "wild and woolly" Northwest. You must seek him out where he dwells in a charming, if solitary, retreat on the border of the great Oregon forest five miles from the village of Sheridan.

High up on a wooded hill overlooking the town and with a far-reaching view of the fertile Yamhill Valley, back two miles from the highway, stands the Jesuit Novitiate of St. Francis Xavier, the training camp of the young members of the Oregon Province of the Society of Jesus. It is here in this secluded spot that Father Moffatt lives his busy, if hidden, life as Master of Novices.

Father Moffatt was born in Spokane, Washington, Oct. 9, 1894. His father, James Moffatt, an immigrant from County Sligo, Ireland, was a prosperous building contractor. His mother, Mary Teresa Barry, who was left a widow when John was two years old, and who was revered by her children as a saint, was a native of Philadelphia, Pennsylvania.

Father Moffatt was the fourth of five children, all of whom eventually became priests and religious. There were two boys and three girls. Henry, the first born, studied for the secular priesthood and in 1942 celebrated the Silver Jubilee of his Ordination. John's three sisters, Mary Teresa, Margaret Irene, and Catharine Agnes, each after a brief teaching career in the public schools of Washington, entered the Congregation of the Holy Names of Jesus and Mary. The eldest, Mary Teresa, for many years held the responsible position of Mistress of Novices at the Novitiate of the Oregon Province of the Congregation at Marylhurst, Oregon.

When John was not more than three or four years old he began to go daily with his brother Henry to the parish school conducted by the Sisters of the Holy Names, where, as he often recalls with amusement, until he was old enough to be enrolled as a regular pupil in the lowest class, he spent most of the day sleeping beneath the teacher's desk on an improvised couch made of the generously offered coats of the older boys.

On the completion of the primary grades and one year of high school, John went to work for a neighborhood pharmacist, in whose employ he remained for the next five years. This interruption of his schooling was necessary due to the fact that by this time his elder brother, Henry, who for some years had helped to support the family, had entered the Seminary to begin his studies for the priesthood, and his eldest sister, Mary Teresa, had entered the convent. So John had to take his turn as bread winner.

During this period John did not completely set aside his studies. Intent on resuming his schooling with a view to pursuing his secret ambitions to become a Jesuit, the young pharmacy clerk spent his spare moments in the none-too-busy apothecary shop reviewing and perfecting his Latin and even introducing himself into the mysteries of Greek, the latter with the aid of a tattered grammar which he remembers having purchased for ten cents in a second-hand book store.

When conditions at last made it possible for John to return to school, he enrolled in the high school department of Gonzaga University, conducted by the Jesuits in Spokane, where he remained until he entered the Society of Jesus two years later. It was during this time that the youth's latent literary talent began to manifest itself. Several contributions, both in prose and verse, appeared in *The Gonzaga,* the University student publication, and brought much favorable comment.

However, John was not ambitioning a writer's career. His dream was to become a Jesuit. This dream was realized on the 24th of May 1917, when he was received into the Sacred Heart Novitiate, Los Gatos, California. Here, following the customary routine in the training of young Jesuits, he remained for four years. From Los Gatos the young scholastic returned to Spokane to pursue the usual three year's course on philosophy at Mount St. Michael's, a few miles outside the city.

Thus far, with the exception of the few literary efforts during his high school days, John did not give any evidence of an urge to use his pen. But now there awakened within the soul of the young philosopher a strong desire to "get into print." It was not that he found any special delight in writing for writing's sake. Writing was and has ever remained a laborious task for him. Nor did he seek the distinction of authorship. To this day Father Moffatt disclaims any right to the title of author. He styles himself a "pious scribbler."

By vocation the young Jesuit was an apostle. He had a mission. He had a message. He saw his pen as a powerful instrument in carrying out that mission, an efficacious means of delivering that message. As an apostle he must help men to find God, to find God everywhere, in the beautiful things of creation, in all the happenings and circumstances of their lives. He must help men realize their purpose in existence. He must teach men to think prayerfully of their eternal destiny. He must help men to be supernatural in their outlook on life. Some day as a priest he would preach of these things in the pulpit of the Church. But that day was far distant. While awaiting its coming, he would preach with his pen. He had no misgivings as to

his ability. He was not yet a theologian. He would take care
not to go beyond his depth. He would make a humble beginning in the field of simple devotional writing. From childhood
strongly attracted to the tabernacle, his first impulse was to write
on the Blessed Sacrament. Accordingly, a series of brief Eucharistic essays written during the spare moments of his well-filled
student days, was offered to the *Sentinel of the Blessed Sacrament.*
The Series was accepted, and for the next three years the young
Jesuit's offerings appeared in each monthly issue of the magazine. During these same years there were frequent contributions
in verse both to the *Sentinel* and the *Messenger of the Sacred
Heart.*

Unlike the ordinary beginner, Father Moffatt was spared the
painful experience, too often disheartening to the young writer,
of having to pass through the rejection slip period. His first
offerings were accepted. He never considered this as an indica-
tion of superior ability, but simply as due to the fact that in his
choice of subjects he did not go beyond his depth and that he did
not disdain the *labor limae,* so essential for literary finish.

Encouraged by his initial success, John decided to give greater
permanence to his work and accordingly gathered his already
published essays and verses with numerous additions into a set
of five small books which appeared successively during the next
few years under the title, *Thy Kingdom Come* Series.

Having once "smelled printer's ink," the young Jesuit Scholastic could not put down his pen. The next several years of his
training, three of which were devoted to teaching in the high
school department of Seattle College, Seattle, Washington, and
the following four to the study of theology at Weston College,
Weston, Massachusetts, in preparation for his ordination and
priestly career, were crowded with the varied and numerous
duties of the teacher and student. However, by a careful harvest-
ing of the fragments of time, John was able during these years to
write and publish several books and booklets. It was during
this period that there appeared the volumes 3, 4, and 5 of *Thy
Kingdom Come* Series; two booklets on the Mass, *The Morning
Sacrifice,* and, *Pray the Mass;* a pamphlet on *The Forty Hours*

Devotion; two booklets of meditations for children, *God's Wonderland,* and, *Another Visit to God's Wonderland,* a book, *The Sanity of Sanctity,* which was an outgrowth of the young Jesuit's Master's Thesis on the immortality of the soul, written during the days of his philosophical studies; a small volume of meditations on the rosary, *Ave Maria;* and a book of readings on Christian devotedness entitled, *God's Minutemen,* which was later translated by a fellow Jesuit into Chinese.

Following his ordination to the priesthood in June 1930, and the completion of his theological studies the following year, Father Moffatt returned to Seattle College High School to assume the duties of Student Advisor. Two years later, he was transferred to the Novitiate of St. Francis Xavier as Assistant Master of Novices, becoming Novice Master in 1936. In this office he is still employed.

The important duties assigned to him after ordination left even less time than had been available during his student days for the use of his pen. However, through a happy habit formed in his younger years of putting to use all the "moments in between," Father Moffatt has been able during the busy days devoted to the constant care of his novices to continue his devotional writing. *Taste and See,* a book of meditations on our daily prayers, was published in 1934, and *Echoes Eternal,* a book of devotional essays in letter form appeared in 1936. Then followed a series of seven small books of meditations, the *Minute Meditation Series.* Next was begun a new series of meditation books, the *Ignatian Meditation Series,* the first two volumes of which, *Matters of Moment,* and, *Knight of Christ,* have already appeared. Father Moffatt's *Watch and Pray,* a set of readings and meditations for Religious for the Monthly Day of Recollection appeared in 1942.

While writing has always been a laborous task for Father Moffatt, it has not been without its compensations. The evidence of strength and comfort for souls derived from his books has ever proved a spur to persevere in an undertaking that entails a deal of drudgery. One instance out of numerous of a like character that, in his younger days, left a deep impression upon

Father Moffatt and has ever urged him to continue writing even under the serious handicap of increasingly busy days, might be cited. It is the case of the fallen-away Catholic woman who was found dead in her bed with a copy of Father Moffatt's meditation booklet, *Thoughts on His Words and Ways,* open in her hand. She had evidently been reading the story of God's love and mercy when death called her away. The hope of being an instrument in God's hand for just such work has been Father Moffatt's motive in using his pen.

The standard of spirituality set in his writing is always high, and the demands made on the soul's generosity in its dealings with God are at time heroic, but one always finds a note of hope and encouragement in Father Moffatt's meditations. He is convinced that all souls are called to perfection in their various states of life and he deems it his duty to show the way to the summit of the mount of perfection to those who would follow his guidance. But the soul is always made to realize that the painful climb is a glorious thing.

Convinced of the power of the pen in advancing the cause of truth, Father Moffatt has done all in his power to develop a like conviction in others. Young writers, especially, who come to him for counsel, are always sure of sympathy and encouragement. Not a few youthful aspirants to a literary career have found their way into print as a result of his assistance in their initial efforts. It is seldom that you would not find on his desk the manuscript of one of his young clients in the process of revision.

With the aspiring young Catholic writer Father Moffatt is ever insistant on the almost sacerdotal character of the Catholic writer's vocation and the serious responsibility that rests upon all who use the pen. He would have them ever mindful that writing, to be worthy of the Catholic pen, must lift the hearts and minds of men above the sordid things of earth, and set them hungering after their true destiny. Hence he insists that their own ideas be drawn only from the pure founts of the most wholesome literature. He requires of them that in their literary endeavors they aim at the highest excellence. When they lay down their pen and consider their work complete, it must be only after repeated revision and most careful polishing. As Father Moffatt sees it, writing is labor and the beginner especially must be ready for a deal of drudgery. He must also possess or develop the virtue of humility whereby he will be ready to seek advice and to meet criticism without discouragement. He must have a spirit of perseverence that will carry him through the painful "rejection slip" period.

Although his duties keep him almost constantly at his desk, Father Moffatt is a great lover of nature. An occasional walk in the woods is almost the only form of relaxation he allows himself, and he always returns from these sylvan rambles with a fresh supply of illustrations for his writing. He is of a buoyant, optimistic disposition and is enthusiastically confident in the sterling worth of American Catholic youth to whom his life is dedicated.

The Guide to Catholic Literature, 1888–1940, includes twenty-five of Father Moffatt's works. Since its publication he has written *The Knight of Christ* (Ignatian mditations), 1940, Bruce; and *Watch and Pray,* 1942, Bruce.

REVEREND CHARLES J. MULLALY, S.J.

The Story of a Boy's Dream

DO YOU LIKE to write? Many young people do. If you dream that some day you will be an author and have your name on a book or at the top of a newspaper or magazine article, then this biographical sketch should interest you. It is of one who dreamed, as you dream, and whose dreams came true.

As a boy Charles J. Mullaly was an insatiable reader. Fiction and lives of the great or near-great were his delight, with occasional browsing among the poems of Longfellow, Tennyson and Wordsworth. He would often read four or five books a week, and on many a night, his mother would awake at 2 A.M. and, seeing his light, find him deeply absorbed in a tale by Cooper, Scott, or Dickens. The book would be taken away, the light in his room turned off, and the youngster ordered to bed. This constant love of books made him yearn to write, to be an author, some day in the distant future. In his youthful dreams he even found himself working at the plots of stories. He did not then suspect that he would become one of the leading

Catholic editors of the United States, and would be prominent in the development of the Catholic Press Association.

That boy, now the Rev. Charles J. Mullaly, S.J., smiles reminiscently if asked when he first appeared as an author.

"That was long ago—back in the Fall of 1893, when I was sixteen. Old Gonzaga in Washington, D. C., was having a celebration in honor of the golden jubilee of Father Francis McAtee, S.J., as a Religious. I was chosen to write a poem and to read it in honor of this Civil War chaplain. The poem was thought good enough to appear in the *Catholic Church News,* of Washington, but without any remuneration to the author. Though this weekly newspaper ceased to be published later on, I cannot say that its demise was entirely due to my verse."

When in charge of the *Messenger of the Sacred Heart,* Father Mullaly was known as the "kindest and most encouraging of editors." He ever strove to be helpful to young writers, for he never forgot the encouragement he received from that great pioneer in American Catholic literary effort, Father John J. Wynne, S.J., founder of *America* and of the *Catholic Encyclopedia.*

In 1899, while still a student in the Jesuit scholasticate at Frederick, Maryland, the future editor had the thrill of knowing that his first short story was to appear in print. He must have shown talent for writing, for his professor, Father A. J. Elder Mullan, S.J., of Marian Sodality fame, assigned him to write a story to be sent to Father Wynne, then editor of *The Messenger of the Sacred Heart* and of *The Pilgrim of Our Lady of Martyrs.* Though the student had long dreamed of being an author, the assignment came as a surprise.

"Father Mullan," he protested, now really frightened, "I couldn't write a story that Father Wynne would accept! I have had no experience, and——"

The reply was blunt and to the point: "Do as you are told. You'll now get real experience."

The story was written and was sent to Father Wynne, in New York. Back came the kindest and most encouraging letter. The story had been accepted, and Charles J. Mullaly, S.J., was launched on his literary career.

Though the young Jesuit's name was henceforth to appear frequently in print, it took a bloody revolution to win him a recognized place on the newly established review, *America*. In July 1909, Spain suddenly became the scene of an anti-Catholic uprising. In the name of "liberty," churches and convents were set afire by the radical element under the leadership of Francisco Ferrer. The *Semana Tragica* (The Tragic Week) became seven days of blood and horror. The revolution, confined to Catalonia, the ancient northeastern division of Spain, was suppressed; Ferrer was captured, found guilty of treason, and executed. At the same time the American press was being fed the usual distorted propaganda from anti-Catholic sources, and Ferrer was represented as a martyr. In the midst of all the trouble, an article on "The Spanish Situation" reached Father Wynne for his review, *America*. It was vivid in its description and came from an American student of theology in the Jesuit Scholasticate at Tortosa, in turbulent Catalonia. Father Wynne flashed the word for "more and more copy," and the name of Charles J. Mullaly, S.J., soon became familiar to American Catholics.

In 1917, while engaged in missionary work in the island of Jamaica, B.W.I., Father Mullaly was recalled to New York to become assistant editor of *The Messenger of the Sacred Heart*. Three years later he became its editor-in-chief, and national director of the Apostleship of Prayer. That trip from Jamaica was an eventful one—five days through waters infested by German submarines, with the steamer being chased for hours and escaping in the darkness of night. It was such incidents in his travels by train and boat in many lands that made Father Mullaly's articles "On Land and Sea" welcome to his magazine readers. He used everything he saw in life as matter for articles and stories.

"Young people," he often remarks, "ask what they should write about; where they can find material. Tell them to use the scenes and things with which they are familiar."

An editor has to be versatile. The versatility of this Jesuit
editor brought approving comment from such writers as Rev.
James J. Daly, S.J., Rev. Francis P. Donnelly, S.J., Enid Dinnis,
and others, when they saw ascetical articles, fiction, apologetics,
book-reviews, and verse flow from his pen. So great was the
output that, at times, he wrote under three names: his own, and
the two pseudonyms, Paul Winslow and Francis Goodwin. In
his nearly twenty-five years of editorial work, Father Mullaly
acquired an expert's knowledge of engraving and printing that
showed in the beauty of each issue of *The Messenger* and caused
the magazine to hold its remarkable monthly paid circulation
of 300,000, even during the critical years of the Depression.
During those discouraging days he seemed to be immune to discouragement. He added to his heavy duties as editor and national director of the Apostleship of Prayer the task of personal
supervision of the great office and printing plant which he had
built in 1923. Despite prolonged illness he carried on, and his
spirit inspired his loyal assistants. His spirit can be seen in a
quatrain he wrote after leaving St. Vincent's Hospital, New
York, where he had been close to death:

A LESSON

Weak, ill of health, I passed a shattered tree,
Its verdant boughs full ripe with wingéd seed.
Disheartened, lo! its lesson I can heed:
A shattered frame may still God's toiler be.

Father Mullaly's books, published by the Apostleship of
Prayer Press, 515 East Fordham Rd., New York City, have received an enthusiastic welcome. So great is the demand for
Spiritual Reflections for Sisters that 102,000 copies have been
printed, and it has been translated into Tamil, the idiom of the
ancient race in Southern India and Ceylon. *Could You Explain
Catholic Practices?* has enjoyed a sale of 65,000 copies. Though
most publishing firms hesitate to issue an edition of short stories
in book form, *The Priest Who Failed* and *The Bravest of the
Virginia Cavalry* have been popular, the former requiring 7,000

copies and the latter 5,000. When your dreams come true, will
you be satisfied to see your name on 179,600 books?

Some one, with a mathematical bent of mind, figured out the
circulation of Father Mullaly's innumerable articles in *The Messenger* during 25 years. The answer is breath-taking. Multiply
the average paid monthly circulation of 300,000 by the number
of month in the year, and then by twenty-five, and the result
reads as ninety million copies spread into every corner of the
world. This does not take into account his many articles in other
magazines and newspapers. The dry-as-dust mathematician
heaped his data together, then added 200,000 copies of various
booklets and reprints, and announced the complete total as close
to one hundred million. Is it not worth striving to become a
writer?

Father Mullaly's advice to youthful writers is to start with
the short story. His formula is easily remembered: "Catch immediately the interest of your reader; hold the interest; have
suspense, and sustain the suspense until the climax; and have
the climax, if possible, in the very last sentence." He warns
against hackneyed plots and against those where the climax can
easily be foreseen. Success comes as a result of hard work and of
not being discouraged by rejection slips. If you wish to write
for a certain magazine, study its contents, the length of its
articles and stories, the nature of the material used. To do otherwise, is to write your own rejection slip. Write or type only on
one side of the paper, and enclose postage in case your manuscript is rejected.

Even iron wears out. The years of incessant toil at last broke
the already "shattered frame" of the tireless editor of *The
Messenger*. He had fulfilled his boyhood dream of being an
author and he had seen another dream come true: of securing
the consecration of two million families to the Sacred Heart and
of introducing the First Friday Communion of Reparation into
every parish in the United States. He had completed his forty-
sixth year as a Jesuit when his great work was finished. In
July 1941, he was forced to retire from the toil he loved. His

superiors assigned him to a new field of lighter labors. Richard Reid, former president of the Catholic Press Association and recipient of the Laetare medal, expressed the sentiments of many when he wrote in *The Catholic News,* July 19, 1941:

"Catholic press circles in the New York area lose one of the leading editors of the nation with the retirement of the Rev. Charles J. Mullaly, S.J., for three years assistant editor and for nearly twenty-two years editor of *The Messenger of the Sacred Heart.* Father Mullaly, a native of Washington, D. C., has had a career as a Jesuit which brought him to Maryland, to Spain, to Jamaica in the British West Indies and to Fordham in New York City. As editor and as national director of the Apostleship of Prayer with six million members, he is one of the most widely-known priests in the nation. Father Mullaly has always been the soul of consideration, the personification of kindly courtesy to those fortunate enough to be associated with him. The Catholic Press Association, which he served as treasurer for some time, owes him a towering debt of gratitude for his effective service and wise counsel. He is above all a priestly priest, and he carries with him to his new post as spiritual director of the Jesuit scholastics at the Novitiate of St. Isaac Jogues, Wernersville, Pa., the most cordial of good wishes from thousands of friends."

Father Mullaly's two collections of short stories, *The Bravest of the Virginia Cavalry* (1937) and *The Priest Who Failed* (1936), are published by the Apostleship of Prayer, as is his *Spiritual Reflections for Sisters* (1938).

REVEREND EDWARD
FRANCIS MURPHY, S.S.J.

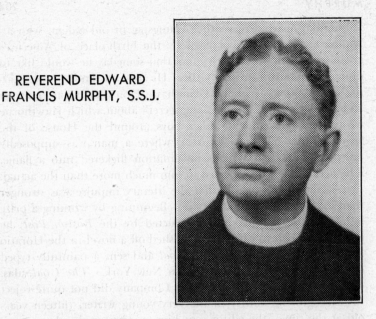

BORN IN SALEM, MASSACHUSETTS, back in 1892, Edward Francis Murphy grew up in an atmosphere of history and literature. Yes, and sanctity too! Three people most affected his life: a great saint, a famous writer, and a little Sister of Charity. The saint was Peter Claver; the writer, Hawthorne; the Sister— Marie Concilio.

Right across Salem Harbor, opposite Derby Wharf where Edward Francis used to swim in boyhood days, stretches the shore of Marblehead. Sister Concilio told him that the first slave-ship sailed from that port long ago, beginning a traffic in human misery which was to result in the Civil War and leave a trail of problems still unsolved. Too, she told him of the meek saint who made himself the slave of slaves and tried so hard, with personal sacrifices, to atone for the mistakes of men. The boy, looking out on the hills of Marblehead when they were an emerald blur in the after-glow in the evening sun, and listening to the Angelus from St. Mary's Church on the Salem side, dreamed of being another Claver.

But like nearly every other youngster in old Salem, who attended St. Mary's School hard by the birth-place of America's
greatest novelist, he thought, too, that someday he would like to
draw magic out of an ink-bottle. He used to stand in awe, gazing at the doorway of the Grimshawe House on Charter Street
and pondering the story of "the secret" about which Hawthorne
wrote. He played with other boys around the House of the
Seven Gables on Turner Street, where a man was supposedly
murdered by a ghost. His imagination flickered into a flame.
The fictional world appealed to him much more than the actual.

It seemed, for a while, that the literary impulse was stronger
than his plan of spiritual service. Beginning by winning a prize
in a juvenile letter-contest conducted by the *Boston Post,* he
grabbed his pen in earnest and dashed off a novel in the Horatio
Alger manner. Called it *The Goal* and sent a painfully typed
copy of it to Benziger Brothers in New York. *The Goal,* alas,
did not make the grade. But the Company did not quite reject
it. Recognizing ability in the very young writer, (fifteen years
old at the time), the editor sent him an encouraging letter, suggesting certain changes in the script. These were promptly
made, but not to the entire satisfaction of the Company; so *The
Goal* lay unpublished until the author was inspired to send it,
without any further revision, to the *Sunday Companion,* the
favorite weekly paper of Catholic school-children. Promptly accepted it caused something incredible to flutter into our embryo
Hawthorne's hand: a cheque for $100. He rubbed his eyes;
indeed, and rubbed them the more when a regular snowstorm of
letters from delighted readers came to him, begging for more.
The Goal, up to that time, was the most popular serial story the
Sunday Companion had ever published. It was sheer consequence that Edward Francis sat down and confected another
imitation of Nathaniel Hawthorne (and Horatio Alger) which
certainly did not steal a single leaf from the great American's
laurels but, happily, brought home a larger cheque and still
more epistolary appreciation. Entitled *The Tale of Two
Brothers* this second story fitted right into Catholic young
America's heart. Then came a third juvenile, called *The*

Triumph of George, just as successful as the others. Father Francis Finn, S.J., dean of writers for Catholic youth, wrote a glowing letter of commendation to this rising young fellow craftsman.

But Edward Francis was growing up and away from juveniles. He had discovered O. Henry and was trying his hand at short stories. Wondrously, the very first one he ever wrote was accepted by the very same Company that had rejected his first novel. It netted him $25, but many times that amount in encouragement. About this time, *Extension Magazine,* making extraordinary effort to develop Catholic writers, became more interested in his work. The Managing Editor, Mr. S. A. Baldus, turned the benefits of a rich and varied literary experience his way; and story after story, each one an improvement on its predecessor, sprang from the Murphy pen to the Extension pages.

Now in college, Edward Francis Murphy was discovering the utter seriousness of life. World War No. I was in progress, and the shadow of it lay on every thinker's thought. So he wrote an article to express what he conceived as possible results of the gigantic fray on civilization. Sent it to the Jesuit Weekly *America* and promptly received a cheque with a request for further efforts. A variety of articles followed on subjects that ranged from tuberculosis to birth-control. The young man was on his way to becoming a two-legged encyclopedia. He had discovered that the world of reality is after all, more challenging than the realm of fiction.

His out-put appeared all over the country, mostly in the religious press; but he was quoted widely in secular journals.

At the Catholic University in Washington, he became interested in medieval history and civics and was able to draw a remarkable parallel between the Declaration of Independence and the political theories of Saint Thomas Aquinas. For this original work, he was awarded a Ph.D.

The *Commonweal,* the *Ecclesiastical Review,* the *Sign,* the *Rosary,* the *Preservation of the Faith,* etc.: all have carried the products of his pen.

But life has not left him any too free to transcribe his impressions. Thirty years ago, the boyhood dream that he used to cherish when the hills of Marblehead were fading in the mists of evening and the Angelus from Saint Mary's was solemnly speaking of another world, had superseded the desire for a literary career. He abandoned the star of literary success for that of Bethlehem, and the inspiration of America's finest novelist for that of Peter Claver. Now, as pastor of the Blessed Sacrament Mission in New Orleans and Dean of Philosophy and Religion in Xavier University, the only colored Catholic institution of its kind in the U. S. A., he is actively devoted to the cause of the lowly and to the Society of Saint Joseph concecrated to the ideal of Negro evangelization. It is only in rare moments that he can pick up his pen and plunge into a labor which he loves only a little less than the far greater one to which he is giving his life.

Nevertheless, while winning distinction in the missionary field, he has somehow managed, in recent years, to publish three important books: *New Psychology and Old Religion,* a critique of Behaviorism, which holds place in the Catholic-revised list of Professor Adler's famed selection of "the world's greatest books." *The Tenth Man,* a humanized essay on the American Negro. And *Handclasps with the Holy,* a series of charming introductions to the lives of the Saints.

Though he has abandoned the short story, he still believes it to be the medium most alive and suitable to the expression of a truth of life or a comment on it. He is impressed that the Greatest Teacher used this form, and feels that Catholic pencils are best sharpened to this point: especially in a day of general education like ours when everybody reads at least a little, and fiction is the language that all can understand with interest.

"You see," he explains, with a twinkle in his eye, "I never really did get over that first cheque for $100!"

Father Murphy's books include *A Tale of Two Brothers,* 1922, O'Donovan; *Just Jack,* 1924, John Murphy Co.; *New Psychology and Old Religion,* 1933, Benziger; and *Handclasps with the Holy,* 1941, Catholic Literary Guild.

MRS. ESTHER W. NEILL

Novelist

THE DESIRE that I have always felt to write is quite easily explained. My mother, Mary T. Waggaman, author of so many children's books was a professional writer, working under contract for the secular press long before she began her Catholic work for which she became so well known. Since all children are imitative, writing in our house was considered an interesting part of life to us all. There is a tradition in the family that I began my literary career at the age of three lying on my "tummy" beneath my mother's desk.

Nearly everyone in the house took to writing as a sort of natural pursuit. Even one of the Irish cooks tried her hand at it saying, "Shure it's an easy way to make a living, just shoving a pen along."

To live in a world of make believe and to create characters to my liking seemed to me a most satisfactory sort of existence. From my earliest childhood I planned and prayed for the power to write. I neglected my lessons at school and won the forgiveness of my teacher by giving her stories to read to prove that I had not been altogether idle during my study period. Fortunately, she was an understanding person who seemed to realize that the cultivation of an imagination might prove more important in after life than the boundary line of states or the dates that marked the reigns of dead and forgotten kings.

But a happy marriage to Charles P. Neill, who then occupied the chair of Economics at the Catholic University, diverted my ambition for a time, and later on four lively sons rather interfered with intensive work. Literature had to be pushed aside for more important maternal duties which seemed to have a prior claim. But in spite of many distractions the urge to write persisted and I tried to find some time each day to spend at my desk.

Father John Burke, C.S.P., former editor of the *Catholic World,* became interested in my work and published nearly everything I could send him. My first book *The Red Ascent* was first published by him as a serial before appearing in book form. My next, *Barbara's Marriage and the Bishop,* was published by Macmillan. It is a story dealing with the inviolability of marriage. The next books, *Miss Princess* and *The Tragic City,* were brought out in *Ave Maria* and then published in book form. I have contributed to many magazines and I have found great joy in my work; but I would advise no one to go into the writing game unless he or she has a real flair for it and unless as O. Henry says—"You have the tenacity of a bull dog," for I must admit the Catholic press is not supported as it should be. Catholic authors are poorly paid and I have known of more than one author of real ability who have confessed that they could not afford to do Catholic work since they had family responsibilities.

This deplorable fact should lead our young people to take an active interest in the apostolate of the press. We need more

Chestertons, more Bellocs and we need wholesome Catholic fiction to offset the immoral standards and filth of so many popular novels published today and which we find difficult to keep out of our libraries because—as our young people argue—"Everyone is reading them."

EDITOR'S NOTE: Instead of including here a full record of her literary background, Mrs. Neill has given it in her chapter on her mother, Mrs. Waggaman, which appears in this series of *The Book of Catholic Authors*. Mrs. Neill's books include: *Barbara's Marriage and the Bishop*, 1925, Macmillan; *Miss Princess*, 1929, Kenedy; *The Red Ascent*, 1914, Kenedy; and *The Tragic City*, 1932, Kenedy.

MISS COVELLE NEWCOMB

Children's Books

THERE ARE THREE QUESTIONS which, I venture to say, have been asked almost every writer: When did you begin to write? Why do you write the kind of books you write? and How do you write? The third generally means Under what conditions do you write? Is it hard? Are you ever discouraged? etc.

To reply: I began writing with my first lesson in penmanship. Not books, to be sure; but I believe that even then I got the *feel* of letters and words, primer words like hen, cow, cat, all the one-syllable words we generally meet in our first introduction to language. Where some children naturally "take" to paints, others to music, others to mud, I took to the alphabet. The actual shaping of the ABC's and mixing them up in hopeless scrambles, like alphabet soup, fascinated me more than anything else. Thus, I believe I can legitimately say that my love of letters, if not for *belles lettres,* showed itself at an early age. This attraction to the alphabet grew into a love for words, reading, composition, and even spelling!

Born in San Antonio, Texas, I spent most of my early life on my father's sand country ranch where I got acquainted with cow-herders' Spanish, rattlesnakes and coyotes. When the time came, I was sent to school in San Antonio and passed through trials like punctuation and arithmetic with a never-ceasing shudder.

At high school I started out on the essay track. The first essay submitted to a contest brought back $25.00. A million could not have looked bigger. More essays and, with time, some feeble poetry, worked their way off my pen. Most authors say "roll." Not I. There was then, and still is, perspiration and effort behind every word I manage to get on to paper.

Somehow I got to college—and took degrees. I went successively to Incarnate Word College (San Antonio), Washington University (St. Louis), Hunter College and Columbia University (both New York City). Along the way I wrote several prize-winning essays. I won a check and a four-year scholarship to the Texas University. But I used only the check.

By the time I was ready for a Master's degree I was faced with a different kind of eassy, the Master's thesis. It was during the struggle of writing that thesis that I believe I knew I was destined (condemned, if you prefer), to a career of writing. My own persistence in the face of three rejections convinced me. The fourth writing of the thesis gave me the degree. But it also gave me something more important: experience for which I have always been grateful.

While being educated I sailed away my summers, mostly in the tropics: Dutch Indies, Haiti, South America, Mexico, Guatemala. I like to move around. To recuperate from the effects of having my Master's thesis accepted, I took a freight boat to Haiti and South America. I had a limited wardrobe, but plenty of note pads and pencils. On my return to the States, I tried writing stories with a Haitian background. Having had no training outside of essay writing, my stories always came back. My failures sent me to writing classes at Columbia University, New York University, and to privately conducted classes. On the verge of giving me up, one of my instructors said: "Your stories are always about children or told from a child's angle. Why don't you try writing for them?"

I took his suggestion and went to Columbia University to enter Dr. Mable Robinson's famed class in Juvenile Fiction Writing. I went without an idea, but my Haitian notebooks soon provided me with a biography,—the life of Henri Christophe, the slave-king of Haiti. The book became *Black Fire,* published in 1940. I next tackled my favorite churchman (my favorite even before I became a convert from Anglicanism in April 1925), John Henry Newman. I wrote his life for young readers in *The Red Hat* (1941). My third hero is the author of Don Quixote, Miguel de Cervantes: *Vagabond in Velvet* (1942).

I write biography because I prefer it to fiction. I find the lives of great men and women of never-failing inspiration. And why do I write juvenile biography? Because I like writing for that audience. The range of interest and subject is limitless. Further, juvenile books allow illustration. And I believe in combining one art with another whenever possible. (It seems a great loss that adult books are so rarely illustrated.)

I have two hobbies: water colors and ancient musical instruments. Can only splash with the one and only peck with one finger on the other.

I am not especially temperamental, but I write best in hot weather—being a Texan. I work on a studio couch, propped up with pillows. I hold the typewriter on my knees. The more they ache, the faster I think. I prefer a room with a north light; a neutral color on the walls; and no furnishings other than plenty of shelves for books and paper. Waste baskets I find useless. I prefer the floor. At the end of several days I harvest the crop of papers I have recklessly thrown about and store them away for next winter's fire. I work six hours a day when not rushed (by nature I'm lazy), and eighteen to twenty-two hours a day toward the end of a job. I write *every* day, no matter how bad the output is.

Have I any advice to give budding authors? Yes. If you love words and are willing to learn how to use them, willing to give up three-quarters of your social life, willing to cherish rejection slips, willing to turn yourself into a hermit for six to nine months out of the year, willing to lock your door against visitors and fun, willing to take discouragement and bob up like a cork no matter how far you sink in depression (for you will), willing to work day after day, for ever and ever, you will almost surely grow into a writer. However, there is one ingredient which is somewhat necessary: a grain of imagination. Writing is more than a craft, it is an art. But with discipline and training, even a little imagination can do big things. And don't worry about wondering whether or not you've got what it takes. You'll find out. If your best friend won't tell you, you'll find it out for yourself. Above all, if you think you want to write, *try*. The pleasures of completing a difficult task which will, in time, find itself in print, far outweigh the discouragement that precedes it. If once you experience that joy, you'll never stop!

Miss Newcomb's books for young readers include: *Black Fire* (the story of Henri Christophe), 1940, Longmans; *The Red Hat* (the story of Cardinal Newman), 1941, Longmans.

MARY PERKINS

SOME PEOPLE seem to know what God wants them to do almost as soon as they know anything. One of my sisters is this kind of person; when she was ten, she knew that she wanted to be a country doctor, and now she is one, beloved of God and man. But I am of the other kind, the people who never know exactly what they want to be or do, until they find themselves doing it— rather like the debutante whose answer to the question "What do you think about modern art?" was, "How can I tell what I think till I hear what I say?"

At school and college, people kept telling me that I should Write; but I could not think of anything to write about, and also I had to earn a living. So after graduation, I took a secretarial course. In the middle of this, to me, incredibly penitential procedure, I was offered a job with Sheed & Ward, who had just come to this country to found their American office. As soon as I grasped the Sheed & Ward idea of a book, I knew that I wanted to help that idea in any way I could. For Sheed & Ward's purpose is to publish books which will help contribute towards forming in their readers a truly Catholic mind, that is, a mind which is so deeply possessed by the truths of the Faith that it can see everything else in the light of that knowledge.

But it soon became all too clear to everyone that my enthusiasm for Sheed & Ward's books did not compensate for my hopeless inability to be an efficient secretary. So I had to leave, and for two years wandered around working at all kinds of jobs. Then I came home to Boston and spent an unhappy winter trying to write short stories, at the end of which I found myself spending four months in a hospital and several more as an invalid at home.

When I was allowed out again, I went down to New York for a visit, and there I saw the author, Fr. Leonard Feeney, S.J., whom I had known when I was with Sheed & Ward. He asked me what I was going to do next. I said I didn't know. I wasn't well enough to take a job, and I would like to try to write something, but I didn't know what to write about. So he said "I'll tell you. Every convert, and Catholic too, wants a book to tell him all about the little things—when to get up and sit down in church, how to use a missal, when he may eat meat on Friday, what to call a Bishop—all that kind of thing. You call it *At Your Ease in the Catholic Church*—and I'll give you a list of books right now with all the information."

So it was done. As I read the books he had listed, I became more and more fascinated to find the reason and purpose behind all the ceremonies and regulations of the Church. I came bursting down to lunch every day with entrancing new items of information for my patient family. "Did you know that a Patriarch is called Your Beatitude?" "Did you realize that the priest washes his hands during the Offertory because they used to get sticky with handling of real loaves and jugs of wine?" My family learned a lot that autumn, and so did I.

When the manuscript was finished, I submitted it to Sheed & Ward and went hurrying down to New York to await the verdict on the spot—a thoroughly reprehensible practice for a writer. But one morning I telephoned the office as usual, and was told that *At Your Ease in the Catholic Church* had been accepted.

I rushed over to my brother and kissed him on both cheeks before I realised that he was not only astonished, but completely covered with shaving-cream. Of course that was not the happy end of it, by any means. The manuscript was given to a Canon lawyer, who looked it over with the greatest care and kindness, and when I had carried out his suggestions, it was sent to England to have another authority check on it there. For in this kind of writing, originality of presentation is fine, but if you find that you are original in your ideas, you will probably find yourself a heretic too.

While I was writing *At Your Ease,* it had been gradually dawning on me that we should all be infinitely more at home in the Church if we really understood her language. Then I began to wonder if an adequate reading-and-hearing knowledge of the Latin of the Church really was as difficult to acquire as people made out. And I soon became convinced that it wasn't. So I planned a book about Latin using the words of the Mass itself as the text, which would lead the reader by his own common sense, curiosity, knowledge of English and familiarity with the text of the Mass, to a real understanding of the language of the Church. And in due time, with infinite trouble to the publishers, the printers, and myself, *Your Catholic Language:* Latin with the Missal, was finally published, and to everyone's surprise found and is still finding readers. Which proves that Catholics really do want to learn Latin if they are shown a not too boring method of doing so.

In the meantime, I was writing monthly articles on the Liturgy for *The Catholic Woman's World,* and I had been meeting various people interested in the Liturgical Movement. Between their knowledge and my own studying, I began to realize that I had had practically no idea of what it was all about, that I had been only on the outside edge of the inexhaustible riches of the Church. But until I went to the first Liturgical Week, held in Chicago in 1940, I still hung on to a lingering suspicion that the Liturgical Movement was made up of nice people who only wanted less horrible statues and more appropriate music in our churches. Then I found to my confusion and delight that I had been all wrong. I saw the "Liturgical Movement" was a too easily misunderstood name for an amazing reality, a wave of spiritual vitality renewing all things in Christ, a movement in which everybody, clergy, religious and laity, had a part to take. And at the second Liturgical Week, in St. Paul in 1941, I began to understand that this part is only incidentally a matter of organization, spreading of information and so on, and essentially our share as Christians in the Work of Christ Our Lord, in His Mystical Body the Church.

So I do not think I shall ever need to worry again about a subject. I have enough subject for several lifetimes—to do anything I can to clear away the misunderstandings and prejudices and lack of information which keep so many Catholics away from the fullness of life in the Church which is their inheritance.

And here is a work in which every Catholic who wants to write can find a place. You have to find it yourself; nobody else can tell you which of the wonderful works of God you can best declare, or in what sort of language you are to talk about them. But there could be no more interesting subject to think about, no more glorious field of knowledge in which to spend your life, and no greater privilege than to be allowed to write about the beauty of the Truth—whether you do it in articles or stories, biographies or poems or novels. Such writing has also this great advantage: it prevents you from taking yourself too seriously as A Writer. You can never pat your mind on its back for its bright ideas, for the brighter the idea, the less it is yours. You can never grow soft by indulging in self-expression, for your self is the last thing you want to express. And, at the same time, the truth and goodness and beauty of what you are trying to write about almost forces you to be as careful and conscientious a craftsman as you possibly can be. Who would dare to write sloppily or carelessly about anything connected with the mysteries of God? Moreover, you are always subject to authority, which is good for all of us; for however much you know, the Church always knows more and better than you do.

Of course you will never get rich at this kind of writing; which some may consider a disadvantage. Another drawback is that few of your friends will understand that you ever do any work at all. They will think that you have undertaken the easiest job in the world, for most people are convinced that writing is Such Nice Work. Nothing will change their minds, so the first time you meet somebody who says gushingly "My dear, how lovely, it must be Such Fun to write . . . why I've always wanted to be a writer myself!" don't hit her over the head with the handiest heavy object. Just smile. The truth is that writing is not Nice Work at all; it is one of the hardest kinds of work in the world—exasperating, fatiguing, often monotonous, always lonely—and dirty. If you want a white-collar job, don't try to write, because if you start your day's work with a white collar on, you will have thrown it across the room before lunch time anyway. So if you can possibly take any other share of the World's Work and be happy at it, go and do that, and forget all about writing.

But—if you have something to say, and want to say it badly enough to take all the trouble necessary to say it well, you will find compensations unknown to safer and easier jobs. And besides, St. Thomas says that there will be a special reward in heaven for those who spend their lives in trying to communicate the truths of the Faith to their fellow-men.

Sheed & Ward published Miss Perkins' *At Your Ease in the Catholic Church* (1938) and *Your Catholic Language* (1940).

REVEREND CHARLES J. QUIRK, S.J.

Poet

A POET OF OUR times who can "much in little show," and this do with power and effectiveness is Father Quirk. Born in 1889 in picturesque, romantic old New Orleans, a city which owes him an accolade for his sonnet celebrating "The Old Quarter," he received his early education in the schools of his native city. In 1905 he became a convert to the Catholic faith, and in the following year he entered the Novitiate of the Society of Jesus. Later he pursued higher studies at Columbia and Louvain Universities. It was at Louvain that he was ordained to the priesthood in 1922.

Study and extensive travel had their broadening and cultural effects upon the young priest whose poet soul found inspiration in old-world beauties, natural and historic, for some of his finest verse. As, for instance, after having been enthralled by seeing:

> The argent moonlight shining clear
> Upon the whispering waters as they fall

in the Place de la Concorde, he wrote "Fountains in Moonlight."
Or when, at the grave of Keats, he wrote:

> Only a sad and lonely dream-led boy
> Who sought in green cool woods
> To catch the farewells of a fleeting joy.

On his return to the United States, Father Quirk was made
head of the English Department at Springhill College, Mobile,
Alabama. Here he founded poetry and dramatic societies whose
objectives were the furthering of literary appreciation and taste
and the fostering of native talent. He then studied and taught
at St. Louis University and, in 1939, returned to New Orleans to
become a member of the English faculty at Loyola University
of the South, the position he now holds. Continuing here his
literary apostolate, he has organized the Pegasus Poetry Society,
with aims and activities similar to the Springhill societies.

Our poet is a member of the Gallery of Living Catholic
Authors, the Poetry Society of America, the International Mark
Twain Society, the Modern Language Association, is an honorary
member of the Alabama Poetry Society and a founder of the
Pi Chapter of Delta Epsilon Sigma, a scholastic organization
corresponding to Phi Beta Kappa.

He has written five volumes of verse: *Sails on the Horizon*
(1926), *Interludes* (1929), *Candles in the Wind* (1931), *Gesture
before Farewell* (1934) and *Full Circle* (1936). Many of the
poems in these volumes first appeared in such magazines as
*The Catholic World, Studies, The Dublin Review, The Month,
The Sign, The Commonweal,* and *The New Review* (India.).

Just how Father Quirk first came to write poetry, he himself
cannot definitely say. Ever a "feeling observer," with eye, ear,
mind and heart attuned to beauty, he saw that beauty at which
we so often look with unseeing eyes; that beauty which shines
through all the faces and forms of things. And because a poet
is an individual who, happily, cannot "keep counsel," where
this question of beauty is concerned, but "must tell all," he began to dash off little lyrics, the overflow of exalted emotions.
A day came when he mustered up courage enough to send one

of his pieces to a magazine. Then, in trembling expectancy, he
awaited the result. It proved to be—not a rejection slip! He
experienced the thrill of seeing himself for the first time in
print. There was probably nothing very startling, either in
style or in subject matter about the verses that he wrote. As a
matter of fact, he can not even recall the title of the poem. A
discerning editor saw, however, that the lines held promise and
his acceptance heartened the young poet to write again. Other
editors were not so indulgent. But a beginning had been made.
Confidence had been established.

To struggling young poets, Father Quirk's earnest admonition
would be, If you have the urge to write, write. Submit your
work to some honest critic, humbly accepting his comment and
correction, and abiding by his advice. Poetry belongs to youth.
As life advances one loses that freshness of outlook which accom-
panies youth, that poetic curiosity,—loses the glory and the
dream. Satisfy, then, the urge to write!

He cautions against sentimentality while, at the same time,
advocating sentiment. There is a difference. Sometimes aspiring writers whose effusions have been unwisely and unduly
praised think that they have done something great, and so are
led to offer their tears for sale and to betray their high calling.
On the other hand, he begs of young writers not to allow seeming
failure, in the guise of rejection slips, to in any way dismay or
deter them. They may be more successful than they know. The
Muse does not bestow her favors lightly, but she is well worth
being sought after, striven for, agonized over.

The very sense of accomplishment is for the poet ample compensation, even should he receive little or no acclaim. Walt
Whitman's dictum, "to have great poetry we must have great
audiences," must be taken with reservations. Keats simply had
to write, even though no eye were ever to light on his verses;
and Gerard Manly Hopkins had an audience of but one—Robert
Bridges.

To develop appreciation as likewise style, and become poeti-
cal-minded, he advises the reading of all that is best in the work
of the established poets. Poets are born, however, not made.

The poet writes on inspiration, and true poetic inspiration is from God. Great poetry is an infinitesimal mirror of the Deity. What are the sources of this inspiration? Everything that the good God creates. If God, the Poet of poets, thought to create (and all creation is thought wrought out by God), then big things and small,—the deep-damasked wing of the moth, the cosmos of the ant, the blue wonder of the cathedral universe,— all are potential matter for poetry. The poet will see the wonders of God's might and love and will endeavor to give a meaning to the universe. He will seek to find the key to creation. This Father Quirk does, unlocking, especially in his quatrains, hitherto closed doors through which we may glimpse in one shining moment vistas undreamed of. He gives us to see beauty in all and all in beauty. Persons, places, things are used to raise our thoughts to spiritual realities. He is not concerned with the surface of life merely. He has not, however, cloistered himself from the world of reality. Much of his poetry is religious, true, but none of it is pietistic. Rather, it combines a whimsical tenderness with stalwart Catholicity.

Poetry, he claims, to be authentic, must be lyric, because lyric poetry is the expression of the poet's inmost being; of his own personal reaction. For which reason, he defines poetry as "the ecstasy of a moment snared in words." Where we are inarticulate, the poet becomes the mouthpiece of humanity. To effect this, he makes use of rime, rhythm, onomatopeia, connotation. And by some inexplicable power, the divine right of poets, as it were, he not only makes us see beauty, but interprets its message and deeper spiritual significance.

While there is at times a wistful strain in Father Quirk's poetry, he is by no means a sad singer. There is humor and whimsicality in so quixotic a fancy as that which addresses the grasshopper as "the Don Quixote of the grass;" sees in Jack o'lanterns the aeroplanes of Elfland; and tells of the smallest prince of the fairies (fit mate for Queen Mab) whose palace is a rose and whose henchmen twain are a butterfly and a bee.

Father Quirk handles varied forms and meters, sonnets, vers libre, dramatic episodes. It is, however, in the brief concentrated forms, notably the quatrain, that his art is at its best. "Like us all," a noted critic once said of him, "every once in a while he gets an idea; but he differs from most of us in condensing rather than in expanding the gift."

Father Quirk's own effects are gotten through intense concentration, arresting contrasts, sincerity and, its concomitant, simplicity. These last are the hall mark of all he writes. Poetry in the Greek manner he deems the best, and the Greek manner means simplicity of expression and profundity of thought. Such poetry as gives us

> To see a World in a grain of sand
> And a Heaven in a wild flower;
> Hold Infinity in the palm of your hand
> And Eternity in an hour.

EVA J. ROSS

Sociologist

EVA JEANY ROSS was born in Northern Ireland. She was the first of the three children of Charles Alexander Ross and Eva Elizabeth (Woodland) Ross, who had married in the Church of England in 1902. Her father was a Highland Scot, who did not marry until he was middle-aged, and who professed no particular religious affiliation. He was a much traveled, scholarly man, a talented musician, a proficient artist in water-color and oils, a skilled engineer, and knew thirteen languages well, including Greek, Latin, Hebrew and Sanscrit. He had no business acumen, however, and although he was at one time very well to do, the family often had to struggle to make ends meet. Eva's mother was English, and more than twenty years younger than her husband. She was a member of the Church of England and Eva was christened at home by the minister of that Church.

When Eva was about four years of age, she was taken to Scotland, where the first of her two brothers, Donald Alexander, was born, when she was nearly five. Then the family settled down in England, where another brother, Colin Edmund, was born two years later. Eva's early education was haphazard. Sometimes she was sent to school, and then for months she would be kept at home, or went to stay with her grandmother who lived by the sea. Between the ages of eight and ten she spent most of her life in London, where she was often taken to visit museums and picture galleries. Religion for her at this time was confined to attending a Unitarian Sunday-School, to which a friend of the family belonged, and to singing in the children's choir of that Church.

When she was about ten years of age, the family moved to the outskirts of a Lancashire town and she was sent to a Catholic school, partly because it was near her home and partly because her parents thought she would there get stronger discipline than they had given her. The first World War broke out while she was at school, her younger brother died at the age of seven before it was over, and a young uncle was drowned in a British submarine. In successive years, Eva passed the Oxford University Junior and Senior school examinations, the London Matriculation, and the Higher School Certificate Examination, winning a University scholarship on the results of the last-named examination.

During the last two years she was at school, when she was sixteen and seventeen years of age, one of the subjects taught was a survey of the principles of economics and social ethics. This course, which took the place of religion for the six students in the class, stressed particularly the peace letters of Pope Benedict XV and the Rerum Novarum encyclical. At the time, however, she was much more interested in literature than in social questions, and her ambition was to become a novelist. When she left school, she went to Bedford College for Women, London University. She studied English, Latin, French and Spanish during her first year there (going to King's College for her Spanish studies), and intended to take an "honors degree" in French, with Spanish as her minor. To perfect her pronunciation of French, she lived in a French school in London and also spent a short time in a convent school in St. Omer, France. Before she had completed her university career, however, she decided not to spend anymore of her family's depleted finances on her education, but to earn a living for herself. It was at this point that she wished she had had some expert "vocational guidance," for that would have saved her from much wasted effort and uncongenial work. She hired a typewriter, bought a book on how to type by the touch method, and how to write Pitman's shorthand, and within a few weeks had secured a position as secretary in the personnel department of a large engineering works.

In her first position she learned much about how to deal with workers and about factory layout. In the evenings she studied various office subjects and four months later secured a position as foreign correspondent with an affiliate of the Niger Company (Lever Brothers) in Manchester. The hours were long and the pay unsatisfactory, so after teaching herself some bookkeeping she left the Manchester company to become the private secretary of the Managing Director of an automobile spring manufacturing company in Leeds, where again she had an opportunity of dealing with men in the works. Long hours of confinement in a noisy works office was too much for her health or liking, however, and so after eighteen months there she took a position as Spanish appeals director of a charitable organization for the mental deficient for about three months. Then she went to London to look for a position. This was in the autumn of 1925. Although she had been emotionally attracted to Catholicism during her school days, it was not until this period that she became intellectually convinced of the truth of the Catholic faith.

Within a month of being in London, she was engaged as assistant to the Manager of the newly opened office of Moody's Investors Service. She became an Oblate of St. Benedict at St. Augustine's Abbey, Ramsgate in 1926, and a monk of that monastery interested her in making a deeper study of theology and philosophy. After two years at Moody's Investors Service she left this organization in January 1928 to become the head of the Information Department of the newly-opened Paris office of Dillon Read & Co., investment bankers. Her father died at the beginning of February 1928. At Dillon Read's she wrote a daily news digest and a weekly economic review, did statistical and research work and had charge of the filing department. She did not have the time to do the literary writing which it had always been her ambition to do, and so she completed work for a Bachelor of Commerce degree from London University in 1930. She specialized in labor economics in this examination, because she thought that this study would amplify her economic knowledge, which had been centered on banking and finance for several years. At this time she also passed the final examination of the Chartered Institute of Secretaries, London. Then, in September 1930, she came to the United States to teach economics at Nazareth College, Michigan, with the idea of writing a novel during her first summer vacation and returning to England within two years. She stayed at this college for the two scholastic years of 1930–32.

Realizing the need of a Catholic textbook in sociology, and finding a middlewestern summer too hot for creative work, Eva Ross began her first book, *A Survey of Sociology,* in the summer of 1931. The book was published in September 1932, at which time the author took a position teaching economics and sociology at Maryville and Fontbonne Colleges, St. Louis, and began to study for an M.A. in sociology at St. Louis University, which she secured in February 1934. She returned to England for a summer vacation in 1933, and visited Belgium, becoming interested in the Jociste and the Grail youth movements. In the summer of 1934 she traveled in Canada and the West. The Bruce Publishing Company published her second book: *Rudiments of Sociology,* a high school textbook, in September 1934. Wishing to secure a degree of Doctor of Philosophy in sociology, Miss Ross left her position at Maryville and Fontbonne Colleges in June 1935. She spent the summer in England and on the Continent, and a short series of lectures which she gave at the summer school of the Catholic Social Guild in Oxford was published in 1936 by Sheed & Ward under the title: *Social Origins.* In September, 1935, Miss Ross registered at Yale University, New Haven, and taught for the 1935–36 year at Albertus Magnus College in that city. In the summer of 1936 she again went to

Europe, doing research for her doctoral dissertation on Belgium
Rural Cooperation in Italy, Belgium, and Great Britain, and
attending the *Semaines Sociales* at Versailles. In September
1936 she took a position as professor of sociology and economics
at the College of St. Elizabeth, New Jersey, where she taught
until 1939. During the 1936–37 year she went weekly to Yale
University, and received her doctor's degree there in June 1937.

Between 1936 and 1939 Miss Ross wrote two books: *What is
Economics?* and *Fundamental Sociology,* both of which were
published by the Bruce Publishing Company in 1939. She left
the College of St. Elizabeth at the end of January 1939, with the
idea of taking about six months' vacation and then doing other
work. After visiting friends in the middle-west and giving lectures in various colleges and seminaries as far as Winnipeg, she
went to Europe in March 1939. There she traveled in Great
Britain, France, Holland, and other countries studying Catholic
youth movements and completing a book on Belgium. The war
upset her plans, and so she returned to the United States at the
end of 1939, lectured in various colleges and seminaries, and
began work on a high school text on the problems of American
Democracy. Her book *Belgian Rural Cooperation* was published in 1940, and a second high school text on sociology: *Sound
Social Living* in 1941. Since September 1940 she has been a
professor of sociology and economics at Trinity College, Washington, D. C., and in the summers of 1941 and 1942 she taught
at the rural priests' summer school at St. John's Abbey, Minnesota.

Miss Ross considers that it is not so much intellectual com-
petence which is required for the writing of a textbook, as a
broad background of experience and facts, and the physical
ability to stand the strain of long hours of work. She writes a
book only when she believes that it will fill a real need. She
still looks forward to having time to devote to creative literature,
but says that she is not sure that she has now the requisite
talent to do this type of writing. She considers *Belgian Rural
Cooperation* to be her best work.

REVEREND J(OHN) ELLIOT ROSS

*Sociological and Religious
Works*

IF SHAKESPEARE'S WORDS,

> "The evil that men do, lives after them,
> The good is oft interred with their bones,"

could be applied to the books they write, then mine are certainly
not evil, for there is no probability that they will live after me.
Indeed, my books ought to be good; for most of them have been
buried without waiting for the interment of my bones. But even
the traditionally fond prejudices of literary parenthood cannot
deceive me into believing that my books make such an important
contribution to human thought that they deserve immortality.

What I have written is partly in the field of social reform and
partly in the line of apologetics. St. Paul calls himself a Jew
of the Jews, and what attracted me to the Paulists was the fact
that they were Americans of the Americans, one of whose principal purposes was to convert non-Catholic Americans. Both
my grandparents had been converts and I had numerous non-
Catholic relatives. As an additional formative influence should

be reckoned the fact that I grew up in Maryland with the traditions of the founders and the example of Cardinal Gibbons regarding religious tolerance. Newman confronted similar problems of a Catholic minority facing a non-Catholic majority and did in England what, *mutatis mutandis,* American Catholics should do in America. Moreover, he has been selected as patron of the work for Catholic students in non-Catholic colleges, to which work fifteen years of my priestly life have been devoted.

So when the publisher, W. W. Norton, asked me to write a life of Newman for a series of biographies he was publishing, I gladly consented. The book does not profess to be original historical research; but I think it is a good short life based on published material.

This fundamental vocation of presenting the Catholic Church to the American people, fitted in with giving credit courses in religion at non-Catholic universities,—Texas, Teachers College (Columbia University), Iowa, Illinois. And in 1934 I was glad to accept the invitation of the National Conference of Christians and Jews to tour the country with a rabbi and a Presbyterian minister in the interest of a better understanding between these three great religious groups. Rabbi Lazaron, Rev. Dr. Everett Clinchy and I traveled about 10,000 miles together, addressed some scores of thousands of persons in sixty or more meetings in half the States of the Union, besides speaking over two national hook-ups. To some extent, the book, *Religions of Democracy* (Devin-Adair), in which Rabbi Louis Finkelstein expounds Judaism, Professor William Adams Brown, Protestantism, and I, Catholicism, carries out the same idea. It was published under the auspices of the National Conference of Christians and Jews.

As a boy in college, I was strongly attracted to John Ruskin. He turned my thoughts in the direction of social reform and at the same time convinced me that at bottom the social question is a moral question. Neither Ruskin, however, nor the Catholic authors I read, seemed to me to present any convincing solution. What was the use of writing about the right to work or to a living wage when 13,000,000 persons were unemployed and could not find any work at any wage? I felt that Catholic commentators on the social encyclicals had failed to point out how the admirable principles of these encyclicals could be applied so that the problem of unemployment would be met and everyone would have work at a living wage.

So, having been paralyzed in 1936, and unable to do any active parochial or missionary work, I used much of the time in trying to think out a possible solution to this problem. It may be a fond parent's self-delusion for this Benjamin of his old age, but I think that my *Co-operative Plenty* (Herder) is the first Catholic book showing how the principles of the social encyclicals can be applied gradually, peacefully, without revolution, without politics, so that each one will have enough and no one too much.

Some of this book was written a page a day, because I was not strong enough to do more, at any one time. Years before my stroke, I had acquired habits that enabled me to work in this way and was thoroughly convinced of the truth of the old proverb, "many a mickle makes a muckle." Fifteen minutes a day adds up to over five thousands minutes in a year, or thirteen working days of four hours each. Or, put in another way, 125 words written each morning and 125 words each afternoon, would mean two five-minute sermons in a week, or a year's such sermons in twenty-six weeks. And though I had a second stroke in 1941, incapacitating me even more than had the first, I hope, God willing, to write a little more in this nibbling way. Doubtless it is an uninspiring procedure and accounts to some extent for the mediocre quality of my authorship. But I am no genius, and I am sure that I have accomplished more by this steady plodding than if I had waited till I felt inspired. And perhaps it will be an encouragement to some others who are not geniuses.

Besides this system of doing a little bit at a time with regularity, I have trained myself to write *currente calamo*. Once I have started, I deliberately force myself to write without stopping. There is something almost hypnotic, I find, in keeping on. One idea leads to another and thoughts come that would never have occurred if I had stopped to chew the end of a pencil. Then after I have finished the first copy of the manuscript, I go over it to make changes. This practice goes back to writing letters home as a young man. Often I found that though I did not know where I could get material for a reasonable long letter when I started, by not stopping I wrote a longer and more interesting letter than if I had paused between sentences and paragraphs.

My books have been in addition to my other work as a priest—parochial, preaching, teaching. For instance, *Sanctity and Social Service* (Devin-Adair) was a course of sermons showing how saints had been responsible for some of the most successful social work. *The Right to Work* (Devin-Adair) was based on a sermon dealing with the parable of the laborers hired at different hours. *Ethics* (Devin-Adair) was written because I was giving a supposedly non-sectarian credit course in religion at the University of Texas and could not find a suitable text-book. *Five Minute Sermons* (Herder, 4 series) were short sermons I actually preached. *Truths to Live By* (Holt) was based on a credit course in religion at Teachers College (Columbia University). Being thus tied in with actual work, I believe my books, whatever they lack in literary polish, have a certain practicality. Whether I can do any more writing is in the hands of God. But I would rather wear out than rust out.

RIGHT REVEREND JOHN AUGUSTINE RYAN

Social Ethics

THE DATE of my birth was May 25, 1869; the place, Dakota County, Minnesota, about twenty miles south of St. Paul. My education was received in an ungraded country school; and in the Christian Brothers High School, St. Thomas Seminary, and St. Paul Seminary, all located in St. Paul. During the four years immediately following my ordination on June 4, 1898, I took post-graduate courses at the Catholic University of America, where I received the degree of Doctor of Sacred Theology, May 31, 1906.

The first productions of mine that got into print, written while I was in St. Paul Seminary, appeared in *The Northwestern Chronicle,* the Catholic weekly paper published in St. Paul. They dealt, for the most part, with socialism. My first magazine article was published in *The Catholic World,* November, 1900, and received the honor of first place in that magazine. It was entitled "A Country without Strikes," and dealt with the recently-enacted compulsory arbitration law of New Zealand. A few months before that date, the Catholic University accepted my dissertation for the licentiate in theology on "The Moral Aspects of Speculation on the Exchanges." In the fall of 1900, I began to write my dissertation for the doctorate, the subject of which was "A Living Wage: Its Ethical and Economic Aspects."

The titles of these first publications of mine are sufficiently indicative of my principal interest as a writer, namely, social and economic problems. The sources of this interest were mainly: *The Irish World,* which came to our home weekly for several years before I went to college; and, later on, the works of Archbishop John Lancaster Spalding, Canon William Barry of England, Mr. W. S. Lilly of the same country, and Dr. Richard T. Ely, then head of the Department of Economics at the University of Wisconsin; and last but not least, the speeches of the brilliant author, agitator, and economic reformer, Ignatius Donnelly, whose home was about ten miles from my own.

My doctoral dissertation, *A Living Wage,* was not finished until 1905. It was published for the general trade by the Macmillan Company in the spring of 1906, and almost immediately achieved wide circulation. The greater part of what I have written since can be found in germ in that work. My subsequent books and articles were written to a great extent as developments of what is contained in *A Living Wage,* although they were called forth by particular occasions and situations. For example, my debate with Morris Hillquit on *Socialism: Promise or Menace?* occurred because *Everybody's Magazine* desired to publish such a discussion in the years, 1913–1914. At the completion of the debate, all the articles were published in book form by the Macmillan Company. My most important work, *Distributive Justice* (of which a thoroughly revised edition was brought out in the spring of 1942, twenty-six years after its first appearance) was undertaken in order to apply to the whole field of industrial distribution the principles which I had expounded and defended in *A Living Wage.*

Perhaps the most important exception to the statement made above concerning the relation between the latter work and subsequent volumes of mine, is *Catholic Principles of Politics,* of which Reverend Dr. Francis J. Boland of Notre Dame University and I are joint authors. That book is, of course, in the general field of politics, rather than of economics. It is a revised edition of *The State and the Church,* by Reverend Moorhouse F. X. Millar, S.J., and myself, first published in 1922.

I am asked to offer some suggestions "for the aspiring young writer." In all probability, more than one of the other contributors to this Series is competent to, and will, provide a more helpful and comprehensive response to this request than I could produce. Only one observation occurs to me as worthwhile: Whatever success I have had in obtaining readers for my books and magazine articles has been mainly due, I think, to my preoccupation with the qualities of clearness and directness of expression. From the time when I began to write, I have always believed that clearness is the most important and effective of all the qualities of style.

What I have called "directness" is, in my opinion, the next most important requisite. So far as I can recall, "directness" is not explicitly included among the formal qualities of style set forth in manuals of rhetoric, although it is undoubtedly implicit there. But I believe that it should have explicit recognition and constant attention on the part of any writer who desires to be effective. What I mean by directness is the practice of choosing the best word or expression rather than one that is "about as good," straight-out rather than roundabout language, concrete and specific rather than abstract and general phraseology.

These two qualities will, of themselves, be sufficient to command the reader's attention, provided that one has something to say. Forcefulness and brevity are obviously useful qualities of style, but they are almost automatically involved in clearness and directness. Ornament and rhetoric are likewise important, especially in some forms of writing, but they are not adequate substitutes for the two qualities that I have stressed. Moreover, they can easily be over-done, causing the reader to lose sight of the thought, in his preoccupation with the decorative side of the production.

EDITOR'S NOTE: Rt. Rev. Dr. Ryan is Professor of Social Ethics at the Catholic University of America and Director of the Social Action Department of the National Catholic Welfare Conference. His best known books are: *A Better Economic Order*, 1935, Harper; *Declining Liberty*, 1927, Macmillan; *A Living Wage*, 1906, 1920, Macmillan; *Social Reconstruction*, 1920, Macmillan; *Catholic Principles of Politics*, 1940, Macmillan; *Distributive Justice*, 1916, 3rd edition revised and enlarged, 1942, Macmillan; and his autobiography, *Social Doctrine in Action*, 1941, Harper.

DANIEL SARGENT

Poet and Biographer

DANIEL SARGENT is a Bostonian. He was born in Boston, Massachusetts, when Boston's literary enthusiasms were dying out. The year was 1890, the day August 22nd.

His paternal grandfather had been a Bostonian man of letters, who wrote Byronic verse which nobody read. This was in the 60's. But his immediate parents were not interested in literature. They were Bostonians who went to a Unitarian Church, and who were very conscientious, and who were busy with their seven children, of whom Daniel was the fifth. The father was busy also with his occupation as a cotton broker. The mother had been born Jane Welles Hunnewell. The father's name was Francis Williams Sargent. They thought that young Daniel might well become a soldier, for his Uncle Daniel had been an officer in the Civil War.

Daniel received his first schooling at Noble's School, which boasted of its "classical" character, and which was installed in a brown free-stone house on Beacon Street. He was quick to learn the names and dates of the English Kings, and he was keen to be best at Latin grammar. At this time he began to argue, and his parents decided he was more fit for the law than for the army.

At thirteen he was sent to a boarding school, which was under the auspices of the Protestant Episcopal Church. It stood on the hills thirty miles north-east of Boston, in the town of Groton, and was called Groton School. It had a pretty Gothic chapel. He ceased to be so keen about Latin grammar while at Groton, but he read a good deal of history, and gained, through a remarkable teacher, an appreciation of Homer. Before six years were up he had written at least two poems in imitation of Browning. He did not consider himself, however, nor was he considered, literary. If there was anything in which he shone, it was in debate. It was expected that he would enter politics. He left the school, a more defiant Unitarian than he had entered it, in spite of the Gothic chapel.

In 1909 he went to Harvard College. At school, until the very end, he had been frail and small, but suddenly he now grew to six feet, and almost became an athlete, almost a member of the Varsity Crew. This added a certain exuberance to his life, especially in the way of companionship. He also relished his studies with an aroused appetite. In spite of this general happiness, however, there welled up within him an inquietude which may be called religious. This was a wonderful life, but what was it all about?

It was not that he broke with Unitarianism. There was little in it to break with. He merely wanted to find out more. He studied philosophy in order to discover more. He found nothing. It was in studying the deeper traditions of European literature that he began to be aware of the great meanings of life. Even Chaucer opened his mind more than any philosopher. But most of all, Dante's *Divine Comedy* made him awake. In it he discovered the Church. It was Professor Barrett Wendell who was his chief guide in these readings.

At the end of three years he had fulfilled his requirements for an A.B., and was ready in the eyes of the college to go on to the Harvard Law School, but in other ways he was not ready. Politics did not seem to him so high a calling as formerly, nor one

for which he had been made. Lyrical poetry rather than parlia-
mentary oratory had become his mode of expression. So he resolved to stall for time, and spent a fourth college year taking
an A.M. in English literature.

The end of the year found him still in perplexity. Barrett
Wendell came to his help by offering him a position as his assistant in teaching Comparative Literature. This he accepted,
for though he was averse to the law, and wished to write, he did
not wish to accept the label of writer. From now on he could
write as he wished and be classed as a teacher.

Before he began to teach, he went abroad for a summer of
study. This was not his first trip to Europe. He had crossed
the Atlantic in both June 1912 and June 1913, and had wandered
widely. But this trip was different. In the first place, he meant
to study more systematically. In the second place, during that
trip, the first World War broke out. From a midnight window
in Hanover he watched Germany mobilizing.

This war did not fade from his mind during his year of teaching at Harvard 1914–1915. It made him restive. Another thing
made him restive: the fact that he had published a book of
lyrics, *Our Gleaming Days*. Teaching seemed tame. He decided
to quit the academic atmosphere, as if to seek real life elsewhere.
He would write. He might paint at the same time. He thought
painting would make a good vocation for a poet.

But it was hard to learn a craft with such exciting head-lines
in the newspapers, and he determined to take some part in the
conflict. He sympathized with France, and blamed the war on
German philosophy. Therefore he would try to help France
by driving an American Ford ambulance for the French
wounded. In March, 1916, he started across the Atlantic, and
before it was April, had been torpedoed in the English Channel.

Yet he got to France, and to the front, as they say; and began
to pass through experiences, some of which (those which have to
do with the actual commotion of battle) can be imagined, but
others of which cannot. It was something new to be a part of
French villages. It was a great discovery for him when he came
on the books of Ernest Psichari, and Charles Peguy. He shall

never forget how he was sent to Macedonia and to Thessaly, and
how he reread his Groton School Homer under Mount Olympus
when the Sengalese French were bathing in the Peneus River.
It was a revelation to him to see the work of the French chaplains
with the wounded. It was not merely that he found out how
admirable they were as men. He found out what an admirable
thing was their priesthood.

In the spring of 1917, his own country, which seemed far away,
declared war on Germany. He straightway joined the American
army, as a first lieutenant in the artillery of the First Division.
This rewedded him to his own people, through seeing their valor
and their suffering in the French background.

When the Armistice came in November 1918, he found himself
no nearer than before to knowing what he wanted to do as a
life's work in this new peace in his own country. But one
thing he did know. He wanted to become a Catholic. He was
baptized in April, 1919, at the Immaculate Conception Church
in Boston by Father Martin J. Scott.

The easiest thing was to return to Harvard as a teacher, which
he did. He became an instructor in the department of History
and Literature which had been instituted by Barrett Wendell.
He opened again many a book which he had not seen for five
years. Many things looked different. The Middle Ages looked
different. Professor Maurice de Wulf, a Belgian refugee who
had a room next to him at Harvard, introduced him to the importance of the medieval scholastic philosophy. He started once
again to write poetry; long narrative poems, somewhat epic.

During his resumed teaching, Barrett Wendell did him another and greater favor (the last, for he was soon to die). He introduced him to Louise Collidge of Boston, a convert like himself, who had discovered the Faith while nursing the wounded
in France. In June of 1920 he married her and henceforth had
double strength in all he did.

After a year off in Europe, he went on with his teaching work,
even for fifteen years. All these years he was in love with the
new-found beauty of the Church. He occasionally did something by way of apostolate, such as helping to found *The Com-*

monweal, and lecturing before Catholic groups. In 1925, when on a visit to Europe, he encountered Jacques Maritain who became to him an inspiration.

All these years also he wrote poetry. A minor part of it he published. A volume of lyrics, *The Door,* appeared in 1921. In 1925 he published—more noteworthy—*The Road to Welles-Perennes,* a symbolic poem shadowing forth some of his spiritual Odyssey in France during the war. Five years later he published at the St. Dominic's Press in England a long poem which he illustrated himself: *My Account of the Flood.* It was a laconic warning of the calamities impending in our de-christianized society. In 1931 another of his poems, in a small brochure illustrated by Philip Hagreen, appeared, also from his friend Hilary Pepler's St. Dominic's Press: *The Song of the Three Children.* In 1934 Longmans Green published for him a series of lyrics, *God's Ambuscade.* Two years later, he was elected President of the Catholic Poetry Society of America.

Up till 1933, he had written very little prose. But in that year he published *Thomas More,* a biography of the English saint not then canonized. He might never have written the book if he had not on a visit to England in 1930 come upon the American Jesuit poet, Leonard Feeney, who was then studying at Oxford. Father Feeney urged him to write more prose.

Since then he has been a busy writer of prose; so busy that after three more years he resigned from his teaching position at Harvard.

Before 1940 he had written *Four Independents, Catherine Tekakwitha,* and, *Our Land and Our Lady.* Before 1942 he had two more books in print, *Christopher Columbus,* and, *All the Day Long.* He had turned his attention from the Middle Ages, and English and French literature, to the general subject of the New World in its relations with the Old; which subject is none other than the epic of the spreading of the Christian Hope, once in the catacombs, round the world. In 1936 he had been elected President of the American Catholic Historical Association, and in 1942, a member of the Advisory Board of the Catholic Book Club.

He now lives with his wife and two children on the banks of a river at South Natick, Massachusetts. It seems that his main work is to continue to write historical biographies of characters whom he discovered when writing *Our Land and Our Lady,* a book of his which he prefers. Occasionally the poet in him makes it difficult for him to write prose, and he slips into verse. Even his prose has a poetical aim: it tries not only to tell the truth and interpret, but also to celebrate.

Longmans published Mr. Sargent's *Catherine Tekakwitha* (1936), *God's Ambuscade* (1935), *Our Land and Our Lady* (1939), and *All the Day Long* (a life of Bishop Walsh, co-founder of Maryknoll) 1941; Sheed & Ward issued his *Four Independents* (Peguy, Brownson, Claudel, Hopkins) 1935, and *Thomas More* (1935); Bruce Humphries issued his *Song of the Three Children* (1932) and *My Account of the Flood* (1930); his *Christopher Columbus* was published by Bruce in 1941.

MONICA EDITH SELWIN-TAIT

Novelist

BORN IN LONDON, ENGLAND, and educated privately there and in Scotland and on the continent, I recognize the difficulty of explaining how I manage to write popular American novels with the sort of background I possess. Possibly the best explanation is that I have traveled and lectured here a great deal and thus have come to know this country quite as well as my own.

My father, James Selwin-Tait, of London and Washington, was a banker and a financier, but he was also devoted to literature, wrote really lovely poetry, and was the author of four novels. He read charmingly, and was always reciting; so naturally I absorbed a good deal of serious literature while very young.

My mother, Augusta Edith Meynell, was a cousin of Wilfred Meynell, the husband of Alice Meynell. My mother's translation from the French of a work by a Pole, *The Two Chancellors*, is a standard work on German affairs. She was a linguist, musician, and artist; so that even as a child I was quite used to hearing four languages being spoken in our drawing-room at Greystoke, and being asked to sing and to recite.

It happened that I was an only daughter with four brothers, an only niece with four young uncles, and an only granddaughter. While not spoiled, I was featured quite a bit. I became so used to meeting people that I have never been shy or self-conscious in my life.

When I was six years old, something happened that changed the whole current of my life. My father met with sudden business reverses. Our lovely home was broken up. My brothers were sent to Scotland to my grandmother, and I was taken with my parents down to Kent, to a very modest cottage. Only an English child can understand what it meant to be free from the strict rules of the nursery! I had my father and mother all to myself. They were young and brave: I never saw a cloud on their faces. They went fishing and hiking, and I went too, of course; and when I grew tired, papa would carry me on his back.

Without going into the details of that wonderful summer, I must tell what bears on the subject of this article. We visited many historic places, and I was never left in ignorance of what those places meant. Throned on my father's strong young shoulders, I had no fear of the darkest dungeons, and in one house I rode on a shabby old rocking horse that had belonged to King Charles First,—of course after that he was real! However, it must be remembered that I had a family background for all this both in England and Scotland; it was part of my countries, for my father was Scots from the Border.

But soon, business took my father to Edinburgh, and life took on its ordered sequence with my brothers back home. But Edinburgh is a city of romance, and I was fertile ground. My mother had her own ideas of education. Whenever I was to see some interesting place, she tactfully introduced a fascinating book or story that made it all so real. Such as the *Lay of the Last Minstrel* before we visited Melrose (in the pouring rain).

By the time I was ten I was writing poetry (it was the natural outcome) and at twelve I was embarking on real stories, dramatizing everything I saw or read, and victimizing my poor brothers (who had no dramatic leanings). I even made my dear mother say with a gentle sigh that she would like to come into the schoolroom just once and find her own little daughter instead of Mary Queen of Scots, complete with court.

Though I wrote piles and piles of stories at this time (with no thought of their publication), private theatricals were my chief diversion. I dreamed of the stage, till one evening my mother, looking at me after an especially successful performance, said gently: "I hope my little daughter will not want to go on the stage." I was just sixteen at the time. A few months later my delicate mother was gone. And I turned to the lecture platform and to writing.

Once while in the country, I was seized with the urge to write. And although I had all day long for it, I felt that to get up at five o'clock in the morning insured success. Now I had a bad habit (which I regret I still have) of reading in bed. This being but a country house, I had only a candle. I carefully borrowed the kitchen clock, set the alarm for five, read a few minutes, and then went peacefully to sleep. It seemed that I had hardly closed my eyes before that fiendish clock went off! I gave one frantic clutch, gathered it into my arms and smothered it under the bed clothes. I awoke peacefully at my usual time, 8 A.M. The clock was standing quietly on the chair and a very much mussed up candle was clasped to my heart!

Well, I finished the story. It was not a success at the time, but has been published since, and been liked. But many things happened to put me off fiction. The return of the soldiers from the War inspired writing that attracted favorable notice. Then I had a loss, and when I recovered I devoted myself to research work. It paid very well; and I thought I was off fiction for life.

Then something remarkable happened. I made an eight days Retreat at a convent; and when it was over, I said to the Mother who had given it to me and whom I had known for some years: "Mother, perhaps I could write a pamphlet to help others know what I have gained from this Retreat." So it began. Mother gave permission for certain spiritual assistance and the writing became, not a pamphlet, but the triple love story, *Three Ships*

Come Sailing. The story is especially popular with the younger set. For gracious counsel in revising the story before publication, I am indebted to Father Talbot, S.J.

This, my advent into Catholic literature, was followed by a broadcast over the Yankee network, with the permission and special blessing of Cardinal O'Connell, always my friend.

All my succeeding books *(Uncharted Spaces, Wings of Lead,* and, *Winding Ways)* were published serially in *The Ave Maria* before coming out in book form. All have made me happy with the happiness that is greatest to a Catholic: I have not made money at the expense of what I wanted to live after me.

Some beautiful and unexpected experiences have happened to me through my books, particularly in the matter of lapsed Catholics who read them returning to the Sacraments.

To those of you who want to become writers, I would say: First, learn your own language, and how to write and to spell. It is a rare accomplishment, believe it or not! Secondly, learn how to make up a manuscript so that it will attract at the first glance,—good paper and good typing. Thirdly, do not be discouraged at returned manuscripts. If at first you do not succeed, learn the reason why. Then perhaps you will not have to try and try and try. Fashions in writing are changing all the time: watch your market!

EDITOR'S NOTE: Miss Selwin-Tait, now a resident of New York City, is the author of four novels: *Three Ships Come Sailing,* 1931, Benziger; *Uncharted Spaces,* 1932, Longmans; *Wings of Lead,* 1937, Ave Maria Press; and *Winding Ways,* 1939, Ave Maria Press.

INEZ SPECKING

Novelist and Girls' Story Writer

INEZ SPECKING, our "Doc" Specking, lives in a big red brick house in a quiet part of St. Louis, surrounded by books, music, flowers, pictures, and young people. Fifty girls getting ready for a slumber party; eighty Newman Club boys and girls lined up for a wiener roast in the back yard, or spilling over the stairway, the library floor, the living room floor, while they shout "Comin' Round the Mountain," "Susanna," "School Days;" a hundred and sixty for the college bridge party; four hundred for a visiting Cambridge lecturer! Doc's home is headquarters for them all, and for dances, spreads, lectures, meetings, discussions, religious instructions, candlelight teas, pledgings, initiations, club meetings. Here, too, older people meet,—the Shakespeare Club, the Writers' Guild, old-time school friends, faculty members, neighbors. At any time one may hear the blare of the radio, the music of new records, the ping of balls in the basement, the scuffle at billiards on the top floor, the swish and whirl of the dance, the rattle of silver, the clatter of china.

Occasionally, the house and garden are quiet. That is when

Doc is studying or loafing somewhere in Europe, South Africa, Alaska, South America, or when she is teaching students to write themes, or is reading Shelley or Keats or Browning or Shakespeare with her students. For Doc is a full-time college professor of English, forty six weeks a year (Saturdays, too, if you please, and sometimes nights).

When has she found time to write a dozen books and the many essays, short stories, articles, poems, that have appeared in Catholic and secular periodicals and anthologies? Probably during slumber parties!

Doc can and does cook, keep house, garden, ride, play bridge, baseball, ping pong, shuffle board. She reads, too; at least five hours a day; and she walks miles and miles.

How did she come to write? When asked that, she usually says "Oh," rather vaguely and goes on talking about the new fourteen-inch goldfish in the backyard pool or about her R.C.A.F. nephew in Canada. This time, however, the united and persistent plea of her class finally brought: "Why you've been in college for years with me; you must know all about it. I must have told you. Anyway, the *Quarterly* dummy has to be proofed and . . ."

They answered: "The *Quarterly* dummy can wait. No, you haven't said anything. You really have no idea how little any of your students know about your life, how you came to write, where you get your material. Please!"

"All right; but I warn you!—Well, when I was a pig-tailed little girl of eight (the same Missy whom Boy called a clam) I tiptoed into the library one afternoon and told my stern professor Dad that I'd like to write a book, a blue book with gold letters on the back. Dad gave his whole attention for a full half minute to this new and startling freak, (What would his children think of next!), and then returned to his Dante, murmuring wearily: How is the German script coming along, and have you finished weeding the onions?

"Ten years later I came home from my second year at college with the manuscript of *Missy*. How to break the secret to the family I did not know; but at last, when Boy was beginning to

invite trouble (some questions about my use of his typewriter)
I decided to tell my news in the evening when Father Roberts
was making himself at home on our front porch. I could always
count on Father Roberts. He had never believed that I was
the family's black sheep.

"Boy dropped his huge volume on torts and shouted: You
can't do a thing like that! You'd disgrace the family. I'd
never dare show my face again.

"The rest were silent. Daddy looked puzzled, as if he were
searching for something that he had misplaced. Mother, for
once, did not say that she would find the something in a minute.
She merely looked helplessly at me and at Daddy and at Father
Roberts. But Father Roberts smiled across at me and said:
Fine! And then, as Boy began again, Father Roberts lit a ciga-
rette and said: Boy, you *could* go to Siberia. The family disgrace
wouldn't reach you there. And probably they need lawyers in
Siberia. Or perhaps in Southern Patagonia.

"And then came the First World War! *Missy* was forgotten
until I returned from Stanford University with my M.A. in 1923.
I was helping Harry gather and press wild flowers one sultry
afternoon, when I discovered that he was using the *Missy* manuscript in place of newspaper. He said he had found it under the
lumber pile back of the barn.

"I rescued what was left, rewrote the whole thing and sent it
out. It was accepted. The long slim envelope was waiting for
me when I came home from Confession one Saturday afternoon.
Was I excited? I should say I was! I went straight back to
church to tell Father Roberts. And next morning I wondered
why the whole congregation didn't get up and shout for joy.

"That same year I wrote *Boy,* the companion book to *Missy.*
Those two books are the record of my early life. Most of my
other books and stories are records of the lives of others with
whom I have lived. I met Edith at the Benedictine Convent at
Clyde, and, years after, I wrote a book about her: *The Awakening of Edith.* I met Martha Jane at the B.V.M. Academy when
I was a Colorado University student. Martha was a gay and
sparkling girl, and she furnished me with all the incidents for

Martha Jane and *Martha Jane at College.* I spent many days at Fontbonne College with the girls and Sisters, and with that background, I wrote *Martha Jane, Sophomore.* From Stanford University I gleaned *It's All Right;* from Normandy, *Sue Elizabeth;* from foreign travel, *Martha Jane Abroad;* from the German-American scene, *What Else Is There?;* from teaching in southwest Colorado, *Go West, Young Lady.* The short stories are also records of persons, places, incidents. Some of them have been collected into a volume: *So That's That.*

"Do I intend to write more? Am I writing now? Yes, to both questions. What about? Catholic college life at Oxford, college stories with Ohio and Michigan backgrounds, a South American book, a Paris story, a Carmel-by-the-Sea book, a St. Louis society novel.

"Do I write under my own name? Not always. My books have all appeared under my own name. But many articles, stories, essays and poems have been published under six different names, most of which I have forgotten. But wasn't that the bell? It's time for the Romantic Literature class. I'll meet you later in the *Quarterly* room!"

Books by Inez Specking, Ph.D., D.Litt.: published by Benziger, *Missy* (1924), *Boy* (1925), *The Awakening of Edith* (1925), *Mirage* (1926), *Martha Jane* (1927), *Martha Jane at College* (1927); published by Bruce, *Literary Readings in English Prose* (Science and Culture Series, 1935); published by Herder, *What Else Is There?, Martha Jane, Sophomore, It's All Right, So That's That* (all 1929); published by the Catholic Literary Guild, *Go West, Young Lady* (1939).

DON LUIGI STURZO

I HAD MY FIRST experience as an author at the age of eighteen, fifty-three years ago. While still a student, two of my philosophical articles were published in *Il Tomista* (The Thomist) of Palermo, in my native Sicily. I also wrote poems, in Italian and in Latin; and between 1890 and 1893, five of my poems appeared in the year books of the Seminary at Caltagirone. I also composed a piece of religious music which the editor of *Santa Cecilia* (Milan) liked, but which he did not find rigidly liturgical enough for his Review. Since then I have written for many reviews, as well as pamphlets and books. Not a writer by profession, I wrote to accomplish my vocation as a priest, teacher, social welfare promotor, and political organizer.

At twenty I taught literature. Dissatisfied with the text book, I wrote some chapters of *A History of Italian Literature*. Soon afterwards, I went to Rome to obtain a doctorate in philosophy and theology at the Gregorian University and the Academy of St. Thomas Aquinas. Then I was asked to teach philosophy and sociology.

At Caltagirone, in 1897, I founded a weekly newspaper, *La Croce di Constantino* (Constantine's Cross), and helped found a daily paper at Palermo, *Il Sole* (The Sun), in 1899. Journalism, always pressing, impedes or disturbs creative work. Yet I managed at this time to write several plays. (One of them, *An Episode at the University,* was published at Bergamo with so many typographical slips that I stopped its sale.)

Then I began my sociological writing with a pamphlet with the present-day sounding title, *Conservative Catholics and Christian Democrats* (1900), followed by *L'Organizzazione di Classe e Unioni Professionali* (The Organization of Classes and the Professional Unions). Both were published in Rome by La Societa di Cultura. The second title, which appeared in 1901, was very successful. It was dedicated to Professor Giuseppe Toniolo, famous Catholic economist and leader of Christian Democracy, whose process for beatification was just passing its first stage.

Little by little it was good-bye to schools, books, drama, music. Public life was drawing me away, despite my efforts to avoid abandoning my preferred studies. In an article in *The Commonweal* (Sept. 26, 1941), I tried to explain how and under what circumstances my political vocation developed. It is difficult for many to understand the enthusiasm my generation had for Christian Democracy and social welfare in Italy under Pope Leo XIII. "Go to the people" was our motto for meeting all classes, all ages, and all the needs of our workmen and peasants.

In 1899, I was appointed Municipal Councilor of my town, later Provincial Councilor, governmental authority of Caltagirone; and immediately afterwards, Mayor. For twenty years I was also National Councilor, and Vice President of the Italian Communes; and during the same time, often a member of national governmental commissions. I did not, however, drop Catholic and Social Action. In fact, I was appointed a life member of the General Council of the Catholic Economic Union, elected a member of the Executive Committee of the National Catholic Electoral Union, and General Secretary of Catholic Action. It is difficult for me to remember how many appointments I had in my thirty years of public life in Italy.

Yet I continued to write sociological and political addresses on themes that had been or were still the object of my studies: Christian Democracy, the modern state, social labor questions, the relation between Church and State, and morality in public life; and to deliver them often in different centers of Italy.

One of my most important and popular social talks was delivered in Milan in May 1903, and was published under the title, *The Social Struggle—Law of Progress*, by the principal Catholic daily paper of that city. It was also published, along with some of my other lectures, by La Societa di Cultura, under the title *Sintesi Sociali* (Social Syntheses), in 1905. The same publisher issued my *I Cattolici nella Vita Politica* (Catholics in Political Life), in 1906. Both books were very well received.

Public life is selfish: it wants one entirely for itself. My publications from 1906 to 1920 were strictly technical. They dealt with problems of public administration, agriculture, finance, municipal agencies, communal rights, housing, food, public health. How many writings? I do not know. I agreed with a publisher's request to compile a volume of selections of these writings; but could not find time to collect and revise them. On another occasion, Francesco Ferrari, a publisher in Rome, had a friend of mine collect some of my addresses on Italian finance in the first World War, the problem of war orphans, the appeal for peace by Pope Benedict XV in 1917, Jerusalem and the Jewish problem, etc. But I could not find time to revise the proofs and the printing of the book was discontinued.

After the Armistice, I founded a new political party, the Italian Popular Party, composed of Catholic Christian Democrats. To organize the party I left my home town definitely, traveled over Italy most of the year, and established headquarters in Rome. Along with this new responsibility came the obligation of writing articles, addresses and studies, explaining the character, aims, and meaning of the new party. And so rapidly did the Italian Popular Party grow, that in the general political election of November 1919 it won 99 of the 508 seats available in the House (Camera dei Deputati). It ranked second among the parties represented, the first place being held by the socialists with 151 seats. I also aided in founding the Christian Democratic Union. In a few years its membership rose to 1,200,000; while after 30 years the Socialist Confederation had but 1,500,000 members.

I edited a weekly in Rome and continued to contribute to other Catholic papers in Italy until the establishment of the daily paper of our Party, *Il Popolo* (The People).

And between 1920 and 1925, I wrote several books on Sociological, political, economic and polemical subjects: *Dall'Idea al Fatto* (From the Idea to the Fact), issued by Ferrari, in Rome; *Riforma Statale e Indirizzi Politici* (On State's Reform and Political Orientations), issued by Vallecchi, in Firenze. (The celebrated sociologist Pareto wrote that this is a scientific and not a political book); *Popolarismo e Fascismo* (Popolarism and Fascism), issued by Gobetti, in Torino. (Popolarism refers to the theory and practice of the Italian Popular Party as the antithesis of Fascism); and, *Pensiero Antifascista* (Antifascist Thought), issued by Gobetti, in Torino.

La Liberta in Italia (Freedom in Italy), though published by Gobetti in Torino, was written in London where, late in October 1924, I sought refuge from the Fascist persecution by voluntary exile.

Exile is often propitious for an author. After the first months of waiting and observing, I realized I could not soon return to Italy, and so I accepted the offer of Faber & Gwyer (now Faber & Faber) to write a book for them. The book, *Italy and Fascism,* with a Preface by Professor Gilbert Murray, was published in London by Faber (1926), in New York by Harcourt Brace (1927), in Cologne by Volkverein (1927), in Paris by Felix Alcan (1927), and in Madrid by Editorial Reus (1930). The volume was praised by all but the pro-fascist press, as impartial, high minded, and sound in political outlook.

As the political interest in my own country became more distant to me, I turned my mind to international affairs. My book, *The International Community and the Right of War,* with a Preface by Professor G. P. Gooch, was published in London by G. Allen & Unwin (1928) and in New York by Rochard R. Smith (1930), to whom it had been recommended by Professor R. Mc-

Iver of Columbia University. In his Preface to the French edition, Professor Louis Le Fur wrote: "I have never seen an exposition more luminous than this on the various theories of war
from the end of antiquity till our epoch." The book was written
from a sociological point of view.

The last poetry I had written dated back to 1900, and my last
music to 1908. Between 1905 and 1908 I had composed a *Dixit,*
a *Magnificat,* and three pieces of *Jeremiah Lamentations,* all
executed by an orchestra and choir in Caltagirone. Since then
my heart but not my thoughts or my will had returned to poetry
and music. And little did I think that at the age of fifty-seven
I would return to them. But so it was.

Wagner's Tetrology was being performed at Covent Garden,
London. That music has ever had a deep and strange charm
for me. But the librettos are pantheistic and pessimistic: they
deify a humanity that returns to its primitive instincts. The importance of the music had previously made me unmindful of the
meaning of the opera. But now I thought: Why not a Christian
Tetrology, put to music by one with talent. I discussed the subject in an article in the London review, *Music and Letters.*
Then some friends suggested that I do such a Tetrology myself.

My first idea was to write four librettos, but while drafting the
work, I decided that a dramatic poem would be better. It was
published by Bloud & Gay, in Paris, in 1932, under the title, *Il
Cicilo della Creazione* (The Cycle of Creation). It comprised
a Prologue and four Actions or Dramas, titled the Angels, Adam,
the Redemption, and the Apocalypsis. One of the few who ap-
preciated the work in France was Professor Paul Hazard of the
Sorbonne, who wrote me that it ranked first in all the literature
of our time. Only a few copies slipped into Italy, since my name
was on the black list. But *La Civilta Cattolica,* a Jesuit magazine
in Rome, dared to publish an enthusiastic review. A Spanish
version of my Cycle was published in Buenos Aires in 1940,
through the initiative of some friends of mine.

With a view to giving a performance of my Cycle in London,
in 1934 the celebrated French composer Darius Milhaud (who
now resides in Oakland, California), wrote the incidental music

for the Prologue, the Angels, and Adam. But as the society sponsoring the work did not have sufficient funds, the undertaking was not carried through to completion.

Thus freed of the poetic enchantment, I returned to my sociological studies, in particular, to my sociological theory. In Europe sociology has a wider meaning than the word usually connotes in America. By it Europeans understand the general laws of society as a whole. I have had a sociological theory of my own from the time I began teaching the subject in 1900. What I have written since then has been in the light of my theory, delving more deeply into it. After thirty-five years I wrote a book, in French entitled *Essai de Sociologie.* The press in France and England were so favorable that the Institute of Sociology in London appointed a committee to foster a discussion of my theory. But my illness first and then the war put a stop to that. The English translation of a revised edition of the book, titled *New Sociology,* is now ready for publication.

Applying my sociological theory to political and moral problems, I wrote *Politics and Morality* (Burns, Oates & Washbourne. 1938). The French edition was published by Bloud & Gay, in Paris, 1938, and the Spanish version by Editorial Locada, in Buenos Aires, 1940.

American readers are familiar with my book on *Church and State* (Longmans Green 1939 and Geoffrey Bles, London, 1939), which had already appeared in French in 1937. That topic has fascinated me since my university days when in Naples I delivered an address on Church and State under the Bourbons. I worked on this book for seven years; not every day, but most of them. A pamphlet of mine on the same subject was published at Augsburg, Germany, in 1932; but the publishers never paid the royalty. Because my name and my writings are forbidden by the Nazis, I never went further in the matter.

As a diversion I accepted an offer to edit a symposium entitled *For Democracy* (Burns, Oates. 1939), myself also contributing two chapters. It has been quite popular in England, and has been reviewed in the United States by *Thought* and by *The Review of Politics.*

I have been in the United States since October, 1940. Since then I have written *The True Life: Sociology of the Supernatural,* which is now (1942) being published by the Catholic University of America Press; and *Les Guerres modernes et la pensée catholique, et autres essais sociologiques* (Editions de L'Arbre, Montreal. 1942), the Portuguese edition of which is now in the making in Brazil.

I have no idea of how many contributions I have made to periodical literature. I collected eight large volumes of such writings covering the period 1925 to 1936; and now a friend of mine in London is compiling the rest for the years 1937 to 1940.

If God gives me time and energy, I should like to finish my life with one more work on *The Sociological Method.* In it I would complete my theory.

BLANCHE JENNINGS
THOMPSON

Looking for Silver Pennies

WHEN I WAS very little, I had a large linen book which told the story of the Old Woman and Her Pig. I can see the picture yet. The Old Woman wore a mob cap, a kerchief, and a big apron. Her broom was very odd, being circular in shape and obviously home made, and she was gazing with delight at a coin in her hand. The story said, "Once upon a time an old woman was sweeping the floor when she found a silver penny." Many, many years later when I wanted a name for my first book, *Silver Pennies* popped into my head. People often ask where the title came from, and I can only suppose that it came out of that old linen book.

I was born in the small town of Geneseo in New York State. My father was a lawyer and my mother a born story-teller with a strong sense of the dramatic. Everybody in the family seemed to spout poetry on the slightest provocation. My mother read it to us, and my father strode up and down with his hands clasped behind him intoning:

> "I remember, I remember,
> The house where I was born . . ."

I recall thinking that it wasn't much of a feat, considering that he passed the house every day. I also remember well the first poem I ever recited in public. I was about five, and this is the poem:

> "When I was at the party,"
>   Said Betty aged just four,
> "A little girl fell off her chair
>   Right down upon the floor.
> And all the other little girls,
>   They laughed, but only me.
> I didn't laugh a single bit,"
>   Said Betty soberly.
> "And why didn't you laugh, darling?"
>   Asked Mother, pleased to find
> That her dear little daughter
>   Had been so sweetly kind.
> "Why didn't you laugh, darling,
>   Or don't you like to tell?"
> "I didn't laugh," said Betty,
>   "Because it was I that fell."

In school we were especially fortunate in that our reading books contained a great deal of poetry, and that our teachers frequently read aloud to us. We memorized a great deal of poetry, too, so that to-day I can recite long passages from such poems as "The Vision of Sir Launfal," and "Horatius at the Bridge" and any number of short lyrics like "Crossing the Bar" and the poems of Robert Louis Stevenson. Poetry didn't "take" with all of us, however. I had a little brother with deceptively angelic golden curls and a fierce resistance to any form of instruction. To this day he can only recite one passage from the masters. If he happens to be feeling unusually well as he takes the wheel of his car on a sunny day, he begins grandiloquently:

> "Oh, what is so rare as a day in June?"

The family groans in unison, but he goes on relentlessly. It is the one poem he knows, and who shall deny him utterance?

After I was graduated from the State Normal School in Geneseo, I went to Rochester, New York. There I taught first grade for a number of years. Even now after teaching at every level from the first grade straight through the university, I still like the littlest ones best. I left them reluctantly to take my baccalaureate degree at Columbia University, and upon returning was sent to the Rochester City Normal School to teach Reading and Language Methods. I also taught a course in Children's Literature at the University of Rochester, from which institution about the same time I received the degree of Master of Arts. A few years later, after the City Normal School was closed and I had become Head of the English Department at Benjamin Franklin High School, I received the honorary degree of Doctor of Letters from Nazareth College in Rochester, a college for women under the direction of the Sisters of St. Joseph.

Young people often ask, "When did you first begin to write?" Well, I think I was ten. I still have the yellowed newspaper clipping of my first story which was written for a young peoples' prize contest, and for which I received a copy of Thompson-Seton's *The Track of the Sandhill Stag.* Two years later, I received as a prize in a similar contest, Rudyard Kipling's *Kim,* and to this day, I am an ardent lover of Kipling's magic tales. After I began to teach, I wrote a number of poems, short plays, stories, and articles for educational magazines. As I look through my old scrapbooks, I am filled with astonishment at the number of different topics upon which I have uttered the most pontifical pronouncements. Apparently I felt that the world was my field. I have since lectured on all kinds of subjects, and I have even written the music for several songs, although the mouth organ is the only instrument upon which I have ever been really adept. I always play the piano when the family is out.

While I was teaching at the Norman School, I began collecting contemporary poems that children seemed to like. A supervising teacher in the city became interested in them and showed the collection to a friend who happened to be an agent for a publishing company. He asked me if I would consider publishing them. If I would consider! Very much astonished, I said yes and behold *Silver Pennies!* It was as simple as that. But don't get the idea that getting an anthology ready for publication is as simple. I speak as one who knows. Letters! Letters! Letters!

Trying to find elusive poets (for the shadow of prison bars looms over the unhappy anthologist who disregards copyrights), signing innumerable contracts, and paying fees that range from five dollars for the meek and humble poet to fifty or a hundred dollars for the arrogant aristocrat who has arrived. However you look at it, for about a year the anthologist's life, like that of the Gilbert and Sullivan policeman, is not a happy one.

Silver Pennies turned out to be very successful. It never made any money for me because unfortunately I sold it outright. Anthologies are not likely to have a serious effect upon one's income tax, in any case, on account of the royalties on copyrighted material, the expense of which is borne by the compiler. *The Golden Trumpets,* a book of fairy tales and poems came next. In the front of *Silver Pennies* appears the line, "You must have a silver penny to get into fairyland." So many people asked where the line came from that I wrote a poem to quote it from. This poem appears in *The Golden Trumpets* and is probably the only poem ever quoted from before it was written. A one-act play, *The Dream Maker,* had quite a career. It was produced in nearly every state in the union and by every kind of group from an eighth grade in Alaska to the State Federation of Women's Club in Florida. It appeared first in a magazine, and I grew pretty tired of writing out the music to the two little incidental songs, "An April Day" and "Little White Moon of My Dreams" before it was finally published in paper covers. Since which time I have lost track of it.

In 1933, I went abroad. I had been across the water twice before. I had been in Mexico, Canada, the West Indies, and Central America, and had pretty well exhausted the possibilities of my own country—but this was different! I went with a Dominican group on a Holy Year Pilgrimage, one of the most unforgettable experiences of my life. Notre Dame and the Rue de Bac in Paris, the home of the Little Flower in Lisieux, the diamond jubilee of the Apparitions of Our Lady to little Bernadette in Lourdes, Dominican shrines all over Southern France and Italy, full moon on the Bay of Naples, on Lake Como, and on the Grand Canal in Venice were some of the highlights. The greatest moment was an audience with the

Holy Father, Pius XI—surely one of the great ones of this earth.
Upon my return from this pilgrimage I became a member of the
Third Order of St. Francis and began the Catholic anthology
With Harp and Lute, the idea for which came to me while talking to a Dominican nun on ship-board. Soon after that I wrote
Bible Children, the pictures for which were done by the famous
children's writer and illustrator, Kate Seredy. Next came a
rather unusual venture—my prayer book, *All Day with God,* intended chiefly for modern business women, but apparently used
by a goodly number of men. At any rate, I had a complaint from
some policemen that, although I had prayers for lawyers, doctors,
business men, motorists, and a dozen others, I had neglected
them, and they wanted a special prayer, too!

In the last year or two, having finished *More Silver Pennies,*
I have been working on text books for high school, including
Americans All and *Adventures in Reading* (as collaborator). I
write frequently for the *Catholic World, The Ave Maria, The
Commonweal,* and other Catholic magazines. Until the Catholic
public supports its own press more adequately, however, Catholic writers can consider their work only as one of supererogation
and do it in their spare time. It would be almost impossible to
earn a living at it. In fact, writing of any kind, unless one gets
into the "best-seller" class if not a very profitable occupation.
The entire amount that my writings have earned for me in
twenty years is less than three years' salary in the notoriously
ill-paid profession of teaching.

For those who like intimate details—I always wear blue; I
have a very interesting collection of more than two hundred or-
namental crosses from all parts of the world; I would make
every high school student of reasonable intelligence study Latin
(every *Catholic* of course, should be able to read and understand
the language of the liturgy); as for the future, I continue to look
for silver pennies, and in answer to the recent question of a little
girl in Detroit I was obliged to say, "Yes, I really have thought
of *Still More Silver Pennies!*"

Miss Thompson's books include: *All Day with God,* 1939, Bruce; *Bible Children,* 1937, Dodd; *Silver Pennies* (1925) and *More Silver Pennies* (1938), Macmillan. Her fantasy, *Dream Maker,* was published by the Drama League.

REVEREND JOSEPH FRANCIS THORNING

FATHER THORNING stems from the East through his Celtic mother (Julia Theresa Hallissey, of Springfield, Massachusetts) as well as from the West through his Viking father (Cully M. Thorning, of Winneconne, Minnesota). One of four children (two boys and two girls), he was born in Milwaukee and received his early education at the hands of the Dominican Sisters (Sinsinawa, Wisconsin) at St. Rose of Lima School. In eighth grade he won two prizes in Irish history as well as a scholarship to Marquette Academy, where he studied four years. Holy Cross College was his choice for an A.B. course. At Worcester, he wrote verse and prose for the *Holy Cross Purple,* and was elected vice-president of his class of '18.

His studies for the priesthood were undertaken at St. Stanislaus Seminary, Florissant, Missouri, and (1918–1921 and 1925–1929) at St. Louis University. On three occasions at the latter institution he was appointed by the faculty to essay a public defense in Latin of important theses in philosophy and theology. He passed the final examinations in these subjects at St. Louis University, *summa cum laude.*

The ecclesiastical studies had an interlude of three years (1922–1925), which were spent teaching the classics at Loyola University, Chicago. Probably the most noteworthy event of this regency was his founding and organization of the National Interscholastic Basket Ball Tournament that was sponsored by the University. This proved to be an annual event for eighteen years. Knute Rockne never missed this tournament while he was alive.

In 1925, Dr. Thorning received an invitation to write a series of articles on international affairs for *America*. He spent twelve months preparing the first contribution to this series. It was entitled "The Problem of Peace." The series attracted national attention and the author was invited to act as chairman of the Europe Committee of the Catholic Association for International Peace. A longer study, published in *Thought,* was reproduced as a pamphlet (*National Security and International Peace*), by the C.A.I.P. Immediately, Dr. Thorning was invited to join the Foreign Policy Association, the American Academy of Political and Social Science, the American Sociological Society, and other learned societies.

After his ordination to the priesthood in 1928, Dr. Thorning was designated to do research work at Georgetown University and the Catholic University of America. His field of specialization was social, economic and political science. His doctoral dissertation, *Religious Liberty in Transition* (1931), is now a standard work of reference. During this period, he began to write articles on foreign affairs for reviews in India, Australia and New Zealand, as well as the United States.

In 1931, Dr. Thorning received a twofold assignment: study at Oxford University, England, and the post of foreign correspondent of *America*. At Oxford he specialized in international relations, studying under the direction of Sir Alfred Zimmern. Between terms, he flew to Paris, Madrid, Barcelona, Valencia, and Seville. At Berlin, he interviewed the then Chancellor of Germany, Dr. Heinrich Bruening. In France, he consulted with General Edouard de Castelnau, the hero of Verdun, and other French leaders. At Geneva, he was asked to serve as League of

Nations' correspondent of the National Catholic Welfare Conference News Service. His series of dispatches on the so-called
World Disarmament Conference gave a sound analysis of the
character of that assembly. These articles appeared everywhere
in the English-speaking world. At Geneva, interviews for various
publications were secured with Ramsay McDonald, Dr. Joseph
Motta (President of Switzerland), Count Apponyi, Aristide
Briand, and Edouard Herriot.

While in Geneva, Dr. Thorning was invited to be the first
priest to speak over the network of the NBC from Europe. He
gave a number of other lectures at Geneva, in English and
French.

Rome was another center of activity where this scholar can
claim a world record: within a single week he was received by
Pope Pius XI, the General of the Jesuits, and Mussolini.

Returning to the United States, Dr. Thorning was again stationed at Georgetown University and, from 1934 to 1936, he
served as special lecturer on sociology and acting dean of the
Graduate School. He also served as Washington correspondent
of *America*.

Recreation was furnished by long walks in Potomac Park and
by tennis matches with his friend, J. H. Jefferson Caffery, then
Assistant Secretary of State in charge of Latin American affairs.
Summer vacations were spent in Mexico, Cuba, and Central
America, in investigation of social and economic conditions.
The study of Spanish and Portuguese was an indispensable
preliminary for these surveys.

In 1937, Dr. Thorning was appointed by Archbishop Michael
J. Curley to the post of chairman of the department of social
sciences in Mount St. Mary's Seminary and College, Emmitsburg, Maryland. He likewise conducted the courses in church
history and ethics.

The civil war in Spain, with its conflicting reports from both
sides, induced Dr. Thorning to visit the scene of action in order
to gather first-hand information. Early in June, he embarked
on a fast liner for Europe. His arrival in Spain coincided with
the entrance of the Nationalist troops into Bilboa and Santander.

At Salamanca, in the Episcopal Palace, he had his first interview with Generalissimo Franco, leader of Christian Spain against the Leftist forces.

Now began one of the most thrilling episodes in the life of this foreign correspondent. Senor Pablo Merry del Val, chief of the Foreign Press section, suggested a trip to all the battle fronts. Madrid, Toledo, Teruel, Granada, Malaga and Seville were visited in quick succession. High ranking generals, civil administrators, ecclesiastical leaders, chaplains in the armed forces, naval officers, captured prisoners, refugees from the Leftist territory, peasants, factory workers and professional people were consulted and interviewed. The budget of news thus accumulated was filed with the Washington *Post, The Sign,* the New York *Times* and the N.C.W.C. News Service. These reports were recognized as an authentic news source with respect to developments in Spain.

During the same summer, Dr. Thorning visited Norway, Sweden, Denmark, Germany, Finland, Danzig, Leningrad and Moscow. In Soviet Russia he gave special attention to the health services: hospitals, clinics, sanitoria and dispensaries. He was a guest of the Soviet Government at the National Festival of Aviation and was able to estimate the striking power of the Russian air fleets.

During 1937, Dr. Thorning completed his *Primer of Social Justice,* a monograph which has a preface by Archbishop Curley. His address, "Why the Press Failed on Spain," originally delivered before the American Catholic Historical Association was published in pamphlet form by the International Catholic Truth Society.

The officials of the National Broadcasting Company invited Dr. Thorning to describe the International Eucharistic Congress from Budapest in May, 1938. The following account of this activity is taken from the New York *Times* of May 29, 1938:

"Budapest, Hungary—By a record-breaking series of broadcasts to the United States, England, Ireland, Hungary and other countries, an American priest, Dr. Joseph F. Thorning, of Mount St. Mary's College, Mary-

land, has become an outstanding figure at this year's Eucharistic Congress.
Never before in the history of broadcasting has an American priest enjoyed such a vast radio audience as has Dr. Thorning here. Besides
three broadcasts to the United States over nation-wide hook-ups and a
special program to Ireland and England, he also broadcast the congress
proceedings in Hungarian, German, French and Spanish over the other
wave lengths. The congress broadcasts have been carried over all the
world by a score of radio companies."

After the radio work in Budapest, Dr. Thorning made short
visits to Vienna, Prague, Munich and Paris. In France he made
arrangements to enter Spain, where the civil war was still raging.
Successful in his efforts, he crossed the international frontier at
Hendaye-Irun and met Generalissimo Franco at Burgos. This
time, the active fronts, particularly that at Lerida and Tremp,
were reached from Saragossa. With the Army of Navarre, commanded by General Garcia Valino, Dr. Thorning entered Cas-
tellon de la Plana on the Mediterranean, where he celebrated
the first Mass attended by the public in two and one half years.
Thousands of civilians and soldiers were massed in the square
for this occasion.

The next summer, 1939, Dr. Thorning had his meeting with
the head of the Spanish State in Madrid. The war was over
and the work of reconstruction was described in a special series
of seven articles for the N.C.W.C. News Service. Realizing that
war was imminent and that the Balkan area would again be the
cockpit of Europe, the foreign correspondent made a rapid survey of conditions in Jugoslavia, Bulgaria, Rumania, Hungary,
Poland and Turkey, interviewing the prominent personalities of
each country.

A trip to the East coast of South America followed, thanks to
an invitation from the U. S. Ambassador to Brazil, Jefferson
Caffery. Buenos Aires, Montevideo, Santos, Sao Paulo, Bahia,
Pernambuco and Rio de Janeiro were some of the cities visited.
Features of this survey were interviews with those two good
friends of the United States, President Getulio Vargas and Foreign Minister Oswaldo Aranha of Brazil.

In 1940, Dr. Thorning made a survey of social conditions in

Japan, China and the Philippine Islands. His report on the ambitious intentions of the military and naval chiefs of Japan, having appeared in *The New York Times,* attracted Congressional attention.

In 1941, the Mount St. Mary's professor initiated the movement for Spiritual Inter-Americanism. He was appointed by the editors of *The Sign* to direct the first Spiritual Seminar to South America with headquarters at the University of San Marcos, Lima, Peru. His interview with Dr. Manuel Prado, President of the Republic of Peru, was published in many journals in North and South America. The Seminar was successful beyond expectations.

With the cooperation of Monsigor William Barry and the editors of *The Sign,* Dr. Thorning organized the first conference of Spiritual Inter-Americanism at Barry College for Women, Miami, Florida, early in January, 1942. The winners of *The Sign* Las Americas Awards were announced as the climax of this meeting.

In recognition of his efforts to infuse a Christian spirit into the Good Neighbor policy, Dr. Thorning was the unanimous choice of the St. John's University Pan American Fraternity to be the recipient of the initial gold medal award of this organization at a banquet held in New York. Congratulatory letters on this occasion were received from Vice President Henry A. Wallace, Secretary of State Cordell Hull, Under Secretary of State Sumner Welles, and many members of the U. S. Catholic Hierarchy.

In May, 1942, Dr. Thorning was appointed Director of the Spiritual Seminar at the University of Habana. Prior to this appointment he had interviewed Colonel Fulgencio Batista, President of the Republic of Cuba. The interview appears as one chapter of his book, *Builders of the Social Order.*

Any afternoon during the school year, Dr. Thorning may be seen among the Maryland hills, walking over the country roads or playing tennis with the college students. He is a believer in the virtues of outdoor exercise. His mornings are reserved for classes and writing. He reports that it is seldom that he can turn out copy after three or four in the afternoon. He continues to visit Washington frequently, because he regards that capital the center of world affairs.

Father Thorning's principal works are: *Religious Liberty in Transition*, 1931, Benziger; and *Builders of the Social Order*, 1941, Catholic Literary Guild.

MARY THERESA WAG. GAMAN (1846–1931)

By Esther W. Neill

THE MOST ABSORBING STORIES that my mother ever told us were her own experiences when she was a little girl. Her father, John McKee, was born in Ireland. He married Esther Cottrell, his English cousin, the sweetheart of his boyhood; and when she died in her early twenties giving birth to her third child, who survived her only a few days, her young husband, broken-hearted and ill with grief, placed his two little daughters in a convent school because he had no near relatives to make a home for them.

Though we her children judged her trials from our own exagerated juvenile viewpoint, my mother often told us that she found real happiness in her convent home.

Mount de Sales, in Catonsville, was a lovely spot even in the early days of its foundation, though the children were warned not to go out of doors alone for fear that they would "be lost in the woods." The nuns were quick to note the cleverness of mind of this small pupil left in their care, and they wanted to teach her everything they had to offer. My mother was only six years old when her progress in her classes was noted. And since she was motherless, she was called "the child of the house."

There were festive occasions that mother never forgot. Watermelon parties, May processions, picnics, tableaux and theatricals in the odeum, and then the breath-taking excitement of the holidays when her father came laden with all sorts of good things, to take his little daughters to visit some of his friends in New York. These trips sometimes proved embarrassing to a young widower unused to children, for the old nun who watched over them with affectionate care had no way of keeping up with the prevailing fashions; so when she made clothes for them, which was one of her duties, she designed them after the styles of her own childhood.

"I don't know what's the matter with you," my grandfather said to his two small daughters on one occasion when they came down stairs to accompany him to the train. "You don't look like any other children I've ever seen."

As soon as they arrived in New York, he appealed to the wife of his best friend. She, full of sympathy, but laughing at his helplessness, went shopping next morning and outfitted them in modern garb. An old daguerreotype in my possession proves other startling changes in fashion, for on its mirrored surface is pictured a lovely little girl with dark curling hair, big open eyes, arrayed in a full plaid skirt with long, embroidered pantalettes reaching to her ankles.

My mother was fourteen when the Civil War broke out, and Mount de Sales seemed endangered for it commanded a high view of the city of Baltimore, and Maryland was a border state that might become a battlefield between the contending forces. One excitable school girl confided to my mother, "I wouldn't mind being killed but I'd hate to be scalped." Many parents, alarmed for the safety of their children and fearing that communications might be cut off, came to take their daughters home. My mother went to New York where she was to meet with real tragedy, for her father was arrested as a southern sympathizer and accused of fitting out ships to run the southern blockade. Without any sort of warning, he was imprisoned in Fort Lafayette.

Mother wrote an interesting account of this most anxious period of her life, which appeared in the *Ave Maria*, May 28, 1932, under the title of "An American Bastile." Since she was always so unwilling to inject her personality into her work, it was signed "By a Great-Grandmother."

It describes, in a charming and humorous way, her visits to her father and her skill at smuggling food, tobacco, chocolate and other luxuries into the grim old fortress; and one outstanding day of excitement when she was padded with greenbacks to aid one of the distinguished southern prisoners to escape.

It was during these long months of waiting for her father's freedom that my mother turned to books for comfort and distraction. The friends who had so hospitably opened their homes to her, had a well selected library and my mother who had hithertofore had little time to read, found herself in a new world where her real education for authorship began. She read with eagerness and understanding history, novels, essays, poetry, biography. Dickens was a "new" writer that delighted her; and she often said that she thought he had had great influence on her style, for she tried to pattern her first stories after his.

When my grandfather's unjustifiable arrest was brought to President Lincoln's attention, that fair-minded man ordered his immediate release, and my grandfather returned to his little daughters amid great rejoicing. He had suffered so much for his sympathy for the southern cause, that he feared that he might again become involved, hence he decided to leave the country. So the little family sailed for Liverpool.

In lodgings such as Dickens' stories had made familiar, my mother established a home for her father and younger sister. However, when the war was over, they returned to this country and settled in Baltimore. She was happily keeping house for her father when she began to write her first stories for publication. When she received small checks for them, she was silent about the honorariums because she said she was "ashamed of making money" since ladies in those distant days seemed to desire no economic independence.

In this period belongs her meeting with a young medical student who lived in her neighborhood—Samuel Waggaman, who had been one of Colonel Mosby's daring followers all during the war. After a short courtship they were married quietly and then moved to Washington to live with relatives for a time.

My mother always assured us that these in-laws were very kind to her; but they were practical minded people, extraordinary housekeepers, trained in all the domestic arts. So that my mother was sensitively aware that, in spite of their goodness, there must have been times when they looked upon a girl who wanted to write poetry as a helpless wife for a poor man.

The Christmas before my mother's first child was born, *Harper's Magazine* published a long poem from her pen, profusely illustrated, called "The Legend of the Mistletoe." This success marked the beginning of her professional career. To be able to make money seemed to place the writing of poetry on another plane. She could have her own home; she could pay for shirts and embroidered waistcoats; she could buy furniture and clothes, and a crib for her new baby. She was not a helpless wife after all. She had treasures of her own making; for tucked away in an old desk were stories and poems she had written because of her irresistible urge to write. Now she brought them from their hiding, and sending them away to newspapers and magazines she found that they were all saleable, and that editors were asking for more. So while my father struggled to establish himself in his profession, mother wrote regularly for the secular press: serials which were published under the nom de plume of "Fannie Fairie" and poems under the name of "Queerquill." Most of these verses deal with the domestic difficulties of the day, and were delightfully humorous in character.

It was not until her oldest son was preparing for First Communion that her outstanding work for Catholic children began. She had searched the stores and libraries for some books that would hold a boy's attention and "sugar coat" the piety which she wishes to instill. *Blind Agnes* was the only book she could find, and she knew that would not interest a live boy who had arrived at that age that has "no use for girls." In her maternal need it occurred to her that she might write a book of her own. So she began *Little Comrades: a First Communion Story for Boys.* She read it aloud to her own children, chapter by chapter, and she could see that it held their close attention. Later on it was published and found readers for over forty years.

Her later work for *Ave Maria* was the most productive of good in her long life. Father Hudson, with his wide vision, recognized the need of Catholic books for children. He expressed this vision practically by sympathy and encouragement. He practically appropriated my mother's talents for Our Lady's magazine. Her many serials in the *Ave Maria,* which appeared later in book form, brought her letters of commendation from far corners of the world. Even the great Cardinal Logue, Primate of Ireland, sent word that he liked to read her stories "before going to bed at night." And Louise Imogen Guiney, the well-known poet, wrote Father Hudson, who forwarded the letter, that she approached Mrs. Waggaman's stories "with the eagerness of a child." Some of the books have been translated into French and German, some have been put into Braille, some have been dramatized by convent schools when pupils wanted to see their favorite characters upon the stage.

Book followed book in rapid succession, the greater number brought out by the Ave Maria Press. They were wholesome books full of life and interest, but always teaching the happiness of virtue and the disappointment and sorrow of sin; books that prove the wealth of the author's imagination in creating a host of characters and in placing them in such different environments with an artist's skill.

The Strong Arm of Avalon deals with colonial days in Maryland. *Carroll Dare* is a story of adventure during the French Revolution. *Buddy* is a boy's tale of the first World War. *White Eagle, Carmelita, Billy Boy* are western stories. *The Secret of*

Pocomoke is placed in the coal mining districts. *Lorimer's Light* is a story of the sea.

It is interesting to note that when my mother was seventy-seven she was the winner in a short story contest in which 3,000 authors competed for the prize. Irvin Cobb, who was one of the judges, paid high tribute to Mrs. Waggaman.

On her eighty-fifth birthday, when she was busy on her last book, *The Trevelyn Twins,* she was greatly pleased by receiving a spiritual bouquet, hidden in a bunch of violets, from a group of her small admirers in a Chicago school. One little girl had added, "Dear Mrs. Waggaman, I am praying God that you will live forever." Perhaps this fervent little prayer did not go unheeded for this author's books seem to keep an immortality for her here on earth.

One of these books, which appeared serially in the *Ave Maria* a short time ago under the title of *The Nobodies,* is a story of her own family life with her children, though she fails to mention her own important work as a writer. The manuscript was found in an old trunk in the cellar years after her death. Knowing that it would be of interest to her many readers, I sent it to the *Ave Maria.* That answers the question so many are asking: "How could a new book by Mrs. Waggaman appear so long after her death?"

Mrs. Waggaman found her vocation as a writer of fiction for the developed child mind after years of experiment in the writing field. Likely she had in the storage of her experience the materials of plot and the shadings of character fiction long before she entered into her definite career. Or perhaps one should speak of Mrs. Waggaman's service in fictional writing as a vocation. Her apostolate was to administer to the urges and dreams of youth by supplying holy and wholesome adventure to young, questing minds. She made religion lovely and the practice of virtue appealing and noble. Like Christ, she suffered the little children to come unto her and taught them the sweetness and the light of living in the divine plan. In her maturity she became young, the better to serve youth. That she could do so much in such fine returns is the highest praise one can offer to her memory. Indeed, the character of her work is her assurance of permanent ranking in juvenile literature.

In literature and in life she measured up to the scriptural Valiant Women. So it was fitting altogether that on her tomb, just above her name, should be chiselled the significant line:

HER CHILDREN ROSE UP TO CALL HER BLESSED.

EDITOR'S NOTE: Through the courtesy of *Ave Maria*, Mrs. Neill's chapter on her mother is included here in the same volume in which Mrs. Neill's own autobiographical chapter appears. Mrs. Waggaman's stories for young readers, issued by the Ave Maria Press, are: *Barney's Fortune, Ben Regan's Battle, Billy Boy, Buddy, Carmelita, Carroll Dare, Con of Misty Mountain, Jack and Jean, Jerry's Job, Josephine Marie, Killykinick, Lady Bird, Lil' Lady, Little Mother, Lorimer Light, The Secret of Pocomoke, Sergeant Tim, The Story of Raoul, Tommy Travers, The Trevelyn Twins, White Eagle, Winnie's Luck,* and *The Nobodies.*

REVEREND WILL W. WHALEN

A Writer is Born—Somehow

I BECAME A WRITER the way I became a priest. By accident. Oh yes, I know. There's a Destiny that shapes our ends. Also kicks them! For our own good. Though we may kick back against our destiny.

I was an actor. Started as a kid star, "The Boy Patti," with the marvelous soprano voice. I lost my voice completely, every note, every word. Then, no longer deafened by the music of me own throttle, I had time to heed the wee sma' voice of Vocation.

I'd seen the lonely death of actors, with only a priest to console the poor gypsy about to end his earthly wanderings. I knew that the Mass is the greatest Drama on earth. I realized that the priest plays a bigger role than any Booth or Barrymore.

So I started on the thorny road that leads to the sanctuary. More thorny for me than for most brats, because my earlier career hadn't fitted me for solitude and silence. In fighting down my frequent desire to leap from the candlelights back to the footlights, I wrote and wrote. Just for meself. To git the restless divil outen me system.

And I had good luck from the jump. My stuff was bought by papers and magazines. My bad luck came later. When fan letters complained to staid and steady (and dry) publications that I was too too flippant, irreverent, realistic, theatrical,—too much the candid camera and not enough the monastic paint brush. I came near saying whitewash brush! I dared to write of people and things as I saw them. As they are, not as they should be.

Good luck makes fat. Bad luck makes muscle. I've survived. Perhaps I was born too soon, or something. Though some of my knockers think it were better for Catholic literature, had I not been born at all. I'm called a moon-calf of a writer. My nineteen-year-old Dad, anyhow, when he first beheld me said, indeed I was a fine broth of a boy. So I delighted him and my eighteen-year-old Mother. Ever since then lambasting critics seem to get in my hair; but really they do not. I don't give a wheeple of a whoop for 'em!

My first story was published when I was sixteen. Though before that I had little bits in newspapers. Always things I picked up around me own feet like a cockerel. I had never traveled far in my scribblings from my own little barnyard. I penciled my first squib about my Dad. Proving Shakespeare right: it is sharper nor a sarpint's tooth to own a thankless child who writes up his "old man."

Poor young Dad tried to raise chickens. And a rat played the divil with his peeps. Daily a chick or two vanished to furnish funeral unbaked friers for Monsieur Rodent. Dad grimly poisoned scraps of bread and planted those bombs around the murderer's hunting grounds. It would soon be good night to that stabber in the back. Alas, even then Pearl Harbor had its prototype! I heard a sound too strong for just a groan. Dad was collapsed on the woodpile, his dead dreams around him. Old Biddy and her birds were all on their backs, their drumsticks in air, pleading against the deep damnation of their taking-off. The rat was complacently picking his teeth with his tail. The wrong parties got in at that lethal feast!

I've published a string of books. I write too fast, I'm told.

Rather, perhaps I publish too fast. Because I always have about three books ready, lying in wait for an unwary publisher to come whistling by. The critics were flabbergasted when I managed to get out a trio of books in little more than twelve months. Of course these books had been writ between priest jobs during the years. For five years ere they saw a printer they'd been in an old box from the mines marked Dynamite! Beware!

Moral: Be ye ever ready, for ye know not when a publisher may come.

I prefer to write plays. Or rather, I like to turn my novels into plays or the plays into novels. There is really more fun (and, if you're lucky, more money) in the plays. This marvelous country of ours, our own United States, why does anybody go to Europe! One of my American-Irish dramas was played by a mixed cast of Slovacs and Poles for a church benefit. My widow, Mary Ann Maloney, was tackled by Judmila Pelmetski. My pie-eyed Irish hero, Dennis Gallagher, was Zigmund Todoroski. And those budding Yank actors gave a far better account of themselves than their playwright did!

The titles of my books scare and shock. I may be wrong. But I do reach the most unlikely readers. *Ex-Nun* threw a chill into Catholic book shops at first—and sold out an edition within a month. *What Priests Never Tell* sold the book and keeps the play a-flickering. A catchy title does help. My *Twilight Talks to Tired Hearts* has been selling for over thirty years.

I aim at comedy and giggles whenever possible. I learnt that from my theatre experiences. Send 'em away laughing. Work in a merry ha-ha whenever you can. And always have an Uplift. You need disagreeable characters for contrast; but for the sake of your unpublished child, don't let cockeyed *dramatis personae* dominate your narrative. Better St. John than Judas. Mary Magdalene is more showy than Martha, but Mattie should be your leading lady.

I carry old envelopes and jot down on them odd and funny sayings I over-hear, and record any queer experiences. I spy in the subway a jeweled or daggered or birded bonnet and sketch it either on paper or in my retentive memory, leaning slightly to burlesque. That coy dowager doesn't dream that the lanky, pale-faced priest sitting opposite is planning to make her helmet immortal if he can.

My plots I get from life: from the newspapers or experiences I hear about. I twist them till they yowl for mercy, and finally make them fit into some sort of scheme. I always have me feet on the ground, if not in the mud, when I start a story. Such a thing has really happened somewhere, though never just as I tell it.

My characters are composite. Out of a three-leaved shamrock I may concoct a black-eyed susan. I use Tilly's one remaining front tooth with Maria's oyster-shell ears which are flamboyantly sporting Lizzie's too moony and too diamon'd ear-rings. I dot in Dottie's freckles and add to them her grandfather's left eyelid which droops. On top of that I set Tessie's weird plateau of a hat with a widowed crow a-mourning. Then I call my misbegoten virgin Gwendolin and have her walk like her sailor brother Jack or Dorothy Thompson. If I name a personage Joe Peacock, he'll eventually turn out to be a bantam rooster.

The Girl from Mine Run was an easy book for me. A beautiful servant maid married her blueblood employer. That gave me a chance to contrast the masses and the classes, and to cry out loud against Divorce. I was in a newspaper office when a society dame, beautiful but dumb (and none too circumspect in her conduct), sailed in and paid through the nose to have her scandal kept out of print. Her tale had already been set up in type, with fetching photographs. Enough to land her a Hollywood contract. Her check, however, was large enough to strangle the story and keep her in Society and the Blue Book. More grist for my *Mine Run Girl* mill. Later I sold *Mine Run* to that very paper as a serial. The editor waxed a-merry: "The high and mighty hussie paid me to keep her out of print. Now we're paying you to put her in!"

Priests have always had and always will have trouble with their relatives. Perhaps we expect too much from the nephews of our clergy. After all, only one in that tribe is wearing the Roman collar. A bishop's brother was robbed late at night and found

to be worth only two bits. Thence was born my *Celebate Father*.
The priest hero tries to raise his dead sister's two wee daughters.
And whew! What a life they led their reverend uncle! Priests
belong to the cloister, not to the hearth.

From my own experiences, I'd say to embryo authors; never
use your imagination when you can draw on your memory of
what you've heard or seen in real life. Work that imagination
no more than you must. Get your characters rough-drawn in
your brain, then develop them as you go along. I never employ
a synopsis. I have one big scene vaguely in mind, and I work
up to that or work back from it. In the heat of composition
you'll beget your people all right. No, I amn't paid by typewriter companies to tootle their wares. But every scribe should
learn to type, even though like me he only hunts and pecks.
Learn to think with your fingertips. It may take time, but 'tis
worth the effort. And the printed page forninst ye talks more
loudly than script. You can see your stuff as others will see it.
And that's a grand eye-opener!

EDITOR'S NOTE: Father Whalen is now living in New York City. Since 1930
he has concentrated on writing plays for the stage and the movies. His
published books include: *Twilight Talks to Tired Hearts*, 1914, Mission
Press, Techny, Ill.; *The Ex-Seminarian*, 1914, Mission Press (republished by
The White Squaw Press, Orrtanna, Adams County, Pa., in 1929); *The Girl
from Mine Run*, 1927, B. Herder Book Co.; *The Ex-Nun*, 1927, Herder; *The
Girl Who Fought*, 1928, Herder; *Priests*, 1928, Herder; *The Irish Sparrow*,
1928, Herder; *The Golden Squaw*, 1928, White Squaw Press; *The Forbidden
Man*, 1929, Herder; *The Celibate Father*, 1929, Herder; *What Priests Never
Tell*, 1929, Herder; *Give Me a Chance!*, 1929, Herder; *Strike; or, Scandal's
Lash*, 1930, White Squaw Press; *Co-Stars*, 1930, White Squaw Press; and *The
Priest Who Vanished*, 1942, Catholic Literary Guild.

MARY MABEL WIRRIES

Children's Stories

THERE WAS A CHILD, back in the early nineteen-hundreds, who carried a pencil and a paper with her wherever she went. A stubby kind of pencil, well-bitten, and a messy bit of paper, both of them thrust deep into the pocket of a checked gingham apron. There was a river hill where wild grape vines made shelter; there was a marsh land where sweet purple violets and wet yellow cowslips grew; there was an old cemetery where blue myrtle, spicy cinnamon pinks and tiny white Stars of Bethlehem were lost under a tangle of berry vines and sassafras and ivy—a cemetery, with tumbled-over grave stones bearing old, old names. And in the cemetery, tucked away under massive cedars, was an old mission church, long since fallen to decay and ruin. In all these places the child dreamed her dreams and put them on the messy bits of paper with the stubby pencil. Undisturbed by her quiet presence, bright-eyed furred and feathered peoples carried on their activities about her, and the songs of the birds, the murmuring of the river and the soft breath of the wind in the cedars were the things she wrote about. "Poems" she called the thoughts she wrote—and perhaps they were. She filled a book with them.

The child grew up and left the river country but she took her dreams with her. The tenor of her "poems" changed. A convent school was hers, now—and she wrote of her new world. Now she cribbled in what her classmates called her "Spasm Book"—and hers were school-girl thoughts, about the "beauties of dill pickles and half a pound of fudge"; about her studies: "rhomboids, hexagons, parallel planes" and "O, Cicero! thou mover of mens' hearts! Could I but look upon thy kingly form and listen to the music of thy voice . . . Methinks I should be tempted to procure . . . A brick! soft as the summit of Pike's Peak . . . And raising it above thy noble brow, smash it to smithereens! Such, Cicero, the love and reverence that I bear for thee!"

Graduation, then—and the sorrowful realization that she must forego the college education which was to prepare her for a writing career. Despairingly (because she was very young and little understanding) she put her pencils and her dreams away. For five years she wrote not a word. And then she was married and the mother of two babies, and suddenly the old urge was upon her. She had to write! Out came the pencils and paper, back came the dreams. It was slow hard work at first. The verse still flowed easily, but she put it resolutely aside and turned to prose. A husband's illness and the pressure of post-war debts forced her to a new practicality. She would write stories, now—stories that would sell, stories that would help the family finances. What if she didn't have a college education? Surely one could go on learning, even without a professor to correct papers. What were libraries for? And in Detroit where she now lived, there was a wonderful library. But where could she find time to write? Oh, she could always find time to write! She found time to breathe, didn't she? And so, in 1920, began the writing career of Mary Mabel Wirries.

Her first story, "Jonquils and Hyacinths," a story of young married misunderstanding and happy adjustment, was written in the hours of a miserable night while nursing her younger baby

through an attack of colic. The baby lay across her knee on a
hot water bottle, while the mother hurried madly to get her
thoughts on paper before the little sufferer's screams began anew.
Peace came to the baby and to the young lovers in the story
about the same time. And a munificent check for seven whole
dollars came a few weeks later to the aspiring young author from
the third editor who read the story. She knew then that she was
at last embarked upon the career for which she had longed.

Stories literally tumbled from her pen in the next few years.
Some of them were very bad. Some of them were fair. Some
were good. "Write about the things you know," the books told
her, "write about the people you meet. Write about the things
you love." So she wrote about young husbands and wives,
about little children, about her dear adopted Catholic Faith.
She made mistakes, but the editors were more than kind. And
soon her name was appearing in the Catholic magazines regularly, and she had written her first book. And it, too, was about
the things and people she knew. *Mary Rose at Boarding School*
and her companies were the author's own friends and classmates
from St. Ursula's Academy, Toledo, Ohio, masquerading under
new names. Her old teachers came to life on its pages. "We
have no difficulty recognizing ourselves," they told her, laughing,
"No trouble at all. Sometimes, dear, you are almost too truthful. But we like being immortalized by one of our old students."

As I sit at my desk today writing of the child, the girl, and the
younger woman I once was, I think in all humility that little of
the credit for what I have accomplished belongs to me. People
who have to write have to write. I was born with the writing
urge in my heart. God planted it there for His own Divine
Purpose. And then he placed me in a position where writing
was not so much pleasure as necessity. An animal, threatened
with death by drowning but endowed with all his limbs swims,
doesn't he? And I, beset by financial difficulties and faced with
the needs of a growing family but endowed with the gift of expression and the urge to use it, wrote. Often, writing, I was
battling against my own inclinations. For I loved poetry and
wrote prose, wanted to do adult novels and compromised
with juveniles. The checks had to keep coming, you see. Five

little girls eat an amazing quantity of food, wear out countless pairs of shoes. And editors know what they want and pay for that and that only. I never had time to gamble with my talents. And now I am glad I lacked the time. Because—and this is a good thing for young writers to remember—writing what you don't wish to write and doing it well is the finest kind of discipline for a writer. Writing is one of the most exacting of all professions, perhaps. Social activities and even the needs of the writer's family give way to the printer's deadline. But it is also the most satisfying. There is joy in a phrase well-turned; there is glorious sense of achievement in every manuscript completed to an editor's satisfaction.

My record of work accomplished? Although it now runs over a long period of twenty-two years, it is not too impressive, because I reared a family and managed a home as I wrote; and many times sickness, death and misfortune have stepped in to turn me aside from my typewriter for varying intervals of time. I have lost my mother, my oldest daughter Rosemary, and my youngest daughter Barbara Lou, in the past decade of years. But I have published a few hundred short stories, poems and articles, several book-length serials, and fifteen books, and for seven years I have done a weekly column "The Weekly Post-script" for the *Ave Maria*. This latter is, to me, the most enjoyable work of all. And now, in 1942, the old urge to write is back again, after many months during which it seemed gone forever. I pray that it will not leave me again. And perhaps— just perhaps, mind you!—I shall sandwich in, between the tasks the editors set me and the whirl of family activities which beset me (my family now consists of a married daughter, her husband and little daughter; a college daughter; a high school daughter; an adopted one-year son; an eighty-seven-year-old grandmother and my husband) perhaps I shall find time to write a few more poems, a few adult novels. For unlike other people, writers never grow too old to work, and an itching pen will not be stilled.

Benziger published Mrs. Wirries' Mary Rose, Patsy, and Paula books for young readers. Her *Shadows on Cedarcrest, Wayside Idyls,* and *The Road Is Long* were issued by the Ave Maria Press. The author published her lyrics for young readers, *Gay Witch April.*

RIGHT REVEREND PETER M. H. WYNHOVEN

Him of Holland, by Reverend Edward F. Murphy, S.S.J.

BORN IN HOLLAND fifty-seven years ago, Peter's eyes looked out on tulips and up into the sweetest of mother-faces. This gracious fact was to color his whole life. Early he decided to spread beauty and wholesomeness in the lives of such as had known only the opposites.

Coming to this country, he finished his studies at Kenrick Seminary, St. Louis, and in 1909 was ordained a priest. Starting out with a modest desire to renew the face of the earth, he presently found himself limited to a few but very needy corners of it; and, in no time, his tulips of blessings were brightening those corners as they had never been brightened before. His mother's eyes were on him, and he could never let them be dimmed with disappointment.

A popular speaker from his very first years in the priesthood, he never did any writing for publication, and never dreamed of doing any, till he was fifty years old. Once he began, though, he worked like a wind-mill, and, as yet, is far from ceasing. Already he has achieved ten neat little volumes and ranks today as the most widely read columnist of the American Catholic Press. His weekly articles appear in forty-eight papers.

It was his innate practical sense that originally drew his eye to the typewriter, although he has never used one. All his writing comes in longhand. Why? This is his answer: "Never do what someone else can do just as well or better. The woods are full of good typists. So why?" Ribbons, carbon copies and mechanics would only interfere with his spontaneous and catch-as-catch-can moods. He likes the personality of a pen.

Pastor of a large city parish (Our Lady of Lourdes, in New Orleans); editor of the highly progressive weekly, *Catholic Action of the South,* which circulates in four dioceses; Director of the Diocesan Council of Catholic Women; State Chaplain of the Catholic Daughters of America; labor consultant for the United States in the South; he finds all the more urge, if less and less time, to apply his pen to paper. His variety of experiences simply demands an inkwell.

Merely to describe his social achievements would be to fill many pages. And yet these are the things about which he never writes. But, at the same time, these are the things that represent an abundance of life which has to overflow, in some form or other, into expression. "To live much," he says, "is to write at least some."

Founder of St. Vincent's Hotel and Free Labor Bureau for the Unemployed; organizer of the Associated Catholic Charities and its first Director; founder of *Catholic Action of the South;* member of the Boy Scout Directory; Secretary of the Child Guidance Clinic of New Orleans; founder and general manager of Madonna Manor and Hope Haven, institutions for dependent children: Peter M. H. Wynhoven has certainly lived!

Wherever he has walked, the charm and appeal of old Holland seem to have blossomed in America. Naturally, he kept his mother—his inspiration—happy to the very end of her days.

Public appreciation of his efforts is proven by the fact that Madonna Manor and Hope Haven, conceived and administered in the spirit of his beloved parent, attracted eighty-five percent of its initial needs from non-Catholics.

These vivid and varied contacts afford him an unusual outlook on life and its problems. Love of God and down-to-earth-iness are his ideals. He writes as he speaks: short, pithy, pungent sentences, remarkably to the point.

Having always dealt with difficulties, he delights in them. "Your style," a critic once told him, "is as personal as a punch in the nose." "Yes," he answered, "and as pertinent." "But," continued the critic, "isn't a punch in the nose apt to be impertinent—sometimes?" "Never," he retorted, "when the nose is that of a problem and not of a person." Few writers have ever combined so much force with so much charity.

When Archbishop Cicognani, Apostolic Delegate, was sailing on the *Rex* in 1939, he chose Monsignor Wynhoven from twenty-four priests aboard to speak on a certain feast day during the voyage. "Now I can better appreciate your type of writing," His Excellency told him at the conclusion of his sermon. "Speaking and writing, you seem to single out one person, and everybody —reader or listener—thinks you are talking or writing for him."

His approximate reason for starting his literary efforts at such a late date in life is that, about eight years ago, he opened a print-shop and bookbindery for his orphan boys. They needed work and there was little of it. Very well. He elected to furnish them a lot. Result: they have been busy with Wynhoven brain-children ever since.

His books are: *Sermon Seeds, Old Gospel Modernly Applied, Sincere Seeker, Sermon Suggestions for Special Occasions, Swim or Sink, Sacerdotal Salesmanship, I Believe—I Battle, Page My Pastor, Wild Wisdom,* and, *Barbarous Babies.* But his greatest success lies in the beauty and wholesomeness which he has given to lives that would otherwise have known nothing but frustration and regret.

That Monsignor M. H. Wynhoven has been true to the tulips of Holland and to the memory of the best of mothers, his buildings and his books give a proof that is little short of golden.

Msgr. Wynhoven's Hope Haven Press, Marrero, Louisiana, published all of his books except *Wild Wisdom,* which was issued by the Catholic Literary Guild in 1941.

REVEREND JOHN J. WYNNE, S.J.

Encyclopedist

THE WRITTEN WORD is the title of a book by Father Humphrey, long deceased. I used to like it because it set one thinking how much good a Catholic writer can do, and it set one acting, that is, writing. It was a written word that arrested the attention of the greatest master of English prose, Cardinal Newman, and ultimately brought about his entrance into the Church. In a later day he stressed the importance of the printed page as against face to face or vocal argument.

How one comes to employ the written word is not easy to trace. To employ it well presupposes preparation which, though serious, has its own pleasures. Indeed, I doubt if the cultivation of any art can be more pleasant.

At school we wrote themes and compositions of all sorts in every class, whether in the Academy (now High School) or College. What really started me writing was the review we had to make on our weekly holiday of all we had heard or read during the past five days in the class of Philosophy. This required clearness, precision and the manual labor of covering some seven or eight pages of foolscap. For this we were helped greatly by a previous drilling in analysis. Every speech, or part of a speech we read in Greek, Latin or English we had to analyze, and we were encouraged to listen to distinguished public speakers in courts or assembly halls, and take apart and tabulate their arguments. After such exercise it became natural to think and to express thought in writing.

Before that final Philosophy year at Woodstock, we had worried our imaginations to create figures of speech, to be graphic, dramatic, and even sensational, to put the poets and orators of the past in the shade. A fortunate part of our training was to laugh one another out of extravagance, bombast, and buncombe.

After leaving St. Francis Xavier College, New York City, in 1876, I thought little of writing as a life work, but I was intensely interested in what others, I mean masters, wrote and how they wrote it. All through my studies as a young Jesuit (for I had entered the Society that same year), I kept the habit of analyzing and summarizing any book or essay which I considered well written, and it was a pleasure to put the analysis or summary in writing. From six years old I had liked to follow magazines, and I recall with gratitude how I used to read *The Catholic World* almost from the year Father Hewit started it. Then it was mostly a collection of cullings from leading Catholic periodicals in various parts of the world, and it opened up to the young mind a vision of what was beyond the immediate scene.

That vision, it would seem, never left me and when, later in life, writing, or rather editing, became an avocation, my chief quest was items of interest in any country from which credible information could be obtained. This bent is, I believe, manifest in the periodicals of which I was one of the editors, in *The Messenger,* in *The Pilgrim of Our Lady of Martyrs,* later on in *America,* and finally in *The Catholic Encyclopedia.* That is one of the influences of Father Hewit, and it shows how far-reaching any good Catholic writing can be.

So it appears that I have been an editor more than an author or writer of books. What I have written is scattered over thousands of pages, difficult now to collect, and very little of it in book form. I wonder if I could recognize some of it as my own.

Part of an editor's task is to discover writers of promise, to suggest subjects, and to outline the content of the essay or book they are to write. He should discern what is of public interest, what is needed to set people thinking, how best to inform, or correct and stir readers to action.

In his *Essays on the Poets,* De Quincy drew a line between literature of knowledge, meaning information, and literature of power, that is, effusions of the imagination as in the poetry he was criticizing. The distinction served his purpose at the time, but it is not a true one. Genuine writing in any field has its own power. Dickens entertained but he also reformed many a crying evil by imparting knowledge of outlaw conditions in schools, courts, prisons and the business world.

Much of an editor's work is criticism, not of books only, but of everything in life; and criticism rightly understood is the highest exercise of human intellect. It supposes knowledge and it imparts knowledge in such a manner as to correct what is erroneous and establish what is right.

It was a criticism in *The Messenger* which proved to be a powerful corrective of an abuse that had lasted for years and threatened to become everlasting. All the old errors about the Catholic Church, its doctrine, its part in history, its priesthood and monastic orders, its achievement in the arts and sciences, in education, had been culled from thousands of poisoned books and summarized in popular sources of knowledge, such as our encyclopedias. Many of these errors had come to be taken for granted since there was no criticism to overtake them. The wells of knowledge were thus poisoned.

A new and attractive edition of one of these encyclopedias was recommended as fair, impartial, unprejudiced. The editors and writers assumed that there was no gainsay to what they published.

Well, once for all, it seemed to me time to call a halt. A criticism of this *Encyclopedia* was written in which some of the most salient errors were scored. It was entitled "Poisoning the Wells." In this criticism there was no controversy, no argument, simply an exposition of error after error. They were so glaring, no comment was needed. And what happened? There was an immediate demand for this criticism in pamphlet form. About 75,000 copies were circulated among Catholic organizations and individuals who cheerfully paid for them. The publishers of this *Encyclopedia* quickly engaged a group of Catholic scholars to revise the articles criticized and the publishers of other encyclopedias promptly followed suit. Indeed, some members of the transgressing firm soon saw the need of a Catholic Encyclopedia and helped no little in its production.

That same summer of 1902 there was an outcry against the Friars in the Philippines. Day after day "The Friars must Go" headlined articles in our newspapers recounting examples of the unfitness of the Friars and their alleged abuses. Sorry to say, the newspapers were in this instance the mouthpiece of our government.

Indeed, the President had already sent a Commission to Rome for the purpose of inducing the Holy See to withdraw the Friars. Again *The Messenger* was ready with the facts about the Friars and their enemies, and an article entitled "The Friars must Stay" was submitted before publication to the President, then Theodore Roosevelt. Indignant at first, he was quick to grasp the real facts; he lost no time in recalling his Commission from Rome. He even strongly urged that the article be published, and offered to provide for its wide distribution. Some of the Friars deemed it advisable to yield to the storm of opposition aroused against them and leave the Islands, but our government indemnified them handsomely for the properties which they were abandoning.

These articles were only a plain statement of facts; there was nothing in them to stir the imagination or arouse passion. Yet they were literature of power. They brought about what they advocated and their effect has been wide-spread and lasting.

De Quincy's own writings would nullify his distinction between literature of knowledge and literature of power. There is power in all true literature, and that is why to write well for publication is a worthy ambition for every Catholic student and scholar.

Of the many subjects on which I have written and encouraged others to write, the two in which I have found most pleasure and inspiration are the *Jesuit Martyrs of North America,* and the crown of their labors and sacrifices, the Indian Maiden *Kateri Tekakwitha,* our "Lily of the Mohawks." They are all really one subject. Away back, when resting after an illness, I was looking for something to do. The good old priest who had admitted me into college had a rare copy in French of Bressani's *Narrative of the Captivity and Tortures of Father Isaac Jogues,* and he suggested that I translate it. I did so. That was in 1889. When three years later, just fifty years ago, I was appointed editor of the *Pilgrim of Our Lady of Martyrs* the translation turned up somewhat mysteriously, and that was the start of numerous articles, pamphlets and some books, which my associates and others and I gradually published with a view to doing our part to bring about the canonization of the eight Jesuit Martyrs of North America.

When it became sure that Isaac Jogues and his Companions would be declared Saints, I urged several who, it seemed to me, should be especially interested in Tekakwitha to take up the Cause for her canonization. As they were reluctant, I decided to attempt it. This again incited more than a score of writers here and abroad to do the Life of this Indian Maiden in books and pamphlets in various languages.

Writing about the good Catherine has been a labor of love. A swarm of witnesses to her goodness has established her renown for holiness. Just a few days before this was written, 12 June, 1942, Feast of the Sacred Heart, Pope Pius XII ratified the decision of the Congregation of Rites that her virtues were heroic and, to proclaim this, authorized the decree in which she will be styled Venerable. The prospect is that she will soon be Blessed.

Shortly before *America* was launched in 1909, at an audience with Pope Pius X, I requested him to give a motto to express what this periodical should be, and what it should do. In his witty manner he replied: "No, no motto; but after you lay down your pen as Editor, if you can truly say you have never written one harsh word, let me know and I shall send you a pair of wings." I never got the wings, but in his wit there was a world of wisdom.

MARGARET YEO

By Right Reverend Ronald A. Knox

MRS. YEO was a granddaughter of Charles Blomfield, Bishop of early Victorian London; and therefore first cousin of another convert-authoress, the late Dorothy Gurney, who will be remembered, not altogether adequately, by the hymn "O Perfect Love," and the too-often quoted lines about "You are nearer to God in a garden." The two cousins were close friends and admirable foils; both came into the Church somewhat late, with a rich background of miscellaneous culture; both, through their respective husbands, were in close touch with the stage; they differed in that Dorothy Gurney had been a devout High Anglican, and might well have been a devout Quaker, whereas Margaret Yeo boasted that she was a converted pagan, and was honestly bewildered by the existence of other Christianities. I first met both of them in Plymouth, as members of that charmed circle which revolved round the Church of St. James the Less; Mrs. Yeo was an ardent Jacobite even in those days, before the first World War, but professed a complete want of religion.

Then she did the Lough Derg pilgrimage (to see what it was like, was her own story), and came straight out of the lake into the Church. That was in 1906.

Her husband, who remained a delightful pagan, was a chronic invalid and no bread-winner. They lived almost in the precincts of St. Alban's Abbey, in narrow circumstances, for a couple who seemed so born to enjoy things, yet dispensing a memorable hospitality.

Margaret Yeo could write. She had written a few stories, not wanting in atmosphere. I made a joking compact with her that one day we would collaborate, and write a sort of Catholic *John Inglesant;* she would work up the setting, and I would provide the theological interest. As time went on, and I never did my part, I encouraged her to write the book by herself. The result was her first novel, *Salt.* Its readers will admit that it is a more red-blooded story than *John Inglesant;* but the authoress was too much carried away by her story to leave room for philosophic diatribe. Meanwhile, the atmosphere of the sixteenth century had gripped her. The death of her husband left her with more freedom to write, and more need of royalties. She was inexhaustibly plucky, and a cancer of the throat, which threatened to be fatal, but was fortunately cured, never interrupted the activity of her mind.

Like *Salt,* her other novels are perhaps more distinguished by the richness (sometimes almost lusciousness) of the setting than by the intrinsic interest of the characters, and she will be most remembered by her biographies of St. Francis Xavier and St. Charles Borromeo, clear-cut achievements which combine much grasp of detail with an inflexible honesty in the pursuit of history.

Her circle of readers welcomed in her novels and biographies the work of a mind incapable of being tedious, and refreshingly candid.

She was a loyal and active Catholic, without a trace of the fussiness and stuffiness which sometimes dim the lustre of good example. Her friends found in her a pungently amusing com-

panion, a fearless mind, and a generosity of character undis-
mayed by circumstance.

Margaret Yeo died on May 13, 1941, in her sixty-fourth year,
at Uxbridge, near London.

Mrs. Yeo's books include: *Don John of Austria,* 1936, Sheed; *Full Circle,*
1933, Burns; *The Greatest of the Borgias,* 1936, Bruce; *King of Shadows*
(James II), 1929, Macmillan; *Reformer: St. Charles Borromeo* (published in
England as *Prince of Pastors*), 1938, Bruce; *St. Francis Xavier,* 1932, Mac-
millan; *Salt,* 1932, Sheed; *These Three Hearts* (published in England as
Claude de la Colombiere), 1940, Bruce; *Uncertain Glory,* 1931, Sheed; *Wild
Parsley,* 1929, Simpkins.

CECILIA MARY YOUNG

MY FIRST STORY was published serially at the age of twelve in a school paper and was afterwards brought out as a book.

I began writing in the first grade. We used to have drawing projects and I accompanied my "picture" with a story, usually of a blood-curdling character.

Five years later, after handing in a composition, the Sister asked me to remain after school. I feared a reprimand for my arithmetic, but it was only to tell me: "Your *forte* is writing!" I was bitterly disappointed, for I had hoped that I might become a musician. I practiced music before I went to school and preferred to practice during recreation rather than to play games. I practiced when I returned home, doing my home-work between times and leaving my arithmetic (the bane of my existence!) until the last task.

I was five years old when I was taken to see my first play. Ever since the spell of the footlights has been in my veins.

At that tender age, my sister and I were drilled in little home performances by my mother, for both my parents loved amateur theatricals.

"Mama's birthday" was the great dramatic event in our family calendar. I wrote the plays and drilled the neighborhood playmates behind closed doors, fondly believing my mother would have no inkling of the coming performance. Friday nights, when we had no home study, we were brought to see some worthwhile play, and thus were introduced to the work of outstanding actors and actresses.

However, music continued to be the ruling passion of my ambition. My sister now played the violin very well. Our greatest joy was in playing duets by the hour and in singing songs from the light operas. We appeared on club programs and in all the school entertainments.

When I was tall enough to reach the pedals of the large concert harp at the convent, I studied harp, continuing with piano, harmony and counterpoint. The great event of my school life was when I was selected to play the title role of Joan of Arc for the Commencement program. I studied every book I could find concerning Joan, so that I might give a faithful interpretation. This research opened up a vista; for since that year, when I was fifteen, I have been interested in research. At the preliminary elocution contest, I had given my own arrangement of the death of Sebastian from Newman's *Fabiola*. The judges, now at the Commencement, went out to consult during a long orchestra number, and when they handed in their decision the gold medal was awarded to Joan. Thus began an impetus towards amateur theatricals. A drama club was formed that summer. We gave a "parlor-version" of *Mikado*, which I arranged and directed. That winter, during the holidays, we presented my play, *On a Kentucky Staircase*,—the stage our own staircase, the audience being seated in the front hall. We gave several other performances in the ensuing five or six years. Our most ambitious attempt was *Hamlet*, given in a large attic in the suburban home of the boy who played Hamlet.

School days over, we talked of my going away to college. But my mother was not strong, so I decided to remain at home, specializing in music, languages and writing plays. I attended a school of journalism where I was urged to send some sketches to an editor. Then I received my first check. Selling several more sketches encouraged me to embark forthright upon a writing career.

I had begun a correspondence with Brother Dutton of Molokai and wrote some sketches about him. One of these appeared in the Philadelphia *Catholic Standard and Times,* as "The Lone Soldier at Molokai." After Brother Dutton died, I wrote "He Knew Damien" for *The Commonweal.*

We went abroad for three years after my father's death, chiefly to see the Oberammergau Passion Play, to which he had been planning to take us that year. Due to this trip, I conceived the idea of studying the drama of other countries.

By this time I had formed a drama library of my own, having accumulated about two thousand volumes relating to the theatre. I also read all the plays I could find, thus forming the nucleus for the drama catalogue I was to compile.

A year's course in the Literature of the Drama, at Loyola University Extension was followed by an intensive Drama Institute, attending classes given by teachers from Northwestern University and professional theatre-men who taught stage technic, design and production.

My research leanings led me to write *The Illini Trail,* a pageant-play of Catholic Illinois, which I put on in two parochial schools. In one of the schools I had a cast of 500 children, and taught them the music and dancing and directed all the performances.

Then for three years I became a recluse, reading and classifying plays for *The List of Plays for Catholics,* suggested by Father Daniel A. Lord, S.J. I worked for a new type of classification, suggesting the character of each play in special lists and devised a system for finding the number of characters required. This was the first time a play catalogue had been arranged in this form. This system has since been adopted by all play publishers. The book was first brought out in paper covers. When that edition was exhausted the work was issued in leather binding, in 1924.

In that year I organized a Catholic Book Exhibition, the first of its kind, at least in the Middle West.

In connection with the drama course at Loyola, I founded a laboratory theatre at St. Ignatius College, the Sock and Buskin Club, from which emerged the Footlight Club and the Garret Theatre. Both rehearsed and gave performances in the attic of our home which we built into a theatre.

During this time, deciding to combine my three predilections (music, writing, and acting), I evolved a solo-theatre under the rather cumbersome title, Miniatures in Musical Monologue. These recitals, based on historical impersonations, embody the music of the period as background for the dramatic unfolding of the story, making use of the concert harp or the small Irish harp. I have given "The Empress Josephine" in many convents and clubs in many parts of the United States.

In 1928 we sold our home in Chicago, the city in which I was born and lived most of my life, and went abroad, spending three months in Italy and two years in France. Here I became correspondent for the National Catholic News Syndicate, and on my return to the United States continued writing a weekly column for N. C. W. C. News Service called "Women in the News" for several years.

While in France, I had prepared a book on Lourdes. We had felt the need of a volume supplying the concise history in brief summary for the pilgrim. An editor was reading this manuscript while making a trip through Germany just before the first World War. It was my only copy and it was stolen from him and never recovered. (Doubtless some gestapo is still trying to figure out the secret code of the Visions!). I rewrote completely, and the book was published in 1932 under the title Lourdes in the High Pyrenees.

The Franciscan (Paterson, N. J.) published my serial, The Sword of the Russian Prince. Later it was translated into Russian for the periodical The Voice of the Church.

I have contributed to The Catholic World, Extension, America, Rosary, and other Catholic magazines; The Etude, Caecilia, and other music and drama magazines; and have been conducting a monthly column of play suggestions for *The Faculty Adviser* since 1937.

My last book, *Ring up the Curtain,* provides an historical survey of the amateur drama, offers practical suggestions for staging amateur shows, and concludes with a selected list of plays suitable for amateur production.

My advice to young writers is to stick at their chosen avocation through every obstacle; to view the world with a note-book mind, so well disciplined that every impression will prove of writing value. Then to write of what they know. We have need of many Catholic writers who will write as Catholics. I would also advise the young writer to aim high, come down gracefully, and then rebound by easy stages.

Miss Young's books include: *Catalogue and Review of Plays for Catholics,* 1923, 1924, Loyola University Press, Chicago; *Lourdes in the High Pyrenees,* 1932, Buechler Publishing Co., Belleville, Ill.; *The Sword of the Russian Prince* (the story of Demetrius Gallitzin, a Russian prince, who became a priest and a missionary in early Pennsylvania), 1937, St. Anthony Guild Press; *Ring up the Curtain,* 1942, Library Service Guild, St. Paul, Minn.